Our Heritage of Faith
Volume 2

Volume 2

*Our*

# Heritage of Faith

by
Merlin L. Neff, Ph.D.

Pacific Press Publishing Association

Mountain View, California

Omaha, Nebraska        Portland, Oregon

TITLE PAGE PHOTO BY THREE LIONS

# Contents

## Contents, Continued

# III

# Our Heritage of Heroic Faith

(Continued)

# Moses, Heir to the Throne

*Exodus 1 to 10*

chapter 1 ❧

OF ALL the leaders in the ancient civilizations, none
stands higher in talent or intellect than Moses, a slave
at birth. Trained as a general of the armies of the
Egyptian Empire, schooled in the wisdom of the universities
of his day, this man broke from the path to the throne to deliver
his slave-cursed people from their oppressors. He was patient,
courageous, and visionary. He was a lawgiver, a writer of great
history and poetry. And most of all, he was a man of God.

Moses was born at a poor time in history. His parents were
slaves, and he, a boy baby, was decreed to die by the edict of
Pharaoh. But wait, let us see the whole picture.

The children of Israel had been in Egypt about a hundred
and fifty years, tending their flocks and herds in the land of
Goshen. They had once been highly favored by the pharaohs,
but now they were despised slaves. A new line of kings had
come to the throne who did not remember Joseph, who once
saved the country from famine.

Amram, a descendant of Levi, the third son of Jacob, hated
the word "slave." He knew the history of his people—how
Joseph had been sold as a slave by his brothers; how father
Jacob, a brave pioneer, had made the long journey to Egypt
with his family to save them from the famine in Canaan; how
God had told Jacob that his children would someday return to

Moses, a prince of Egypt, was carefully trained to lead the nation's armies, and eventually to be the pharaoh.

JOHN STEEL, ARTIST            © P. P. P. A.

1

their promised home. But the years had dragged on and the Israelites were still in Egypt. No longer could they live in peace as shepherds, for now they were bondservants who must obey the decrees of a heartless pharaoh.

Jacob's family had been only about seventy in number when they came to Egypt, but they had increased marvelously until they filled the land of Goshen. The king was afraid of these strong, clever foreigners. If they were not crushed, he was afraid they might someday possess all Egypt. Therefore, Pharaoh's soldiers were ordered to march into the homes of the Israelites and force the men to do slave labor, building temples and royal cities and toiling in the fields where wheat, barley, and flax were grown.

When the guards came for Amram, he left his house with a heavy heart. He and his wife Jochebed had two children,— a daughter, Miriam, and a younger son, Aaron,—but they were expecting another baby soon. The father was distressed, for he knew that Pharaoh had decreed that every son born to the Israelites should be thrown into the river where the hungry crocodiles swam. In this way the growth of the Israelites would be stopped and they would no longer be a danger to Egypt.

Amram went with a gang of slaves to the brickfields. Sweat poured from his aching body as he kneaded the mud, shaped the bricks, and laid them in the hot sun to dry. There was no rest for the Hebrews, for a guard stood over them with a whip ready to lash the back of any shirking workman. Some of the men were sick, and when a beating could not force them to work any longer, they were left to die. From the slaves went up a cry that Amram knew well. It was a prayer asking God to remember His people and deliver them from the tortures of their Egyptian masters.

Days and weeks dragged slowly by before Amram was allowed to return to his home. He hurried along the road, his mind troubled and perplexed. He longed to see his wife and children; but he dreaded to think of the evil news that might be waiting for him if the new baby was a boy!

2

It was night when he reached his home. As he entered the door, Jochebed ran to meet him, quickly whispering her secret in his ear. Yes, they had a new baby—a handsome son! She led her husband to the hiding place and showed him the chubby youngster, but the worried man scarcely glanced at his child. He knew that the soldiers would soon pound on the door, and he was powerless to stop them.

Now, Amram and Jochebed believed God's promises, and they prayed that the Lord would protect their baby. It was only a short time until Amram had to go back to his work, and the mother was left with Miriam and Aaron and the baby. The courage of Jochebed in the hour of desperation is a tribute to motherhood.

When the child was three months old, he cried so lustily that the mother knew she could no longer hide him in the house. She called her daughter, Miriam, and together they worked out a cunning plan. They took a basket made of reeds, covered it with tar and pitch so that it would be watertight, and set it in the sun to dry. As Jochebed went about her work in the house, she could not forget the basket in the yard. When she looked at it she wondered if it would be possible to save her little son in this strange way.

Early the next morning Miriam and her mother carried the basket to the Nile River and put it in the water. Jochebed watched breathlessly to see if it was watertight. The work had been well done and the snug boat-cradle remained dry. The girl ran back to the house and soon returned, carrying her baby brother in a blanket. Tenderly the mother tucked him into the basket and covered him snugly. Would she ever see her little son again? After praying for God's protection for her child, she bravely pushed the boat out among the tall papyrus grass and reeds where it rocked gently. Well she knew that if the basket floated into the strong current it might overturn.

Miriam sat down near the bank of the river to play and to watch the precious basket. Jochebed did not dare remain, for her presence might attract the soldiers.

3

## Moses Is Discovered

Then it happened! While Miriam was playing, the royal princess came down the path to bathe in the river. Before the princess reached the river's edge she stopped and pointed to something in the water. The basket had drifted into plain sight. Perhaps Pharaoh's daughter thought it was an idol that someone had set afloat in the river as a gift to the god of the Nile. She commanded one of her maids to bring the basket to her; and when she opened it, there was a baby crying! The princess took the child in her arms and rocked him gently. She knew that a desperate mother was attempting to save her baby's life in this strange way.

"This is one of the Hebrews' children," she said.

Now Miriam, who had been watching the princess, came close to her and asked, "Shall I go and call you a nurse from the Hebrew women to nurse the child for you?"

"Go," said Pharaoh's daughter, surmising that the child might bring the baby's mother to her.

So Miriam ran and told her mother all that had happened, and Jochebed hurried to the river and bowed before the king's daughter. The princess must have read the love in Jochebed's eyes, for she placed the baby in the woman's arms, saying, "Take this child away, and nurse him for me, and I will give you your wages."

Jochebed and Amram were thankful to God for His wonderful answer to their prayers. Now they were able to love and care for their own son under the protection of the royal family. But time was precious, for soon the child would be taken from them by the princess. Therefore, the mother spent many hours teaching her son about the true God who created the earth. During his formative years she told him of the pioneers, Abraham, Isaac, and Jacob, who had loved and obeyed the Lord. Over and over again the boy listened to the promise of how the Israelites would be delivered.

When the boy was about twelve years old, Jochebed took

The daughter of Pharaoh discovered baby Moses in the crude basket. She loved him and made him her own son.

JOHN STEEL, ARTIST     © P.P.P.A.

Prince Moses, a Hebrew, saw the task-masters beating his people, and he determined in his heart to save them.

JOHN STEEL, ARTIST                    © P. P. P. A.

her son to the palace, and the princess adopted him. She gave him an Egyptian name, Moses, "because," said the king's daughter, "I drew him out of the water."

A strange, wonderful world opened before Moses. Like Joseph, long before, this young man was suddenly honored in the royal court. Instead of dwelling in a small house, he now lived in a magnificent palace. Here were wonderful statues, rich paintings, and furniture of ivory and gold. Moses, clothed in fine linen garments embroidered in many colors, rode in the royal chariots. He learned to read and write under the guidance of the wisest teachers, and as he grew older he studied history, science, art, and music. He became a military man, carefully trained to lead the armies of the realm. Moses, the prince, educated in all the Egyptian culture, was in line to be ruler of the mighty kingdom of the Nile.

However, all the riches and splendor of the cities and temples of Egypt did not dazzle this youth. He refused to worship the many gods that were honored by the Egyptians; he never forgot his home, and what his parents had taught him concerning God, the Creator of the heavens and the earth. The degrading slavery of his people haunted him. He prayed that they might soon have their liberty, so that they could return to the Land of Promise. But what could he, a prince in the court of Pharaoh, do to help the Israelites gain their freedom? He had visions of being a mighty conqueror; and someday God would make his dreams come true, but in a way that Moses could scarcely have imagined.

One day when Prince Moses was about forty years of age, he made a tour of inspection among the projects that Pharaoh was having constructed by his slaves. He watched gangs of Hebrew slaves dragging huge blocks of stone into place. The torrid sun beat down upon the men and many cried for mercy. Moses went on his way with a sad heart, but he had not gone far when he came upon an Egyptian guard who was beating a slave unmercifully. Moses knew that the tortured man was one of his people, and he became very angry when he thought

of the many times his own father had been whipped while he
toiled for Pharaoh. Perhaps this is the time for me to rescue
my people, he said to himself.

### A Runaway Prince

Acting upon impulse, Moses jumped from his chariot and
grabbed the guard. The whimpering slave fled in terror when
he saw this royal officer attacking the Egyptian. The man with
the whip attempted to fight, but in fierce anger Moses struck
him and the guard fell to the ground. As the prince gazed
at the fallen Egyptian, he realized what he had done. The man
was dead! Moses looked in every direction to see if anyone
had seen him; but the beaten slave had disappeared, so he felt
safe. Quickly he dug a hole in the sand, buried the dead man,
and drove off in his chariot.

The next day, while he was riding through the land of
Goshen, Moses came upon two Israelites quarreling. He

7

stopped and spoke to the one who was hitting his comrade. "Why do you strike your fellow?" asked Moses.

The man who had struck his companion looked at Moses, and recognized him as Prince Moses. Then he replied, "Who made you a prince and a judge over us? Do you mean to kill me as you killed the Egyptian?"

When Moses heard these words, he was shocked. He hurried away, bewildered and panic-stricken. He realized that the news of the Egyptian guard's death had been told everywhere. Returning to the royal palace, he discovered that the account of the murder had reached the ears of Pharaoh and that the angry monarch was determined to take his life. It was whispered in the court that the prince was about to start a revolt and seize the throne. Moses now had to make a fateful choice. He might renounce his people, tell Pharaoh that he was sorry for his impetuous act, and take a permanent place with the Egyptians. In this way he could, perhaps, save himself. Or he could stand with the Israelites, give up his right to the throne, and run away from Egypt. He made his decision quickly. Faith in God's plan made him refuse "to be called the son of Pharaoh's daughter, choosing rather to share ill-treatment with the people of God than to enjoy the fleeting pleasures of sin."

Moses weighed the issues carefully, and that night, under the cover of darkness, he fled from the palace, crossed the Nile River in a boat, and made his way south along the coast of the Sinai Peninsula. The riches, the pleasures, and the glory of Egypt would never be his again.

Tired and hungry after weary days of travel, Moses stopped one afternoon at a well in the land of Midian, a part of the Arabian desert where mountain peaks formed a majestic backdrop. There were no cities and no cruel kings. Peace and quietness pervaded the landscape and God seemed very near. As Moses sat in the shade of a palm tree, he saw seven young women coming to the well with a flock of sheep. They drew water from the well and filled the troughs so that the animals

8

could drink; but some selfish shepherds, who wanted to water their flocks first, drove the sheep away. When Moses saw that the young women were not able to protect their flock, he gallantly came to their rescue and watered the sheep for them.

Returning to their home, the sisters told Jethro, their father, how they had been helped by a traveler. "An Egyptian delivered us out of the hand of the shepherds," they declared, "and even drew water for us and watered the flock."

"And where is he?" said Jethro, a priest of Midian, whose home was noted for its hospitality. "Why have you left the man? Call him, that he may eat bread."

Moses the exile gladly accepted the hospitality of this good man and thanked God for a place of refuge. The family welcomed the traveler, and Jethro offered Moses a home with them. In this way Moses became a sheepherder, living with the shepherds in that desert country.

### Moses Takes a Wife

The prince fell in love with Zipporah, one of Jethro's seven daughters, and the couple were married. For many years Moses was content to live in the desert, far from the threat of his Egyptian enemies. He who had once lived in a royal palace now camped in a little tent and moved from place to place to find pasture for his sheep. The poetic soul of Moses loved the quietness and beauty of the desert. Bare mountains lifted their scarred peaks, and jagged cliffs reflected the heat of the sun. Nature was serene and enduring. Away from the noise and amusements of the cities, this prince of Egypt learned to love God and to understand the wonders of His creation. Having been trained as a soldier, he now learned how to be humble and patient while tending sheep. News finally reached him, however, that Pharaoh had died and that another ruler was on the throne of Egypt. Once more the man thought of his people sweating and dying in the brickfields. Should he not share their suffering and help deliver them instead of hiding in the desert? The divine promises of deliver-

ance that his mother had repeated to him again and again came back from childhood memories.

One day Moses took the flocks to pasture land near Mount Horeb, or Sinai, the mountain he loved. Little did he dream that someday he would climb that peak and stand in the presence of God. On this day, the shepherd saw a bush that was blazing with fire; yet its trunk, branches, and leaves were not consumed. As the man watched the flames and wondered about this mystery, God called to him, "Moses, Moses!"

"Here am I," said he, startled by the voice in the desert.

"Do not come near," said the Lord; "put off your shoes from your feet, for the place on which you are standing is holy ground." It was the custom of that country for people to take off their shoes when they were in a sacred place in order to show reverence.

Moses realized that he was in the presence of God. Therefore, he took off his shoes, knelt down, and covered his face with his hands. Moses trembled as the Voice told him that his fellow countrymen in Egypt were to be set free. "Come, I will send you to Pharaoh that you may bring forth My people, the sons of Israel, out of Egypt," said the Lord.

But when Moses learned that God was choosing him to lead his people he was afraid. He had failed so dismally in his first attempt to set them free. Then, too, he remembered his enemies in the court of Egypt who might be waiting for him, even though the pharaoh who threatened to kill him was dead. Moses was aware of the almost insurmountable difficulties that stood in the way of delivering his people.

"Who am I that I should go to Pharaoh, and bring the sons of Israel out of Egypt?" asked Moses.

"I will be with you," God said, "and this shall be the sign for you, that I have sent you: when you have brought forth the people out of Egypt, you shall serve God upon this mountain."

Moses was filled with awe. Would his people someday live in this desert land free from bondage? He could see them now in thousands of tents, living peacefully in the desert

As Moses beheld the burning bush that was not consumed, he heard the voice of God plainly calling to him.

JOHN STEEL, ARTIST       © P. P. P. A.

11

When Moses and Aaron stood before Pharaoh, Aaron cast his staff on the floor and it became a serpent.

JOHN STEEL, ARTIST     © P. P. P. A.

valleys. But his thoughts returned to the stark reality of the task and he began to make excuses. He said, "But behold, they will not believe me."

The Lord said, "What is that in your hand?"

"A rod," Moses answered, looking at the gnarled stick of seasoned wood.

"Cast it on the ground."

Moses threw it on the ground, and it became a snake. The shepherd ran from it, but the Lord called to him, saying, "Put out your hand, and take it by the tail."

Moses caught the snake by the tail, and lo, it turned into a a staff. This was only one of the signs God gave Moses to encourage the man on his mission. He would use these wonders to prove to the Israelites that his message was from heaven.

Then the shepherd thought of another excuse—he was not a good speaker. But the Lord promised to aid him and give him Aaron's assistance. "I will be with your mouth and with his mouth, and will teach you what you shall do." In addition to encouraging Moses, the Lord told Aaron, the elder brother of Moses, to assist his brother as counselor and speaker.

Returning to the tents of Jethro, Moses told his father-in-law that he had decided to take his wife and two sons to Egypt.

"Go in peace," said Jethro to his son-in-law.

When Moses and his family journeyed toward Egypt, Aaron came out to welcome them. The brothers planned what they would say to Pharaoh, and how they would plan the deliverance of the Israelites. Then Moses and Aaron called the leaders of the people together and told them that the Lord was going to deliver them. Moses performed the wonderful signs that God had taught him, and when the leaders saw the strange wonders, they believed and rejoiced at the good news.

However, Moses was troubled. He must go to the court of Pharaoh and plead for the Israelites to be freed. Would the king listen to his request? Moses knew that he might be put in prison for having killed the Egyptian guard many years before, but he resolved to be true to his divine mission. With

Aaron at his side the shepherd who once walked through the court as a mighty prince now entered the royal palace to face the haughty monarch.

## Ten Plagues Strike Egypt

Pharaoh squinted at the two gray-bearded Hebrews as they walked the length of the stately halls of the palace between rows of soldiers. When they stood before his throne, the king gave them a scornful glance. They were slaves, he thought; why should he listen to them? Why were they not working in the brickfields?

When the visitors arose from bowing before the throne, Pharaoh was deeply impressed by their appearance. Strong and upright, Moses revealed in his face the patience and courage that had developed from long years in the desert. His eyes were keen and intelligent as he addressed the monarch in simple words, "Thus says the Lord, the God of Israel, 'Let

My people go, that they may hold a feast to Me in the wilderness.' "

The angry dictator shouted at the mild-mannered men, "Who is the Lord, that I should heed His voice and let Israel go? I do not know the Lord, and moreover I will not let Israel go."

Moses and Aaron repeated their request that the Israelites be allowed to go into the desert to offer sacrifices and to worship God. Once more Pharaoh refused, and as an excuse for denying their petition, he said, "Moses and Aaron, why do you take the people away from their work? Get to your burdens." He added, "Behold, the people of the land are now many and you make them rest from their burdens!"

If the Israelites were allowed to journey into the desert, the king was certain they would never return. He had tortured and beaten them for so many years that he was certain they would go on to Canaan if once they tasted freedom. When Moses and Aaron left the palace, Pharaoh wasted no time in commanding his guards to increase the tasks of the slaves. Straw, which was essential in making good bricks, was no longer to be supplied the brickmakers. The Israelites would now be forced to go out into the fields and find stubble. Yet in spite of this extra work, they would be required to make the same number of bricks each day. "Let heavier work be laid upon the men that they may labor at it and pay no regard to lying words," said Pharaoh.

Soon the Israelite foremen went to the king and complained, saying, "Why do you deal thus with your servants? No straw is given to your servants, yet they say to us, 'Make bricks!' And behold, your servants are beaten; but the fault is in your own people."

Pharaoh brushed aside this complaint. "You are idle, you are idle. . . . Go now, and work; for no straw shall be given you, yet you shall deliver the same number of bricks."

As the foremen walked down the palace steps they met Moses and Aaron. At once the thought flashed through their

minds that these two men must be the cause of all the trouble. To the leaders they said, "The Lord look upon you and judge, because you have made us offensive in the sight of Pharaoh and his servants, and have put a sword in their hand to kill us."

How easy it is to be misunderstood, especially when you are attempting to help others. Everything seemed to be against Moses. The king had refused his request, and now it seemed that the men of Israel had lost confidence in his leadership. In that dark hour Moses turned to God in prayer for help. An answer came and Moses received this wonderful promise: "Say therefore to the people of Israel, 'I am the Lord, and I will bring you out from under the burdens of the Egyptians, and I will deliver you from their bondage, and I will redeem you with an outstretched arm and with great acts of judgment, and I will take you for My people, and I will be your God; and you shall know that I am the Lord your God, who has brought you out from under the burdens of the Egyptians.' "

## A God-Defying Ruler

Pharaoh had said that the people could not leave Egypt, but the Lord had promised that they would be delivered. We shall watch this struggle between the will of the king of Egypt and the will of the God of heaven. We shall see how God punished the Egyptians for their defiance of the truth and their rejection of the God of heaven.

Once more Moses and Aaron entered the fabulous palace of the pharaoh. When they stood before the golden throne the king demanded that they show him a miracle, a work of magic. Aaron cast his wooden staff on the stone pavement and it became a snake, wriggling and turning as it attempted to crawl away. Amazed by this demonstration, Pharaoh called his magicians and commanded them to put on an equal performance. The men of magic threw their staffs down and they became like serpents; however, the snake that came from Aaron's staff swallowed all the others.

15

Pharaoh refused to see a sign of divine working in the miracle performed by Aaron. The true had been counterfeited by the imposters of Egypt; but the king could not see the difference, even as he refused to discern between good and evil. With a shout of defiance he dismissed Moses and Aaron, and warned them he would never allow the Israelites to leave.

Moses and Aaron made their way to the bank of the Nile River the next morning to meet the king, who went there each day to bathe and to worship the river-god. Moses told Pharaoh that because he had disobeyed God by refusing to let the children of Israel go, a plague would come upon the land. In the presence of the king and his courtiers Moses stretched out his staff, and the water of the Nile turned to blood. This was a calamity to the Egyptians, since they worshiped the river. The fish died, and the river became so foul that the people could get no water to drink except by digging shallow wells near the riverbank. Then, too, the water that was stored in pails and stone jars turned to blood. This plague lasted for seven days, but Pharaoh persisted in his refusal to allow the Israelites to go.

More fearful plagues came in rapid succession. Slimy frogs swarmed over the land, hopping into houses, into beds, into kitchens, and into the dishes of food. Since the Egyptians looked upon frogs as sacred creatures, the pests took possession of everything, even Pharaoh's palace. The king told Moses and Aaron that he would allow the Israelites to leave if only the frogs were removed. But when the frogs died, the king stubbornly refused to fulfill his promise.

Then came a plague which made the Egyptians most miserable. The dust of the ground turned to lice. The vermin crawled on the clothes, on the bodies, and in the hair of the people. The royal magicians could not duplicate this plague, and they said to Pharaoh, "This is the finger of God."

After that the air was filled with clouds of flies, and the land was ruined by them. In spite of all these calamities, Pharaoh refused to free the Israelites.

16

The next plague was a disease which struck the cattle, sheep, oxen, horses, and camels. Although the Egyptians lost much of their livestock, none of the animals belonging to the children of Israel were touched.

The sixth plague brought terrible suffering to the Egyptians. Boils and sores broke out on man and beast, and cries of pain were heard throughout the land.

Then "the Lord sent thunder and hail, and fire ran down to the earth." The hail destroyed many cattle in the field, and it broke down the barley and flax; it tore branches from trees and stripped them of their leaves. Egypt was a desert land where it seldom rained or hailed, and this storm was "such as had never been in all the land of Egypt since it became a nation." The land of Goshen, however, enjoyed sunshine and peace during this fury of nature.

A plague of locusts followed the storm. Great swarms of these insects covered the ground. The grain in the fields and the leaves on the trees that had not been ruined by the hail were eaten by the hungry horde. During all these plagues, though, Pharaoh stubbornly refused to allow the Israelites to leave. A loving God gave the ruler of Egypt striking evidences of divine power, but Pharaoh rejected all overtures of divine mercy.

Bare and desolate was the country when the next plague struck—a plague of fearful darkness. For three days it was so dark that the Egyptians could not see one another nor find their way about. But in the homes of the Israelites there was light.

Now Pharaoh summoned Moses and said, "Go, serve the Lord; your children also may go with you; only let your flocks and your herds remain behind." The shrewd ruler knew that if the people went away without their cattle and sheep, they would be forced to return to Egypt, for they could not make a long journey without them.

Moses refused this offer, firmly standing by his request that his people go with all their livestock and other possessions.

17

"Our cattle also must go with us; not a hoof shall be left behind," he declared. In great anger Pharaoh shouted, "Get away from me; take heed to yourself; never see my face again; for in the day you see my face you shall die."

"As you say!" said Moses. "I will not see your face again."

By this time Moses was the most-talked-about man in Egypt. The king was afraid of his power, and the people stood in awe of this leader who defied the king and overpowered their pagan gods. The Bible record declares that "the man Moses was very great in the land of Egypt, in the sight of Pharaoh's servants and in the sight of the people."

Yet one more plague would fall upon the rebellious nation. It would bring more terrible results than all the nine plagues that had already punished Egypt.

# The Passover Feast

*Exodus 11 to 17:7*

chapter 2 &

THE plagues that fell upon the land of Egypt did not touch the children of Israel. With amazement these protected people watched from their houses. Pestilence, disease, storm, and darkness struck the rebellious nation and the Egyptians were humbled by fearful punishment.

Finally Moses called the leaders of the families and announced that God was ready to deliver His people. At once the Israelites made secret preparations for their journey. They received presents from the Egyptians, gifts of gold and silver, as well as of jewels and clothing. The people seemed anxious to reward the Israelites for their long years of slave labor.

That evening at sundown a special dinner was prepared in every house in Goshen. The father of each family had killed a lamb; and while the mother prepared and roasted it, the head of the house had smeared some of the animal's blood on the doorposts and on the lintel over the door with a brush made of herbs called hyssop. The children looked on with interest and they asked the meaning of the ceremony. The father told them that it was a sign on the house that the family had obeyed God's commands and the death angel would "pass over" and spare the family from the terrible plague of death that would strike Egypt.

Night settled down on the homes of the Israelites, and the

people stayed in their houses. It was the hour for each family to eat the Passover Feast. The father and mother gathered their children about the table. Dressed for travel, the family stood while they ate the roast lamb and the bread made without yeast. With the meat and bread they ate bitter herbs, or greens.

Thus the first Passover supper was celebrated to commemorate the wonderful deliverance that was soon to take place. Henceforth the Passover Feast was to be celebrated every year, for God said, "This day shall be for you a memorial day, and you shall keep it as a feast to the Lord; throughout your generations you shall observe it as an ordinance forever." The Jewish people continue to observe the Passover supper in honor of the Exodus, God's signal deliverance of His people.

The patriarchs—Adam, Abraham, Isaac, and Jacob—had offered sacrifices on altars to show their faith in the promise of a coming Saviour. In like manner the Passover lamb pointed to the time when Jesus Christ, "the Lamb of God," would die, to save His people from sin. The Israelites ate bitter herbs that symbolized the bitter years of suffering in Egypt.

## A Night of Terror

When midnight came, an anguished cry was heard in the land of Egypt. From Pharaoh's palace to the humblest dwelling there was weeping and mourning for the dead. The eldest child, or the first-born in every family, "from the first-born of Pharaoh who sat on his throne to the first-born of the captive who was in the dungeon," as well as "the first-born of the cattle," was struck down by the angel of death. However, there was peace and safety among the families of Israel, for the blood had been sprinkled on the doors of their homes.

Messengers from Pharaoh's palace hurried through the darkness to find Moses and Aaron. The king was determined the Israelites should leave the country before morning. When the leaders appeared before the king, he spoke in a trembling whisper, "Rise up, go forth from among my people, both you

The eldest child, or "first-born," was struck down throughout Egypt, and the royal son was among the dead.

JOHN STEEL, ARTIST                    © P. P. P. A.

and the people of Israel; and go, serve the Lord, as you have said. Take your flocks and your herds, as you have said, and be gone; and bless me also!"

## *Pharaoh Bows to God's Will*

At last the haughty ruler was willing to bow to the divine plan. He knew that all the plagues had come upon his people because of his stubborn refusal to obey the Lord, and his guilt stabbed his heart as he looked at his dead son—murdered by the king's folly.

The message flashed to every family in Israel to start on the journey. Families left their houses so quickly that the women had to snatch up the dough from the bread troughs without baking it into bread. Men and women, boys and girls, hurried down the road in the darkness. Flocks of sheep and herds of cattle were driven from pasture.

In all the excitement of leaving Egypt one important duty was not overlooked. Moses commanded that men carry the coffin containing the mummy of Joseph. It was to be taken to Canaan, the land of his birth. Almost one hundred fifty years before, Joseph had said, "God will visit you, and you shall carry up my bones from here." The faith of this patriarch was rewarded, for his people were going back to the homeland as God had promised!

Six hundred thousand men, besides the women and children, marched out of Egypt. With this cavalcade went huge flocks and herds, which had increased during the years of farming in Goshen. Some of the Egyptians went along, for they were aware of how God had prospered Israel, and they wanted to share in the blessings.

The endless caravan moved south along the edge of the desert for several days until it came to the shores of the Red Sea. Here the people stopped to rest, and here they saw a great cloud of dust rolling up on the horizon from the way they had come. The afternoon sunlight gleamed on chariots and upon the armor of advancing soldiers.

The army of Egypt under the leadership of Pharaoh was coming after them! There was no way of escape, for mountains loomed up on the right and on the left, and in front of them was the Red Sea. Angry voices shouted at Moses, saying, "Is it because there are no graves in Egypt that you have taken us away to die in the wilderness? What have you done to us, in bringing us out of Egypt?" Like the children they were, the Israelites quickly forgot God's promises and His power to deliver them from danger and death.

The dauntless, patient Moses listened to the cry of the frightened thousands, and in that moment courage welled up in his heart. He knew that God would save them. "Fear not, stand firm, and see the salvation of the Lord, which He will work for you today," he said boldly. Then he added, "The Lord will fight for you, and you have only to be still."

Darkness now fell on the terror-stricken camp, and a dense cloud came between the escaping multitude and the enemy army, hiding the Israelites from their pursuers. Moses stretched out his hand over the Red Sea, and a wonderful thing happened in the night!

## *Water for the Thirsty*

Let us go back to the morning after the last plague had struck the land of the Nile and the Egyptians faced tragedy. Their country had been ruined by hail and storm; many of their cattle had been destroyed; and now, there were mourning and preparations for the funeral of the first-born in every home.

Sorrow is soon forgotten, especially when wealth is involved in the loss. As soon as the dead were buried, the people missed their slaves and wished that they had them back to do their work. About this time Pharaoh received messages from his deputies that the children of Israel were marching farther and farther from Egypt. If he did not act at once, they would escape from his clutches forever. The king called his chief officers together. When they heard the news, they said, "What is this we have done, that we have let Israel go from serving us?"

23

Pharaoh summoned his generals, and they quickly marshaled the infantry, cavalry, and six hundred chariots. Commands were shouted and trumpet blasts echoed across the fields as the army started in pursuit of the helpless Israelites.

In the afternoon Pharaoh gave a shout of triumph as he rode ahead of the army in his royal chariot. In the distance, by the shores of the Red Sea, he saw the camp of the Hebrews. Soon we will have our slaves again, he thought. They can go no farther; they will not escape my prowess.

However, as the chariots and cavalry neared the camp, the cloud settled over the land, and the army was forced to stop for the night.

Now, when Moses had stretched his hand over the Red Sea, God caused a strong east wind to blow all night. The waters of the sea were divided, and they formed a wall on the right and on the left. Between there was dry land. During the night the Israelites marched forward and reached the farther shore of the Red Sea before dawn.

The Egyptian guards gave the alarm when it was light enough to see what was happening. The slaves were escaping through a wonderful path in the sea! Trumpets were blown and the soldiers, with the horses and chariots, rushed forward to attack. But soon the heavy chariots bogged down in the soft ground, and although the horses pulled and tugged, they could not move ahead.

As the sun arose, Moses saw the Egyptian army stalled in the bed of the sea. He stretched forth his hand over the sea, and giant waves unleashed their fury and covered the chariots. Pharaoh and his army were swept to destruction!

Here was complete victory for God's people. The tired and frightened travelers had seen their fierce enemies destroyed before their eyes. Now they would never need to return to Egypt as slaves. In this moment of crisis, faith triumphed and the Israelites obeyed God's command, "Go forward." We may not see the way open before us, but as we trust divine leadership obstacles will disappear.

24

During the night the Israelites marched through the bed of the Red Sea, and reached the farther shore before dawn broke.

JOHN STEEL, ARTIST                    © P.P.P.A.

Moses led the throng in a triumphant song of victory, while his sister Miriam took a tambourine and all the women of the camp followed her, playing on their tambourines and dancing. They sang and praised God who had saved them:

"I will sing to the Lord, for He has triumphed gloriously;
    the horse and his rider He has thrown into the sea.
The Lord is my strength and my song,
    and He has become my salvation;
this is my God, and I will praise Him,
    my father's God, and I will exalt Him.
The Lord is a man of war;
    the Lord is His name.
Pharaoh's chariots and his host He cast into the sea;
    and his picked officers are sunk in the Red Sea.
The floods cover them;
    they went down into the depths like a stone."

Leaving the Red Sea, the Israelites marched forward through the wilderness of Shur, not far from the sandy shores of the Red Sea. For a time they forgot the heat of the sun and the dry, burning sand. They were happy to be free from their slave masters, and they thanked God for delivering them. God's kindly providence caused a great cloud to hover over the caravan by day to shelter it from the fierce heat, and a cloud of fire to glow above the camp at night to give light. The people knew they were on the right way because the pillar of cloud always moved ahead of them, directing their course.

For three days the men, women, and children marched. They found no streams in the desert, but they did not worry, for they carried fresh water in goatskin bottles. In that dry country, however, the water supply was soon exhausted, and the travelers began to grumble and complain. Moses, who had traveled through this wilderness, when he was herding sheep in Midian, knew that they were nearing Marah, where there were springs of water; but his heart sank as he remembered that the water from those springs was bitter, unfit for man or beast to drink.

A shout of joy went up from the people when they saw the

water pouring over the rocks. The men, women, and children ran forward to quench their thirst, but their cries of disappointment soon arose above the shouts. Then the multitude turned on Moses, saying, "What shall we drink?" The Lord showed Moses a tree and directed him to throw it into the water. When this was done, the bitter water became sweet. Then the people and the flocks and herds drank.

While the Israelites rested, Moses talked to them about obeying God and following His commands. Some of the vast multitude wanted to do as they pleased. They did not realize that organization and co-operation were essential if this nation was to arrive safely at the promised home in Canaan.

## The Rock Gives Forth Water

The next stop on their journey was Elim, where there were twelve springs of water and seventy palm trees. Soon the pillar of cloud moved ahead, and the Israelites took up the march again. By this time the people had been on the road for more than a month. Their supply of food was low, and as they looked across the rough, barren country, they knew that they would not find anything to eat in this wasteland. Once more they began to grumble, and soon they came to Moses and Aaron with their troubles.

"Would that we had died by the hand of the Lord in the land of Egypt, when we sat by the fleshpots and ate bread to the full," the Israelites said to them; "for you have brought us out into this wilderness to kill this whole assembly with hunger."

Poor Moses! Here were thousands of his kinsmen who had suffered under the whip of Egyptian taskmasters. They had won their freedom, but now they longed to be back in Egypt as slaves! The patient leader might have scolded them, but again he turned to God for help, and the Lord promised food for the hungry throng. That evening flocks of quail flew into the camp, and there were enough to supply the people with an abundance of food. However, the next morning when the

27

Israelites arose, they found the ground covered with small white objects that looked like seeds.

"What is it?" they asked.

Moses said, "It is the bread which the Lord has given you to eat. This is what the Lord has commanded: 'Gather of it, every man of you, as much as he can eat; you shall take an omer apiece, according to the number of the persons whom each of you has in his tent.'" It would appear six mornings in the week, and each family should gather its share. On the sixth day they were to gather twice as much, for none would appear on the seventh day, the Sabbath.

Fathers and mothers, boys and girls, picked up the strange flakelike food, and they called it "manna." The women ground it into flour and made cakes and baked them. It tasted like wafers made with honey.

Although the people were instructed to gather only enough manna for one day, some persons were selfish. They did not have faith to believe it would come every day, so they gathered more. It was useless to attempt to hoard this food, for in the warm weather it spoiled and had to be thrown away. Yet when the people kept a double supply for the Sabbath, as God commanded, the manna remained fresh and good to eat.

The caravan moved on southeastward and came to Rephidim, a dry, rocky spot in the desert. Here there was no water, and again the people surrounded Moses, shouting, "Give us water to drink."

In his distress Moses cried to the Lord, "What shall I do with this people?" And God told Moses exactly what he was to do.

The patient leader took some of the chief men with him to the hot, bare rocks of Horeb. The thirsty people watched, and some of them probably sneered. Did they think they could get water out of these hot, dry rocks? What were these men going to do? As Moses went forward he thought of the days when he had herded sheep in this desert; he remembered God's promise at the burning bush. When he came to the hot, dry

When the Israelites arose and went outside their tents, they found white objects like seeds. It was manna.

JOE MANISCALCO, ARTIST     © P. P. P. A.

rocks he lifted his rod—the one he had used to turn the water of the Nile into blood—and struck a blow. Instantly a torrent of cold, sparkling water gushed out and flowed down the slope. The thirsty Israelites rushed forward to drink, while Moses offered thanks to God for His love and kindness.

Soon scouts came hurrying to Moses with bad news. A fierce tribe from the desert was coming out to fight against Israel. The Amalekites, cruel, savage warriors, were already attacking some of the camp stragglers. Moses knew that his people were not ready for battle, since they had been slaves, not soldiers. But the military training of Egypt came back to the valiant leader and he commanded his men to prepare for battle. He must hurriedly give them instructions in warfare and send them forth to conquer the enemy before the camp of Israel was attacked and defeated.

# The Law Is Given From Mount Sinai

*Exodus 17:8 to 20:17*

chapter 3 ❧

MOSES picked a man named Joshua, a young and courageous man who could be trusted, to command the army. When the news came that the fierce warriors of Chief Amalek were coming to attack the camp, Moses gave this instruction to Joshua: "Choose for us men, and go out, fight with Amalek; tomorrow I will stand on the top of the hill with the rod of God in my hand."

Joshua gathered young men who could fight, and he supplied them weapons. Probably they were equipped with swords and spears, or javelins, such as the Egyptians used. When the soldiers had been drilled, Joshua led them forward into the desert to find the Amalekites.

While the army of Israel advanced, Moses, Aaron, and Hur climbed the hill to watch the battle. Soon the two armies clashed and there was hand-to-hand fighting. Whenever Moses held up his hand, Joshua and his valiant band of warriors were able to win. When Moses let his hand down, the Amalekites won. After a time Moses grew tired, so Aaron and Hur had him sit on a large, flat rock while they stood beside him and held up his hands. At sunset the army of Israel was victorious and the Amalekites were routed.

It was while the caravan was camped near Rephidim that Moses welcomed a group of visitors to his tent. It was his wife,

31

who, with the children, had sometime previously returned to her home. Now she arrived with the two sons and Jethro, her father. Jethro, who lived in the desert, had heard of the wonderful deliverance of Israel from Egypt, and he was anxious to see the people that were destined to settle the land of Canaan. Moses greeted his family and told them how God had saved the nation at the Red Sea.

The next day Jethro watched Moses hold court for the camp. The people came with their petty problems and complained like spoiled children. During the long session Moses listened to requests and complaints.

"What is this that you are doing for the people? Why do you sit alone, and all the people stand about you from morning till evening?" asked Jethro, after he had seen how Moses was burdened.

"Because the people come to me to inquire of God," said Moses to his father-in-law.

"What you are doing is not good," said Moses' father-in-law to him. "You and the people with you will wear yourselves out, for the thing is too heavy for you; you are not able to perform it alone."

Then Jethro advised Moses to adopt a plan of organization whereby captains would be placed over groups of thousands, hundreds, fifties, and tens. These men would act as judges in all the smaller matters. Only the most serious difficulties would come to Moses for decision. The plan was accepted by Moses, and he chose wise men to assist him. After Jethro had seen the plan functioning properly, he said good-by to Moses and his family and returned to his home in Midian.

About three months after leaving Egypt, the cavalcade of Israel, with wagons, flocks, and herds, arrived at the plains near Mount Sinai. This made an ideal campsite for the thousands and thousands of people. Here they could rest after weary days of march. Lofty, rugged peaks towered above them, the mighty sentinels of nature. By day the pillar of cloud hovered over the camp, and at night the cloud of fire gave

protection. While the people slept, the manna, or bread from heaven, fell gently about the camp.

Soon after the nation had settled on the plain, Moses was commanded to climb the steep, rocky trail up the side of Mount Sinai to receive a divine message. The Lord said to Moses, "Now therefore, if you will obey My voice and keep My covenant, you shall be My own possession among all peoples; for all the earth is Mine, and you shall be to Me a kingdom of priests and a holy nation. These are the words which you shall speak to the children of Israel."

When Moses came down from the mountain and told the people what God had commanded, they answered, "All that the Lord has spoken we will do."

A momentous command was issued by Moses. The Israelites were to prepare for a very special occasion. They were to wash themselves and their clothes and be alert, for God was going to speak to the entire nation from the mountain.

### *The Voice of God*

On the third day the men, women, and children looked toward Mount Sinai. The top was covered with a black cloud which swept down the mountainside until it enveloped the great peak. At that moment one of Moses' assistants sounded the trumpet, and the people marched forward to the base of the mountain. From the cloud flashed lightning, followed by thunder crashes which echoed across the plain. The people were terribly frightened and fell to the ground.

Then there was silence. A hush fell upon the vast multitude. The voice of God was heard. In this solemn setting He spoke the Ten Commandments so that every person could hear. What a thrilling day when an entire nation heard God speak the eternal law!

The Ten Commandments are rules of conduct for all ages. They do not apply to one race or one nation; they are not obsolete, old-fashioned or impractical. An English magazine offered a prize for the best new set of "ten commandments." When all the entries had been read by the editor, he confessed that the divine law had all the advantage. There could be no improvement.

Ethics and education are not substitutes for God's law. A noted newspaper correspondent and author once stood on lofty Mount Sinai and surveyed the desert below. Then he penned these words: "Day after day, in this mountain air of crystalline clearness, from heights where one may see fierce and blinding sandstorms raging on the desert below, I have pondered the basic problems of this, our time. With all the honesty of soul I possess I have sought to see straight into the causes and character of conditions I can call to mind."

After reviewing the turbulent state of the world, the lack of moral standards, the upsurge of crime, he says, "Here is the answer to every question. Things have gone wrong because nations and people have departed from this law. They will never go right until nations and people have the clarity of

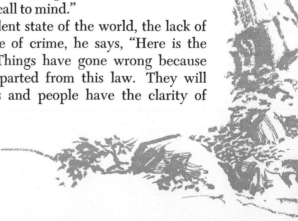

vision and the courage to return to the keeping of the Ten Words spoken on Sinai."

## *The Law in the Heart*

Take the law of God from the hearts of men and we would have savages. There would be no allegiance to a higher being; there would be no regard for the laws of nation or community. Obedience and loyalty to the Ten Commandments help to bring peace and happiness into the home.

The Ten Commandments are divided into two sections. The first four concern man's religious duties and his relationship to God. The last six concern moral duties of man to his fellow men. Jesus Christ summed up the law in this beautiful statement, "Thou shalt love the Lord thy God with all thy heart, and with all thy soul, and with all thy mind. This is the first and great commandment. And the second is like unto it, Thou shalt love thy neighbor as thyself." Matthew 22:37-39.

Consider briefly each commandment as it relates to modern life. The first command declares, "Thou shalt have no other gods before Me."

The instinct to worship something is found in human nature. Western nations pride themselves on a way of life free from idol worship and pagan practices. Yet many a person is guilty of cherishing a second god that steals away the heart and turns him from the worship of the Eternal One. There are gods of stocks and bonds, of houses and lands, of dress and appetite, of fame and position. Can we like Martin Luther stand before the material treasures of life and say, "I obey One greater than all of you"?

The second commandment says, "Thou shalt not make unto thee any graven image, or any likeness of anything that is in heaven above, or that is in the earth beneath, or that is in the water under the earth: thou shalt not bow down thyself to them, nor serve them: for I the Lord thy God am a jealous God, visiting the iniquity of the fathers upon the children unto the third and fourth generation of them that hate Me; and

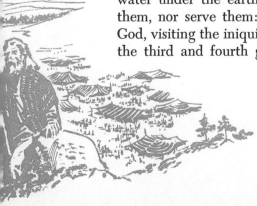

35

showing mercy unto thousands of them that love Me, and keep My commandments."

When we worship the Creator of the universe, the eternal, all-powerful God, we cannot liken Him to images or any human handicraft. "God is a Spirit: and they that worship Him must worship Him in spirit and in truth." John 4:24. Genuine worship is more than forms and ceremonies. Our heavenly Father is so near to us that He can hear and answer our whispered prayer. He never slumbers or sleeps, and His ear is open to the cry of His children. Yes, He is ready to guide us, to bring comfort and peace to our restless hearts if we will only call on Him.

The third commandment states, "Thou shalt not take the name of the Lord thy God in vain; for the Lord will not hold him guiltless that taketh His name in vain."

Cursing and swearing are a foolish person's way of seeking to gain attention and to impress others. Lord Byron described an acquaintance in this way: "He knew not what to say, so he swore." Such language betrays low thoughts and cheap ideals. Taking God's name in a vile oath is an indication that the swearer has no respect or reverence for God or for his fellow men who are God's creatures. It is possible for a Christian to "take the name of the Lord" in vain by professing to follow the Master, Jesus Christ, but denying Him by going on in a deliberate way of sin. We can be Christians in name, but pagans at heart. To be a Christian means that we accept the most sacred privilege offered to humanity—to be a member of God's family.

### The Blessing of the Sabbath

The fourth commandment reads, "Remember the Sabbath day, to keep it holy. Six days shalt thou labor, and do all thy work: but the seventh day is the Sabbath of the Lord thy God: in it thou shalt not do any work, thou, nor thy son, nor thy daughter, thy manservant, nor thy maidservant, nor thy cattle, nor thy stranger that is within thy gates: for in six

days the Lord made heaven and earth, the sea, and all that in them is, and rested the seventh day: wherefore the Lord blessed the Sabbath day, and hallowed it."

The Sabbath is a divine memorial for man to enjoy. Man is to honor the Sabbath and keep it holy, for in so doing he demonstrates his love and loyalty to God. The Sabbath is a sign of the covenant between God and His people. Ezekiel 20:12, 20. The seventh day of the week became the Sabbath because it was the day following the completion of this world. After six days of divine creation, God said the work was finished, and He rested on the Sabbath. This day has a spiritual blessing for mankind. Dwight L. Moody said, "I believe that the Sabbath question today is a vital one for the whole country. It is the burning question of the present time. If you give up the Sabbath the church goes; if you give up the church the home goes; and if the home goes the nation goes."

The Sabbath is a time for physical and mental refreshment after the whirl of a busy week. There is a blessing in work, but there must also be a time to rest—a day for worship and meditation. The Sabbath is to be kept holy. It is not a time to loaf or indulge in amusements and selfish pleasure. It is to be a "delight," a time when we gain the true perspective of life. Why are we here? Where are we going? Is God close to me in my business and in my home? Have I neglected to worship and walk with God? These and a multitude of other vital questions can be answered when we make the Sabbath a day of worship. This is the only commandment which calls men to "remember." Have we forgotten God by disregarding the seventh-day Sabbath?

### Love to Our Fellow Men

The last six commandments set forth man's relation to his brother man. Certainly the fifth commandment is needed today, for we read, "Honor thy father and thy mother: that thy days may be long upon the land which the Lord thy God giveth thee."

This injunction calls for sons and daughters to honor, respect, and obey their parents. How much of the delinquency of youth could be averted if all American homes were founded on this relationship. Lack of respect for parental authority leads to disregard for human laws and irreverence for God.

For parents to be honored, they must be honorable. If they are to receive obedience from the children, they must be worthy of it. The character of the father and mother must be sound for the son and daughter to respect them. A drunken father deserves little honor from anyone. A mother who thinks more of her bridge parties or of earning money outside the home so she can have added frills—all to the neglect of her children—may soon find that she has failed in her greatest privilege, that of training sons and daughters as good citizens and preparing them for God's kingdom.

The remarkable Compton family, whose sons and daughter have served humanity as leaders in fields of education, research, and social work, had a faithful mother who took her responsibility seriously. In revealing the secret of success in her family, she said, "I started each day with prayer, and trained my children with the Bible and common sense." What a splendid prescription to keep the American family spiritually healthy today!

Life, the most precious earthly possession, was given to man by the Creator. To protect the human race from those who would destroy it, God commands, "Thou shalt not kill." This law forbids the direct taking of life, and it also has a broader application. It forbids the indirect taking of life. Our body is the temple of God, and we should do nothing, by intemperate living, eating, or drinking, to destroy it. No habit that injures this body or impairs thought or action should be indulged in by a Christian. He should be "temperate in all things."

God also looks at the motives in our hearts. The Master, Jesus Christ, pointed out that anger and hatred are the beginning of murder. The apostle John declared, "Whosoever hateth

The character of the father and mother must be sound for the son and daughter to have respect for them.

39

his brother is a murderer: and ye know that no murderer hath eternal life abiding in him." 1 John 3:15.

Love puts the law into action in a positive way. "Thou shalt love thy neighbor as thyself" takes away all jealousy, hatred, envy, and malice—the seeds of murder.

"Thou shalt not commit adultery." Exodus 20:14. This divine law calls for purity of life and purity of thought. Marriage is of divine origin, for God said, "It is not good that the man should be alone; I will make him an help meet for him." Genesis 2:18. The first wedding was conducted in the Garden of Eden when Eve was brought to Adam and she became his wife. Jesus Christ placed His sanction upon marriage, declaring that the two "shall be one flesh."

When man fails in his moral responsibility he breaks this commandment. A man or woman is untrue to the marriage vows, and the home is wrecked by divorce, while children are left bewildered without parental care and security.

Immorality usually begins with impure thoughts. Jesus Christ recognized this when He said, "Whosoever looketh on a woman to lust after her hath committed adultery with her already in his heart." Matthew 5:28. Those who would be pure must make a covenant with their eyes and with their thoughts. In a day when our literature, motion pictures, television, and radio feature the cheap and suggestive which lead to moral decadence, the Christian holds to the standards of God's word and heeds the standard of the apostle Paul, "Let this mind be in you, which was also in Christ Jesus." Philippians 2:5.

## Robbing Man and God

"Thou shalt not steal." In these four words are summed up the basic right of private property. It has been truthfully said that in most cases the possession of property is "the proof of merit." Some people have questioned why there are those who amass riches while others live in the slums. Social inequality is often unjust and poverty is a tragedy; but our world would

The family that builds upon the truths of the Bible will be able to withstand the doubts of our times.

4—H.F. 2

soon be chaos and there would be no peace or security if men did not obey this commandment.

We may not steal money or drive off in another person's automobile; but we can break this law by shady business dealings, by not giving our employer an honest day of work, or by robbing God of the tenth (the tithe) we should give Him. There are so-called "good citizens" who think it clever to cheat in their income taxes or to pad their accounts when dealing with the government. True, they are breaking the law; but, worst of all, they are smashing their character for a few tainted dollars.

There are thieves of reputation—those who steal the good character of another person through slander and gossip. The virtue of honesty is to be cultivated in all its forms. If we love our fellow men we will be honest with them in every experience of life.

"Thou shalt not bear false witness against thy neighbor." The ninth commandment upholds the judicial system and forbids perjury in court. Truthtelling is not popular, for many people pride themselves on twisting the truth. Lying had its origin before this world was created, for we read that Satan "is a liar, and the father of it." John 8:44.

Reputations may be murdered by vitriolic tongues, or they may be injured by silence when we have it in our power to defend a person against evil accusations. This commandment is a warning for us to speak "the truth in love," and to control our tongues from all evil speaking.

"Thou shalt not covet thy neighbor's house, thou shalt not covet thy neighbor's wife, nor his manservant, nor his maidservant, nor his ox, nor his ass, nor anything that is thy neighbor's."

To covet means to delight in and to desire to possess something that does not belong to you and that you could obtain only by breaking the law. This commandment differs from the other nine in that it deals with the inner life, where good and evil begins in a person. When the desire has been created in the mind, a person must break another commandment to get the thing he covets. It has been said that this sin leads to all other sins.

This commandment is the acid test of our spiritual life. It strikes at our heart. Is it for God or only for self? The sin of covetousness has destroyed many a Christian. In our world of materialism, when there are so many "things" to be desired, we have the temptation constantly. Jesus Christ said, "Take heed, and beware of covetousness: for a man's life consisteth not in the abundance of the things which he possesseth." Luke 12:15.

The eternal law of God is given as the standard of our relations between our Maker and our fellow beings. The Ten Commandments are beacons to guide us to a happy way of life, a way of peace and security. The psalmist was right when he said, "Great peace have they which love Thy law: and nothing shall offend them." Psalm 119:165.

# Building a Church in the Desert

*Exodus 20:18 to Leviticus 16*

chapter 4 &

GOD had finished speaking, and the frightened people moved back from the mountain. "Do not fear," said Moses to the people, "for God has come to prove you, and that the fear of Him may be before your eyes, that you may not sin."

Once more Moses was commanded to climb to the summit of Mount Sinai, but this time he took Joshua, the leader of the army, with him. Aaron, the brother of Moses, and Hur were left in charge of the camp. Days and weeks passed, and finally the waiting throngs said impatiently, "We do not know what has become of him."

The Israelites grew more and more restless. They wanted to have a celebration. When Moses had been gone almost forty days, the people came to Aaron with their plan. Instead of obeying instructions, Aaron listened to the grumbling throng who had forgotten God, and his tragic mistake cost the lives of thousands of people.

As the children of Israel gathered around Aaron, they shouted, "Up, make us gods, who shall go before us; as for this Moses, the man who brought us up out of the land of Egypt, we do not know what has become of him."

Aaron, who was in charge of the camp while his brother was away, should have stood for the right as he knew it. But

The Israelites offered sacrifices
to the golden calf, and they danced
and feasted in a heathenish manner.

45

he was afraid of the impatient crowd. Finally Aaron said, "Take off the rings of gold which are in the ears of your wives, your sons, and your daughters, and bring them to me." The people soon brought jewelry and heaped it in a pile. Ornaments of gold, which had been brought from Egypt, were given to make the idol.

Taking the trinkets, Aaron threw them into a pot and melted the gold. Then he poured the metal into a mold and made an idol in the shape of a calf. The Israelites were happy when they saw this gold image, for it reminded them of the sacred cow, one of the gods of Egypt.

"These are your gods, O Israel, who brought you up out of the land of Egypt!" shouted the people as they bowed before the idol. When Aaron saw this demonstration, he commanded that an altar be built in front of the golden image. Then he announced, "Tomorrow shall be a feast to the Lord."

The next morning the people flocked to the scene of festivity to offer sacrifices to the gold idol and to dance before it. Afterward they sat down at a merry feast to eat and drink.

During this pagan feast, Moses was talking with God on Mount Sinai. The leader had received the Ten Commandments engraved on two tablets of stone. He did not know what was happening in the camp of Israel until God, who sees all that men do, told him of the terrible sin. The Lord gave this command to Moses, "Go down; for your people, whom you brought up out of the land of Egypt, have corrupted themselves; they have turned aside quickly out of the way which I commanded them."

Holding the sacred stone tablets with great care, Moses made his way down the steep mountain trail. Joshua guided the steps of the aged leader along the treacherous path. Once the two men stopped where they could see the camp spread out upon the broad plain. Joshua listened to the noise coming from the throng of Israelites, and he said, "There is a noise of war in the camp." As the leader of the army, he was afraid that an enemy might have attacked his people.

46

But Moses replied, "It is not the sound of shouting for victory, or the sound of the cry of defeat, but the sound of singing that I hear."

## The Sin of Idol Worship

The two men quickened their steps and soon came in full view of the camp. When Moses saw the people dancing and singing about the golden idol, he could scarcely believe his eyes. In righteous indignation he threw the tablets of the Ten Commandments onto the ground, where they smashed to bits. When the people saw what Moses had done, they stopped singing and dancing. A solemn hush settled over the crowd as Moses marched forward with angry countenance and seized the golden idol. Before anyone dared to protest, he threw it into the fire. Then he had the gold ground into powder and thrown into the water. Moses sternly commanded the people to drink it.

Moses called his brother Aaron to him and asked, "What did this people do to you that you have brought a great sin upon them?"

Aaron tried vainly to excuse himself by saying that the people had forced him to melt the gold. He declared that he had thrown the gold into the fire, and, behold, this strange idol had come forth!

Here was flagrant rebellion against God. Israel had promised to keep God's law, and the first and second commandments declare, "You shall have no other gods before Me. You shall not make yourself a graven image, or any likeness of anything that is in heaven above, or that is in the earth beneath, or that is in the water under the earth; you shall not bow down to them or serve them."

Standing before the camp, Moses shouted for all the people who were on God's side to join him. Most of the people repented of their sin, and they came to their leader with humble hearts; but three thousand of the idol worshipers refused to admit that they had done wrong. Then Moses said to the sons

47

of Levi, the tribe that had not worshiped the golden idol, "Put every man his sword on his side, and go to and fro from gate to gate throughout the camp, and slay every man his brother, and every man his companion, and every man his neighbor." Then the sons of Levi slew some three thousand people because they refused to repent of their wrong.

The next morning Moses said to the people, "You have sinned a great sin. And now I will go up to the Lord; perhaps I can make atonement for your sin." The courageous leader loved the children of Israel. He had given up the opportunity to reign as pharaoh of Egypt in order to lead them out of slavery. He had prayed to the Lord many times for the nation's protection, but now he must kneel and plead that the people be saved from destruction.

Moses turned to the Lord and said, "Alas, this people have sinned a great sin; they have made for themselves gods of gold. But now, if Thou wilt forgive their sin—and if not, blot me, I pray Thee, out of Thy book which Thou hast written."

Here is a wonderful prayer of intercession! Moses was willing to give up the promised reward if he could not share it with his people. When God saw the unselfish devotion of this devoted leader, He forgave the nation's sin.

Soon God told Moses to carve two tablets of stone like those he had thrown upon the ground and broken. He was to bring these new stone tablets to the top of the mountain. Once more Moses remained away from camp for forty days, and during this time the Ten Commandments, engraved in stone, were given to him a second time.

When Moses descended from the mountain with the law, his face glowed, because he had been in the presence of the Lord. When the people in the camp saw the glow on the face of Moses, they honored him and repeated the promise to obey God's law.

Then Moses told the congregation of the plan to build a tent of meeting, or sanctuary, where all the people could worship the God of heaven. Everyone was asked to bring gifts.

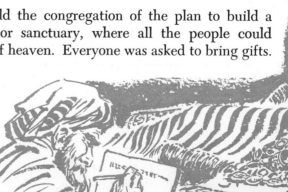

## *Building the Sanctuary*

There was excitement in the camp of the Israelites. Women were searching for little boxes and leather bags in which they kept their treasured gold pins, rings, and necklaces. They were searching for the most precious jewels they possessed. Some of their ornaments had gone to make the golden idol, but now they were giving their treasure for a tent of meeting —the place where God would dwell with His people.

Men were busy sorting the skins of goats and rams, selecting the best as gifts for the Lord. Each morning the people came to Moses with their offerings. Women brought brooches, earrings, necklaces, and all sorts of gold objects, while men came loaded with fine linen cloth, goats' hair, and rams' skins. Children may have brought pieces of acacia wood suitable for the construction, or jars of spices and incense to be used as burnt offerings.

Bezaleel and Aholiab, the two men selected to direct the construction of the tent of meeting, had charge of the weaving, the metal work, and the wood carving. Soon there was so much material on hand that the leaders said to Moses, "The people bring much more than enough for doing the work which the Lord has commanded us to do." So Moses issued this proclamation, "Let neither man nor woman do anything more for the offering for the sanctuary."

Skilled workers were set to the task of spinning yarn, weaving cloth, sewing the curtains and embroidering them. Talented men sewed the rams' skins together for the outer covering of the sanctuary, while carpenters built the wooden frames. Bezaleel constructed the delicately carved gold-covered furniture, and he made the gold and bronze utensils that were to be used in the sanctuary services.

The day came when the sanctuary was finished. The edifice was not large—about eighteen feet wide and fifty-five feet long. Moses inspected the embroidered curtains, the gold-covered boards for the wall, the metal pedestals and pillars, and

49

Skilled workmen were set to the task of spinning and weaving, to hewing an◄

the embossed golden furniture. He placed his blessing on the workers for their faithful service.

On the first day of the month, the sanctuary was set up in the midst of the camp. Curtains were hung on all sides around the tent to form a courtyard. The roof was made of four sets of curtains. The inner draperies were of fine linen, on which were embroidered figures of angels. Over this was placed a covering of woven goats' hair. The third covering was of rams' skins, and the outside covering was badgers' skins. Thick boards plated with pure gold were set on the side to form the wall. These boards were placed in silver sockets and held in their proper position with bars.

The sanctuary was divided into two compartments, separated by a beautiful curtain. The inner room was called the holy of holies; the outer room, the holy place. This outer chamber had three beautiful objects of furniture: a golden

50

rving wood, and to making gold and bronze utensils for the sanctuary service.

table, a richly carved golden candlestick, and a golden altar of incense. On the golden table twelve loaves of fresh bread, one for each of the twelve tribes of Israel, were placed each Sabbath morning. The golden candlestick had seven oil lamps which were kept burning continually. In front of the curtain separating the two compartments stood a golden altar on which incense was burned morning and evening.

In the smaller room, the holy of holies, there was one piece of sacred furniture—the ark of the covenant. This beautiful chest was covered with pure gold on the outside and on the inside. The cover of this chest was a solid piece of gold called the mercy seat. Upon this mercy seat were two angel figures called cherubim, embossed from pieces of pure gold. Their wings were spread in such a position that they overshadowed the mercy seat; their faces were turned toward each other, and their heads were bowed in reverence.

The sanctuary may be better understood by this diagrammatic painting.  Left: T

The two tables of stone on which the Ten Commandments were engraved were placed inside the ark of the covenant. A golden pot containing manna was also kept in the ark, a reminder of how God provided for the temporal needs of Israel. Above the mercy seat, between the golden angels, rested a glorious light, the Shekinah, the sign that God was meeting with his people.

The sanctuary was not a church where all the people could enter and worship. It was a holy tabernacle, where only specially chosen priests could minister before the Lord. Because the tribe of Levi had not worshiped the golden idol, Moses selected the men from this tribe to be the priests in the sanctuary. The priests who conducted the regular service in the holy place wore white robes made of fine linen cloth; but Aaron, the first high priest, wore a beautiful blue robe over his white one. Upon the hem of the blue garment were

52

st holy compartment. Center: The holy place. Right: The outer court and wall.

embroidered pomegranates, and between these hung tiny golden bells. Once a year the high priest entered the holy of holies to minister before the ark of the covenant.

### The Drama of Life

When the sanctuary was complete, Aaron and his four sons were ordained as priests. A cloud hovered over the sanctuary, and the glory of the Lord filled the two compartments. In this way God revealed to His people that He was pleased with the place of worship they had prepared for Him.

The cloud rested above the sanctuary by day and became a pillar of fire at night. When the cloud arose high above the sanctuary, the people knew that it was time for them to move forward on their journey to the land of Canaan.

The sanctuary and its services were to be a drama of life for the Israelites, who had only a few months before escaped from

53

the pagan, idol-worshiping Egyptians. The sanctuary they built was an object lesson of the way to salvation. God showed Moses the glories of heaven and "the true tabernacle," or temple, and then He gave Israel's leader the plan for the sanctuary. Said the Lord, "Let them make Me a sanctuary, that I may dwell in their midst. According to all that I show you concerning the pattern of the tabernacle, and of all its furniture, so you shall make it."

The furniture in this house of worship had a special significance. The twelve loaves of bread on the golden table reminded the people of Jesus, the Bread of Life. The ever-burning light of the seven lamps on the golden candlestick represented "the Light of the world." The incense that arose from the golden altar each morning and evening caused the people to think of the sincere prayers they offered to God. "Another angel came and stood at the altar with a golden censer; and he was given much incense to mingle with the prayers of all the saints upon the golden altar before the throne; and the smoke of the incense rose with the prayers of the saints from the hand of the angel before God." Revelation 8:3, 4. The ark of the covenant in the most sacred compartment, with its "mercy seat" of gold, symbolized God's throne. Even as the ark contained the stone tablets of the Ten Commandments, so the throne of the Eternal One is established on law and justice.

As we consider carefully the services of the sanctuary, we can see how they pointed the worshiper to the coming Messiah, Jesus Christ. To the tent of worship came the people bringing an offering and confessing their sins on the head of an innocent lamb or goat. The lamb was then slain and the priest took some of its blood into the holy place, or he ate some of the flesh of this sin offering. By this service the sinner understood the promise that the Messiah would come to bear "our sins in His body on the tree, that we might die to sin and live to righteousness. By His wounds you have been healed." 1 Peter 2:24.

54

On the solemn occasion known as Yom Kippur, the tenth day of the seventh month of the Hebrew calendar, there was to be a spiritual accounting for the people. All secular work was put aside and the Israelites fasted and prayed. On this day, only once a year, the high priest entered "the most holy place" and stood before the ark of the covenant. On the Day of Atonement there was "a reminder of sin year after year." Hebrews 10:3. Two young goats were brought to the entrance of the sanctuary, and lots were cast to decide which one would be for the Lord and which would be the scapegoat. The goat upon which the first choice fell was slain as a sin offering for all the people who had previously confessed their sins. Now the high priest took the blood of the animal into the most holy place and sprinkled it on the mercy seat. This was a symbol of the cleansing of the holy compartment for the sins that had been brought into it all during the year.

### The Day of Atonement

When this solemn rite had been accomplished, the high priest came out of the tent of worship and placed his hands on the head of the second goat, known as the scapegoat, and confessed over this animal all the sins of the children of Israel. Then the goat was led into the wilderness.

On the Day of Atonement the high priest was the only one who performed the service for the salvation of Israel. He killed the sacrifice and took the blood into the most holy place. He humbled himself before God and obtained forgiveness for his people. His work was based upon the confession and the sin offerings that the people had already made. Thus the work of the high priest was symbolic of Jesus Christ, our Mediator, for we read, "When Christ appeared as a High Priest of the good things that have come, then through the greater and more perfect tent (not made with hands, that is, not of this creation) He entered once for all into the Holy Place, taking not the blood of goats and calves but His own blood, thus securing an eternal redemption." Hebrews 9:11, 12.

55

## *Jesus Christ, Our High Priest*

The blood of the lambs sacrificed in Old Testament times could not remove sin; it simply pointed to the sacrifice of Jesus Christ, who lived a perfect life and died on the cross. He is the "Lamb of God, who takes away the sin of the world." John 1:29.

We have a risen Saviour who has become our High Priest in heaven. "We have such a High Priest, One who is seated at the right hand of the throne of the Majesty in heaven, a Minister in the sanctuary and the true tent which is set up not by man but by the Lord." Hebrews 8:1, 2.

Even as the earthly sanctuary was cleansed once each year on Yom Kippur, the Day of Atonement, so Christ "has appeared once for all at the end of the age to put away sin by the sacrifice of Himself." Hebrews 9:26. We have a Saviour who knows our needs and sympathizes with us in a world of sin. "Because He Himself has suffered and been tempted, He is able to help those who are tempted." Hebrews 2:18.

Thus in their sanctuary and its services over three thousand years ago, the Israelites learned that they should look to the coming of the Messiah who would die for their sins. They would have a High Priest in heaven who would intercede for them and their sins would finally be blotted out. This was the drama of salvation portrayed during the wilderness wanderings of God's people. They looked to the Messiah foretold in the divine prophecy:

> "Surely He has borne our griefs
> and carried our sorrows;
> yet we esteemed Him stricken,
> smitten by God, and afflicted.
> But He was wounded for our transgressions,
> He was bruised for our iniquities;
> upon Him was the chastisement that made us whole,
> and with His stripes we are healed." Isaiah 53:4, 5.

On the Day of Atonement the high priest killed the sacrifice and took the blood into the most holy place.

5—H.F. 2

# Defeat at the Border
# of Canaan

*Numbers 10 to 14*

chapter 5 ❧

O NE morning after the Israelites had camped on the plain
before Mount Sinai for about fourteen months, the
cloud arose over the sanctuary and moved forward.
News passed quickly from tent to tent that the nation was
moving forward. Since the tent of meeting was a portable
building, it was taken down in sections and carried by Levites
assigned to the task. The ark of the covenant was carried by
means of poles that were put through rings in the sides of the
chest. The rest of the golden furniture was carried in the
same manner.

The nation traveled in an orderly formation. The sacred
ark containing the Ten Commandments led the procession.
Priests carrying silver trumpets marched close to the ark, and
they gave signals from Moses and Aaron to the travelers by
buglelike calls. An impressive ceremony marked the start and
the end of a march. Whenever the ark moved forward, Moses
said, "Arise, O Lord, and let Thy enemies be scattered; and
let them that hate Thee flee before Thee." Numbers 10:35.
And when the march came to an end, Moses said, "Return, O
Lord, to the ten thousand thousands of Israel."

The cavalcade moved eastward through desolate mountain
regions. The route was treacherous because of the rocky can-
yons and arid regions. Progress was slow and the journey
tested the stamina of the bravest hearts.

When the children of Israel marched
forward, the ark, carried by priests,
was at the head of the procession.

It was not long before complaints were heard from the rabble. They were tired of eating manna, which tasted like cakes baked with oil. They were hungry for the delicacies of Egypt, and they craved meat. "O that we had meat to eat! We remember the fish we ate in Egypt for nothing, the cucumbers, the melons, the leeks, the onions, and the garlic; but now our strength is dried up, and there is nothing at all but this manna to look at." Numbers 11:4-6.

The weary, disheartened marchers gathered with their families and wept as weariness overcame them. Moses heard the murmuring and crying and he called upon God. "Why hast Thou dealt ill with Thy servant?" asked the patient leader. "And why have I not found favor in Thy sight, that Thou dost lay the burden of all this people upon me?"

Moses was almost cracking under the strain of leadership, and the Lord saw he needed assistants. Therefore Moses was given these instructions, "Gather for Me seventy men of the elders of Israel, whom you know to be the elders of the people and officers over them; and bring them to the tent of meeting, and let them take their stand there with you. And I will come down and talk with you there; and I will take some of the spirit which is upon you and put it upon them; and they shall bear the burden of the people with you, that you may not bear it yourself alone." Numbers 11:16, 17.

## Moses Shares His Leadership

Moses chose strong, efficient men to share his responsibilities. It was their duty to reason with the people and check their violence. Here was a plan of organization that called for co-operation from leaders in all the tribes. Instructions were given for the next day. The people were told that they would have an abundance of meat to eat, not for one or two days, but for a month!

The next morning a brisk wind blew from the sea, bringing flocks of quail near the camp. Soon the Israelites were busy gathering the birds. They worked day and night to garner the

60

game birds for food. Then a feast was prepared and many gorged themselves with the food. Soon they paid for their intemperance and gluttony, and many people died in the plague of food poisoning that struck.

At the next encampment Moses was faced with more trouble —this time from his own family. Aaron, his brother, and Miriam, his sister, had honored positions in the camp organization. The woman was a gifted leader and the people loved her. Nevertheless Aaron and Miriam desired more power and prestige. They said, "Has the Lord indeed spoken only through Moses? Has He not spoken through us also?"

Moses refused to argue the matter with his brother and sister. It was then that God commanded them to go to the sanctuary. While the three stood at the door of the sanctuary God said, "Hear My words: If there is a prophet among you, I the Lord make Myself known to him in a vision, I speak with him in a dream. Not so with My servant Moses; he is entrusted with all My house. With him I speak mouth to mouth, clearly, and not in dark speech; and he beholds the form of the Lord. Why then were you not afraid to speak against My servant Moses?" Numbers 12:6-8.

The glory of the Lord departed and Miriam looked at her hands and arms and, behold, she was as white as snow. Leprosy had struck her! Then in remorse Aaron spoke out, "Oh, my lord, do not punish us because we have done foolishly and have sinned." Moses cried, "Heal her, O God, I beseech Thee."

Then Miriam was shut outside the camp in a state of quarantine for seven days. During those days the Israelites could not march forward; they simply waited until the woman was well again and could return to the camp.

Criticism and jealousy can destroy the happiest families. Where there is fighting for the highest position there is no peace. Miriam, as a girl, had guarded her younger brother when he had been set afloat in a basket on the Nile River to save his life. Now, years later, her tender love had been choked out by envy and hatred.

61

Marching northward again through the wilderness of Paran, the Israelites came to Kadesh-barnea. Here Moses gave the signal to make a permanent camp in the grass-covered valley where streams of water gushed from the rocks. Trees loaded with rich fruit were a promise of good things for the weary travelers when they entered the Promised Land.

## The Report of the Spies

At Kadesh-barnea Moses and his corps of leaders planned how the nation would enter the land of Canaan. Moses chose twelve men, one from each tribe, and sent them to spy out the land, and to estimate the strength of the people. Before the twelve spies started on their dangerous task Moses instructed them, saying, "Go up into the Negeb yonder, and go up into the hill country, and see what the land is, and whether the people who dwell in it are strong or weak, whether they are few or many, and whether the land that they dwell in is good or bad, and whether the cities that they dwell in are camps or strongholds, and whether the land is rich or poor, and whether there is wood in it or not. Be of good courage, and bring some of the fruit of the land."

The men were absent almost six weeks. The waiting people must have gathered in groups and speculated about the country they were going to conquer. Day after day they watched for the spies to return, and one evening their patience was rewarded. A shout echoed through the camp. The spies had returned! The twelve men came before Moses and Aaron, bearing the fruit they had gathered. A giant cluster of grapes was carried on a pole between two men, while other men brought baskets of figs and pomegranates. Moses waited anxiously for the report of the spies' strange adventure.

"We came to the land to which you sent us," the spies began; "it flows with milk and honey, and this is its fruit." A murmur of joy must have swept through the crowd as the people heard the optimistic words of the spies and saw the fruit of the land. But then the men continued, "Yet the people

62

Caleb and Joshua, two men of valor, gave the report that Israel, with God's help, could conquer Canaan.

who dwell in the land are strong, and the cities are fortified and very large; and besides, we saw the descendants of Anak there."

A wail of terror came from the listening throng. Men scowled and women wept. Then Caleb, one of the spies, broke through the crowd to Moses and quieted the people. He said, "Let us go up at once, and occupy it; for we are well able to overcome it." Joshua, the warrior, joined Caleb in his challenge to go forward. These two men had faith that God would help them conquer the enemy.

Then the other ten spies cried out, "We are not able to go up against the people; for they are stronger than we." Allowing their fears to spur their imagination, they went on, "The land, through which we have gone, to spy it out, is a land that devours its inhabitants; and all the people that we saw in it are men of great stature. And there we saw the Nephilim (the sons of Anak, who come from the Nephilim); and we seemed to ourselves like grasshoppers, and so we seemed to them."

All that night there was weeping in the camp. The dreams and hopes of the hundreds of thousands of people had been shattered. The next morning the Israelites continued to grumble against Moses and Aaron. "Would that we had died in the land of Egypt!" the whole community said to them. "Or would that we had died in this wilderness! Why does the Lord bring us into this land, to fall by the sword?" Others said, "Let us choose a captain, and go back to Egypt." The ungrateful throng were ready to turn their backs on Moses and defy the plans of God for the nation.

Moses and Aaron mourned because the people had rebelled against the command of God. Once more Caleb and Joshua stood up before the mob and spoke courageously. They said, "The land, which we passed through to spy it out, is an exceedingly good land. If the Lord delights in us, He will bring us into this land and give it to us, a land which flows with milk and honey. Only, do not rebel against the Lord; and do not

64

fear the people of the land, for they are bread for us; their protection is removed from them, and the Lord is with us; do not fear them."

The stubborn people refused to listen. In their insane rage they picked up stones and rushed upon Caleb and Joshua to kill them. But the evil, rebellious crowd stopped suddenly. The stones dropped from their hands! The glory of the Lord like a flame of fire suddenly appeared over the tent of meeting. With fear and trembling the people bowed their heads. In silence the crowd melted away and the traitorous spies hurried to their tents.

Then the Lord said to Moses, "How long shall this wicked congregation murmur against Me? I have heard the murmurings of the people of Israel, which they murmur against Me. Say to them, 'As I live,' says the Lord, 'what you have said in My hearing I will do to you: your dead bodies shall fall in this wilderness; and of all your number, numbered from twenty years old and upward, who have murmured against Me, not one shall come into the land where I swore that I would make you dwell, except Caleb the son of Jephunneh and Joshua the son of Nun.' " What a terrible fate for the Israelites! They were to wander in the wilderness and die there because they rebelled against God's word. Of the older generation only Joshua and Caleb would go into the Promised Land; but with them would go the youth who had not taken part in the rebellion.

When Moses told the nation what its punishment would be, the people mourned. They had distrusted the power of the Eternal One and thought only of their weakness. The next morning they decided to prove that they had courage after all, for they said, "See, we are here, we will go up to the place which the Lord has promised, for we have sinned." They also declared, "We will go up and fight."

But Moses said, "Do not go up lest you be struck down before your enemies, for the Lord is not among you."

Once more the stubborn people refused to obey the admoni-

tion of their leader. With swords and spears a band of men rushed forward into Canaan; but these soldiers were not prepared to fight, and they did not have God's blessing. The Canaanites were hiding in the mountain passes ready to attack the invaders. Soon the men of Israel were surprised and driven back in a rout. Death and defeat were the result of rushing headlong into disobedience. The tragic defeat gave courage to the enemy and made the later conquest of the land much harder than it would have been if the Israelites had followed the divine instructions.

It was a sad day when the people turned back from the green meadows and fruit trees of Kadesh to the hot desert. In their ears rang the words they had shouted against Moses and Aaron, "Would that we had died in this wilderness!" Now they knew that they would never see the Promised Land. They would die in the desert because they had refused to go forward at God's command.

# The Death of the Rebels

*Numbers 16 to 21:20*

chapter 6 &

DEEP grief settled over the thousands of pilgrims camped at Kadesh-barnea. They had refused to conquer the land which God had given them, and when they had attempted to fight the enemy in their own strength they had been completely defeated. Now there was nothing for them to do but to accept their punishment and live in the desert.

Rebellion smoldered in the hearts of the disappointed Israelites. Two hundred fifty of the chief men became jealous of Moses, and wanted to be priests. The leaders of the rebels were Korah, a Levite who served in the sanctuary, and three colleagues, Dathan, Abiram, and On. These men not only defied Moses and the people, but also they refused to obey the commands of God.

Standing before the whole camp, the rebels shouted against Moses and Aaron, saying, "You have gone too far! For all the congregation are holy, every one of them, and the Lord is among them; why then do you exalt yourselves above the assembly of the Lord?"

Weariness swept over Moses as he declared that there would be a test in which the Lord would decide who was the leader of Israel. He said, "Do this: take censers, Korah and all his company; put fire in them and put incense upon them before the Lord tomorrow, and the man whom the Lord chooses shall be the holy one. You have gone too far, sons of Levi!"

The next morning the rebels appeared, with Korah as their leader. The words of Moses must have echoed in their ears, "You have gone too far!" The men brought fire pans and burned incense in front of the tent of meeting. The whole assembly waited to see what would happen. Suddenly the glory of the Lord appeared over the sanctuary, and Moses shouted for the innocent people to separate themselves from the rebels.

Then Moses spoke to all the people, saying, "Hereby you shall know that the Lord has sent me to do all these works, and that it has not been of my own accord. If these men die the common death of all men, or if they are visited by the fate of all men, then the Lord has not sent me. But if the Lord creates something new, and the ground opens its mouth, and swallows them up, with all that belongs to them, and they go down alive into Sheol, then you shall know that these men have despised the Lord."

When Moses had finished speaking, behold, the ground under the feet of the rebellious leaders broke open and a yawning crack in the earth swallowed them. Fire consumed the two hundred fifty men who were burning incense in front of the sanctuary. The sudden destruction of these wicked men caused the crowds of people to flee from the place in terror. However, some of the people continued to sympathize with the rebels, and the next day a fearful plague destroyed more than fourteen thousand persons who persisted in disobeying God.

To settle the dispute concerning priestly authority that Korah had started, God ordered twelve leaders—one representative from each tribe—to bring a rod to the door of the sanctuary. The name of each leader was written on the rod, and on the rod of the tribe of Levi was written the name of Aaron. The Lord declared, "The rod of the man whom I choose shall sprout; thus I will make to cease from Me the murmurings of the people of Israel, which they murmur against you."

The rods were carefully laid out in the sanctuary, and the

next morning Moses entered the sanctuary to see what had happened. The rods were brought out and displayed to the people and, behold, Aaron's rod was covered with beautiful blossoms and ripe almonds. Then Moses was instructed to place Aaron's rod in the sanctuary as a witness to future generations.

## *Wanderers in the Desert*

Long, monotonous years in the hot wilderness dragged by and the older generation was constantly reminded of God's decree. Those who had left Egypt as children were growing up. They were learning to do what their fathers and mothers had not done—obey the Lord's commands. Thousands and tens of thousands of men and women who could not enter Canaan died in the desert. Miriam, the sister of Moses, died and was buried with honors.

At last thirty-eight years of wilderness wandering were over. The hills of the Promised Land came into view once more. The people camped where the water had gushed from the rocks when they were there previously, but now the springs had dried up. Again the people turned against Moses and Aaron, saying, "Would that we had died when our brethren died before the Lord! Why have you brought the assembly of the Lord into this wilderness, that we should die here, both we and our cattle?"

The two brothers went to the door of the sanctuary to seek divine counsel. The glory of the Lord appeared to them and they received these instructions, "Take the rod, and assemble the congregation, you and Aaron your brother, and tell the rock before their eyes to yield its water; so you shall bring water out of the rock for them; so you shall give drink to the congregation and their cattle."

Moses hurried out to meet the assembly, with Aaron at his side. Moses said angrily, "Hear now, you rebels; shall we bring forth water for you out of this rock?"

Raising his hand, Moses struck the rock twice with his

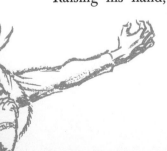

69

staff. The water gushed forth and the people drank. All the flocks and herds had water; but in this moment of impatience Moses had disobeyed the Lord. He had taken the glory to himself by saying, "Shall we bring forth water for you?" and he had struck the rock when God had instructed him to speak to it.

The Lord said to Moses, "Because you did not believe in Me, to sanctify Me in the eyes of the people of Israel, therefore you shall not bring this assembly into the land which I have given them."

Weary and discouraged by the constant complaining of his people, Moses had forgotten to trust in God when he needed Him most. How like our experience today! We face complex problems, our nerves become jangled, and we speak harshly to those we love. It is then we need to pray for peace, for courage, and for strength to see our problems through.

Because of his disobedience Moses could not march with his people into the land of Canaan. He told them what his punishment was to be. He said, "The Lord was angry with me on your account, and would not hearken to me; and the Lord said to me, 'Let it suffice you; speak no more to Me of this matter.'"

Moses had not been guilty of a great sin. It was only a matter of losing his temper and disobeying God one time, but it was enough to keep him from the Promised Land.

It is no light thing to disobey God, for in breaking His laws we actually break ourselves. One sin can keep us out of heaven. But if we confess our sins and pray for forgiveness, Jesus Christ will cleanse our record and make us perfect through His righteousness.

As Aaron grew old, God told him he must die. It was decided that Eleazar, the son of Aaron, would take his father's position as high priest in the sanctuary.

All the camp stood watching one morning as Moses, Aaron, and Eleazar started up the trail to the top of Mount Hor. Here were two brothers, each well over a hundred years of

70

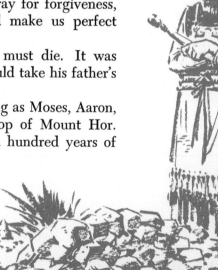

age. Their lives had been spent in the service of God and of
their people. Some time later the people saw two figures
coming down the side of the mountain. Those with keen eyes
saw Moses and Eleazar.

## A Plague of Snakes

Later the news was told of how Moses had stripped Aaron
of his priestly robes and had placed them upon Eleazar. Then
Aaron had died and was buried on Mount Hor. For thirty
days the nation mourned the loss of Aaron, the high priest and
assistant leader, who had served the nation for forty years.

Leaving Mount Hor, the people grew impatient because the
journey was hard, and they were weary. Seeing only the dark
side of life, they complained to Moses, saying, "Why have
you brought us up out of Egypt to die in the wilderness? For
there is no food and no water, and we loathe this worthless
food."

Could the people do nothing but complain? They talked of
Egypt and wished they were once again in the land where
they had been slaves. God had shielded them from sickness,
hunger, and enemies. On this occasion the Lord took away His
protection and allowed the poisonous snakes of the desert to
crawl into the tents and bite the people. These reptile bites
brought inflammation, swelling, and death. Terror struck
the camp of Israel! In almost every tent there were the dead
or dying, for no one was safe from the deadly sting of the
snakes. In their hour of trouble the people became humble
and repentant. They said, "We have sinned, for we have
spoken against the Lord and against you; pray to the Lord,
that He take away the serpents from us." Moses prayed for
help, and the Lord said, "Make a fiery serpent, and set it on
a pole; and everyone who is bitten, when he sees it, shall live."

Moses made a serpent out of bronze and placed it on a pole
where the sick and dying could see it. If they looked at the
serpent, believing that God would save them, they were healed.

The bronze serpent was to teach Israel that they could not

71

save themselves. There was no virtue in the metal snake, but it represented Jesus Christ, the Son of God, who would some-day come to this world and die to save men from sin. When Jesus was on earth, He said, "As Moses lifted up the serpent in the wilderness, so must the Son of man be lifted up, that whoever believes in Him may have eternal life." John 3:14.

It was a momentous day when the cavalcade made camp near the Jordan River. The people could look across the stream and see the land which had long before been promised to their fathers, Abraham, Isaac, and Jacob. At this time Moses took a census of the people, and in all the camp there was not a man of the generation who had refused to go into the land thirty-eight years before, "except Caleb the son of Jephunneh and Joshua the son of Nun." The rejected generation had died in the wilderness because they refused to have faith in God.

Moses, the aged leader, called the people together, and recounted the goodness of the Lord in rescuing them from Egypt and in caring for them during the wanderings in the desert. In one of his great orations he reminded them of how their fathers had died because of disobedience, and he warned that if they forgot God and worshiped idols, they would be scattered among the nations. Moses repeated the Ten Commandments to the people so that all could hear, and then he wrote them on a scroll of parchment. Moses said, "All the commandment which I command you this day you shall be careful to do, that you may live and multiply, and go in and possess the land which the Lord swore to give to your fathers. . . . Know then in your heart that, as a man disciplines his son, the Lord your God disciplines you. So you shall keep the commandments of the Lord your God, by walking in His ways and by fearing Him."

## The Ceremonial Laws

Moses also wrote all of the laws concerning sacrifices, the clean and unclean animals, and the laws of quarantine and sanitation. These were written on a scroll, put in a safe place

Moses had the bronze serpent placed on a pole where the sick and the dying could look and be healed.

JOHN STEEL, ARTIST          © P. P. P. A.

in the side of the ark of the covenant, and the priests were instructed to read these laws to the people every seven years.

There were scores of laws concerning the operation of the camp of Israel, the relation of employer to workman and servant, and the rules of buying and selling. There were laws concerning marriage and social problems. There were many laws concerning the rites and ceremonies of the sanctuary.

The laws of Moses dealing with religious issues have sometimes been confused with the eternal Ten Commandment law given by God on Mount Sinai. They are two separate, distinct codes. The ceremonial laws dealing with the sanctuary services of offering the lamb for a sin offering, as well as a host of other offerings and rituals, pointed forward to the Messiah and His sacrifice for the sins of the world. John the Baptist recognized this when he said of Jesus, "Behold, the Lamb of God, who takes away the sin of the world!" John 1:29.

The death of Jesus Christ made the Old Testament sacrifices and rites obsolete. They pointed to His divine sacrifice, and when that was accomplished the ancient sanctuary had fulfilled its purpose. There were "holydays," special sabbaths, and the feasts and festivals in Israel. The law concerning all of these rules was set aside by Jesus, according to the apostle Paul, and He nailed "it to the cross." Colossians 2:14.

These ceremonial days and the laws of sacrifice and offerings have no connection with God's eternal law. The Sabbath of the fourth commandment originated at the creation of the world, and it is an everlasting memorial of God's work.

The ceremonial law of the Israelites was only "a shadow of the good things to come," says the writer of the book of Hebrews. He points out that "it is impossible that the blood of bulls and goats should take away sins." Hebrews 10:1, 4.

These laws, then, were a temporary code for Israel. Some of the laws dealt with the nation, while the religious laws anticipated the coming of Jesus, the Lamb of God. We need never be confused concerning the two laws. The laws given to Israel as a nation were for that specific time and need.

These religious laws ended when Christ died on the cross. The law of God, the Ten Commandments, is eternal. Jesus declared this when He said, "Think not that I have come to abolish the law and the prophets; I have come not to abolish them but to fulfill them. For truly, I say to you, till heaven and earth pass away, not an iota, not a dot, will pass from the law until all is accomplished." Matthew 5:17, 18. This law is the blueprint for happiness in our world today.

After Moses had reviewed the laws and the blessings that his people would receive if they obeyed them, he gave this beautiful summary: "And now, Israel, what does the Lord your God require of you, but to fear the Lord your God, to walk in all His ways, to love Him, to serve the Lord your God with all your heart and with all your soul, and to keep the commandments and statutes of the Lord, which I command you this day for your good?"

# The Man Who Missed Greatness

*Numbers 21:21 to 25*

chapter 7

A S THE children of Israel marched into the Jordan Valley they gained victories over the tribes that were settled in the land. Messengers were sent to Sihon, king of the Amorites, saying, "Let me pass through your land; we will not turn aside into field of vineyard; we will not drink the water of a well; we will go by the King's Highway, until we have passed through your territory."

The Amorites were stubborn and refused passage through their land. Armies marched instead, and when they met the warriors of Israel they were annihilated and all the cities of King Sihon fell. This was the first great victory in the land of Canaan.

Next the conquerors marched toward Bashan, and they were met by Og, the king of the land. The men of Bashan were tall and strong. Probably they were some of the "giants" described by the spies some forty years earlier. At least King Og was a tall man, for he had a bedstead twelve feet long. But giants no longer stood in the way, for this generation had learned to trust in God. They obeyed the divine instruction, "Do not fear him; for I have given him into your hand, and all his people, and his land; and you shall do to him as you did to Sihon king of the Amorites, who dwelt at Heshbon."

The brave army of Israel invaded Bashan and wrought havoc

Balaam looked from the heights at the camp of Israel, and with inspired words he blessed God's chosen ones.

77

"until there was not one survivor left," and the land was conquered.

When Balak, king of Moab, heard what was happening to the other kingdoms about him, he was afraid and called his chiefs to a special council. "This horde will now lick up all that is round about us, as the ox licks up the grass of the field," said Balak, in colorful language. The king, therefore, planned an unusual strategy. He decided to send for a prophet named Balaam, the son of Beor. King Balak would give this man rich presents to come and place a curse on the conquering nation. Chieftains were sent to Balaam to flatter him and entice him to accept the king's invitation. When the men of Moab arrived, the prophet listened to their story and he asked the visitors to stay all night so that he might find out what he should do. He did not really need the time, for in his heart he knew that he should not go; but he hoped that God would permit him to receive this honor and treasure. The Lord said to Balaam, "You shall not go with them; you shall not curse the people, for they are blessed."

The next morning Balaam arose and said to the chieftains, "Go to your own land; for the Lord has refused to let me go with you." Disappointment was plainly revealed in the prophet's words, for he attempted to place the blame on God for not letting him fulfill the king's request.

When King Balak heard of Balaam's refusal, he sent chieftains of higher rank to Balaam, urging the man to accept the royal commission. When Balaam heard the second request, he said, "Though Balak were to give me his house full of silver and gold, I could not go beyond the command of the Lord my God, to do less or more. Pray, now, tarry here this night also, that I may know what more the Lord will say to me."

God looked into Balaam's selfish heart and then told the prophet, "If the men have come to call you, rise, go with them; but only what I bid you, that shall you do."

In the morning Balaam was so eager to go with the chieftains that he did not wait for them to come to him. One

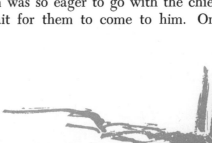

wrong step makes it easier to take the next one, and so the covetous man harnessed his ass and, with two servants, hurried to find the chieftains of Moab.

### Stopped by an Angel

Now the Lord stationed an angel on the road to stop the prophet from doing wrong. When the ass saw the heavenly being standing in the road with a drawn sword in his hand, she turned aside into a field. Balaam struck the beast, and turned her back to the highway. Again the angel stood in the way, and the ass turned aside and crushed Balaam's foot against a stone wall. Ill-natured from the injury, the prophet struck the animal again. Finally the angel stood in a narrow place where the beast could not turn aside. When the animal saw the angel, she lay down under Balaam. The prophet was furious, and he struck the ass again. The Lord then allowed the animal to speak, and she reproved Balaam with these words, "What have I done to you, that you have struck me these three times?"

"Because you have made sport of me," said Balaam, without showing surprise at the animal's speech. "I wish I had a sword in my hand, for then I would kill you."

The ass said to Balaam, "Am I not your ass, upon which you have ridden all your lifelong to this day? Was I ever accustomed to do so to you?"

"No," he said.

Then the Lord opened Balaam's eyes, and he saw the angel standing on the road with the drawn sword in his hand. The unworthy man humbly bowed his head and acknowledged his wrong.

"Why have you struck your ass these three times?" the angel asked. "Behold, I have come forth to withstand you, because your way is perverse before me."

"I have sinned," said Balaam, "for I did not know that thou didst stand in the road against me. Now therefore, if it is evil in thy sight, I will go back again."

79

Certainly Balaam knew by this time his actions did not please God, but even now he hoped he could go with the chieftains and reap the reward.

The angel told Balaam, "Go with the men; but only the word which I bid you, that shall you speak."

So Balaam went with the chieftains of Moab, and King Balak came out to meet the prophet. The next day Balak took him to a high hill overlooking the camp of Israel. Sacrifices were offered, and Balaam said that he would go into a solitary place to hear what God would tell him. He said, "Perhaps the Lord will come to meet me; and whatever He shows me I will tell you."

When Balaam returned to the king and his counselors, he began to speak. Imagine the astonishment of the king when he heard Balaam blessing, not cursing, the nation! Balaam said:

> "How can I curse whom God has not cursed?
> How can I denounce whom the Lord has not denounced?
> For from the top of the mountains I see Him,
> From the hills I behold Him;
> Lo, a people dwelling alone,
> And not reckoning itself among the nations!"

The king was furious. "What have you done to me?" he asked.

"Must I not take heed to speak what the Lord puts in my mouth?" answered Balaam.

The king decided to try again, so he took Balaam to another mountain. Again sacrifices were offered to pagan gods, but once more when Balaam spoke, he blessed Israel.

A third time altars were built and sacrifices offered. Balaam was certain now that he could not curse Israel. He looked down upon the valley and saw the beautiful camp spread out in a perfect pattern of tents. He saw the sanctuary with the pillar of cloud resting over it. Again he blessed the nation, and he also prophesied that the promised Messiah would come, as symbolized by a brilliant star in the heavens. Balaam spoke

80

these beautiful words concerning Jesus, the Saviour of men:

"I see Him, but not now;
 I behold Him, but not nigh:
a star shall come forth out of Jacob,
 and a scepter shall rise out of Israel;
it shall crush the forehead of Moab,
 and break down all the sons of Sheth."

Balak, the king of Moab, was filled with indignation at Balaam, and he struck his fists together. "I called you to curse my enemies," said the monarch, "and behold, you have blessed them these three times. Therefore now flee to your place; I said, 'I will certainly honor you,' but the Lord has held you back from honor."

Balaam might have been a great leader for God, but he went home in disgrace, without silver or gold. We are told by the apostle Peter that the weakness in Balaam's character was that he "loved gain from wrongdoing." 2 Peter 2:15. In spite of his attempt to curse the nation, he had prophesied of the prosperity and growth of Israel. He had foretold the coming of a king who would subdue all his enemies, and that ruler is the Son of God who will establish His throne upon the earth.

### Enticements to Sin

The Israelites camped on the high plains of Moab among the acacia trees. Under the direction of Moses, the leaders of the twelve tribes made their plans to occupy the Promised Land. The cavalcade had skirted the Dead Sea on the march northward, and soon they would turn westward to cross the Jordan River. The heathen peoples lived in the country surrounding the camp, and for a time the conquerors did not mingle with the enemy. But after weeks had passed the women from Midian began to slip into the camp. Then the Israelites were invited to attend the weird pagan services. King Balak had decided on a subtle strategy. If he could not curse Israel he would entice them to join in worshiping his pagan deities. Many of the Israelites accepted the invitation to the pagan feast and they listened to the music, joined in the dancing, ate and drank, and bowed before the idols. The heathen rites soon drew the Israelites into immorality, and the degradation spread rapidly through the camp of God's people.

Instruction came to Moses to move swiftly against the leaders who had failed to obey the divine law. The command to Moses was, "Take all the chiefs of the people, and hang them in the sun before the Lord, that the fierce anger of the Lord may turn away from Israel."

Then Moses said to the judges, "Every one of you slay his men who have yoked themselves to Baal of Peor."

A virulent plague broke out in the camp and thousands of people were struck down by it. Frightened by the judgments that were falling, the people gathered in front of the sanctuary and confessed their sins. In the midst of this solemn service, Phinehas, a priest, saw Zimri, one of the nobles of Israel, bring a Midianite woman into the camp and take her to his tent. With a spear in his hand, Phinehas followed the couple and killed them both.

Loose, immoral conduct has been the downfall of good men and strong leaders. David yielded to the enticements of evil; Samson betrayed his strength. King Solomon, said to be the wisest of men, succumbed to passion. In an age when society scoffs at standards of purity, it is a challenge for every Christian to be pure in heart and life. "Keep your heart with all vigilance; for from it flow the springs of life." Proverbs 4:23.

# The Greatness of Moses

*Deuteronomy 31 to 34*

chapter 8 ✴

MOSES was one hundred twenty years of age. His brother Aaron was in the grave, and the older generation had perished in the wilderness—all except Caleb and Joshua, the two spies who had given a courageous report. Children who had seen the spies return from Canaan were now close to fifty years of age.

One day the Lord said to Moses, "Behold, the days approach when you must die; call Joshua, and present yourselves in the tent of meeting, that I may commission him."

So Moses and Joshua stood at the door of the sanctuary before all of the people. Then the Lord appeared in the pillar of cloud which stood over the doorway of the tent. "Be strong and of good courage," said the Eternal One; "for you shall bring the children of Israel into the land which I swore to give them: I will be with you."

A sign of greatness in a leader is that he can prepare another man to take his place. The work of Moses as a leader of Israel had ended and he once more told the congregation how he had disobeyed the Lord by striking the rock instead of speaking to it. Because of his sin, it was impossible for him to lead the nation to victory in their new home.

As thousands of people looked at Moses, the aged patriarch, they realized it was their own sins of ingratitude, criticism, and faithlessness that had caused their leader to falter. They could enjoy the Land of Promise, but he must die.

Then the Lord said to Moses, "Ascend this mountain of the Abarim, Mount Nebo, which is in the land of Moab, opposite Jericho; and view the land of Canaan, which I give to the people of Israel for a possession; and die on the mountain which you ascend, and be gathered to your people, as Aaron your brother died in Mount Hor and was gathered to his people."

Time and again Moses had been called to go into the mountains to commune with God; but now he must make a one-way trip. He cannot return to the people for whom he lived, suffered, yes, and sacrificed a throne. Now for the last time he stands before the assembly. The grandeur of his language rises to poetic heights as the prophetic impulse possesses him, and he exclaims:

> "Give ear, O heavens, and I will speak;
>     and let the earth hear the words of my mouth.
> May my teaching drop as the rain,
>     my speech distill as the dew,
>     as the gentle rain upon the tender grass,
>     and as the showers upon the herb.
> For I will proclaim the name of the Lord.
> Ascribe greatness to our God! . . .
> He found him in a desert land,
>     and in the howling waste of the wilderness;
> He encircled him, He cared for him,
> He kept him as the apple of His eye.
> Like an eagle that stirs up its nest,
>     that flutters over its young,
>     spreading out its wings, catching them,
>     bearing them on its pinions,
>     the Lord alone did lead him,
>     and there was no foreign god with him.
> He made him ride on the high places of the earth,
>     and he ate the produce of the field;
>     and He made him suck honey out of the rock,
>     and oil out of the flinty rock."

From the top of Mount Nebo the aged Moses was shown the Promised Land, but he was not able to enter there.

JOHN STEEL, ARTIST                    © P. P. P. A.

When Moses had finished reciting his beautiful ode, he again spoke to the people, instructing them as if they were his own children. He told them to trust in God and be of good courage. He blessed each of the twelve tribes and said farewell to all.

He ends with a glorious benediction upon the entire nation:

> "There is none like God, O Jeshurun,
>     who rides through the heavens to your help,
>     and in His majesty through the skies.
> The eternal God is your dwelling place,
>     and underneath are the everlasting arms.
> And He thrust out the enemy before you,
>     and said, Destroy.
> So Israel dwelt in safety,
>     the fountain of Jacob alone,
>     in a land of grain and wine;
>     yea, His heavens drop down dew.
> Happy are you, O Israel! Who is like you,
>     a people saved by the Lord,
>     the shield of your help,
>     and the sword of your triumph!
> Your enemies shall come fawning to you;
>     and you shall tread upon their high places."

Then Moses walked alone out of the camp and started up the trail leading to the heights of Mount Nebo. Thousands of men, women, and children stood watching with tear-dimmed eyes as the solitary figure grew smaller in the distance. How many times they had grumbled and complained against this great man! How many times he had prayed for God to spare their lives! Now he must leave them, and they will go into their homeland without him.

From the top of Mount Pisgah Moses, with undimmed eyes, looked across into the land of Canaan. He saw the green valleys and meadows, the rolling hills and forests. Far to the north loomed snow-covered Mount Hermon. He could see the river Jordan, the Dead Sea, and the rugged mountains to the east. Then God gave him a vision of what would happen to the nation in the centuries ahead. He saw the people settled in the land, the rise and fall of kings, the glory and the sins of the nation. He saw the wonderful day when Jesus Christ would be born in Bethlehem. He saw the Saviour living among men and dying that all might have eternal life. Then he was shown the time when the earth would be made new.

After the aged prophet had seen all this, he was content to go to his rest. The Bible gives this record, "So Moses the servant of the Lord died there in the land of Moab, according to the word of the Lord, and He buried him in the valley in the land of Moab opposite Beth-peor; but no man knows the place of his burial to this day."

If Moses had remained in Egypt, he might have had a royal funeral when he died, and his body would have been embalmed and placed in one of the tombs or in a pyramid. But Moses chose to endure hardships and suffering with his people; he loved God more than the riches and honor of men.

Moses did not long remain in the grave, for God raised him to life and took him to heaven. Satan, the enemy of truth, had caused Moses to sin. It was his purpose to keep him under the power of death. But there was no controversy. We read that "when the Archangel Michael, contending with the devil, disputed about the body of Moses, he did not presume to pronounce a reviling judgment upon him, but said, 'The Lord rebuke you.'" Moses came from the grave glorified, and ascended to heaven a redeemed saint.

The years of education, first with his godly mother, then in the palace of Pharaoh, and finally in the desert as a shepherd, prepared Moses to be the leader of Israel in the epic flight from Egypt. Mighty in intelligence, humble in dealing with others, this man was willing to listen to God. This was the secret of his power. "As historian, poet, philosopher, general of armies, and legislator, he stands without a peer."

# Marching Forward in Conquest

*Joshua 1 to 8*

chapter 9

AFTER Israel had mourned the death of Moses for thirty days, Joshua, the newly appointed leader, commanded the people to prepare to cross the Jordan River. With firm determination, he listened to the word of the Lord to him, "Be strong and of good courage; for you shall cause this people to inherit the land which I swore to their fathers to give them. Only be strong and very courageous, being careful to do according to all the law which Moses My servant commanded you; turn not from it to the right hand or to the left, that you may have good success wherever you go." Officers went through the camp giving this instruction, "Prepare your provisions; for within three days you are to pass over this Jordan, to go in to take possession of the land which the Lord your God gives you to possess."

Joshua knew that he must take the frontier cities on the other side of the Jordan River before he could conquer the enemies that lived in the interior. Therefore, he sent two men to Jericho, the key city in the region, to study the situation. They entered the walled city through the gate and walked along the narrow streets. They felt strange among these foreign people, and soon they discovered that they were being watched. Curious men of the town began to follow them to see where they were going. The Israelites quickened their pace, but so did

When the feet of the priests touched the water, the river parted and they marched ahead on dry ground.

JOE MANISCALCO, ARTIST        © P.P.P.A.

89

7—H.F. 2

the men of Jericho. Someone hurried off to tell the king that spies from the camp of Israel were in the town. Now the two men were running to escape. They turned in at an open doorway and met a woman named Rahab, a harlot of the city. She welcomed the fugitives when they told her that they were Israelites.

"I know that the Lord has given you the land," she said to the spies, "and that the fear of you has fallen upon us, and that all the inhabitants of the land melt away before you." This woman had entertained travelers who told of the conquest of Israel. She knew how the God of this nation had performed miracles in behalf of His people, for she said, "We have heard how the Lord dried up the water of the Red Sea before you when you came out of Egypt, and what you did to the two kings of the Amorites that were beyond the Jordan, to Sihon and Og, whom you utterly destroyed. And as soon as we heard it, our hearts melted, and there was no courage left in any man, because of you; for the Lord your God is He who is God in heaven above and on earth beneath."

Soon officers from the king of Jericho arrived at Rahab's house and said to her, "Bring forth the men that have come to you, who entered your house; for they have come to search out all the land."

Rahab admitted that the spies had been in her house, but she suggested that the officers hurry on and pursue them into the country. Actually she had hidden the spies under piles of flax that were drying on the flat roof of her house. When the officers had gone, she called the men forth from their hiding and said to them, "Now then, swear to me by the Lord that as I have dealt kindly with you, you also will deal kindly with my father's house, and give me a sure sign, and save alive my father and mother, my brothers and sisters, and all who belong to them, and deliver our lives from death."

The men said to her, "Our life for yours! If you do not tell this business of ours, then we will deal kindly and faithfully with you when the Lord gives us the land."

90

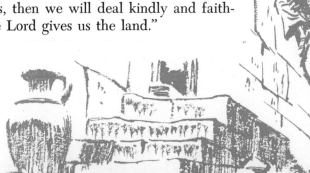

Rahab's house was built in the city wall; and when it was dark, she let the two spies down by a rope from her window. Because of her kindness in sparing their lives, the men gave Rahab this promise before they slipped away in the darkness, "Behold, when we come into the land, you shall bind this scarlet cord in the window through which you let us down; and you shall gather into your house your father and mother, your brothers, and all your father's household. If anyone goes out of the doors of your house into the street, his blood shall be upon his head, and we shall be guiltless; but if a hand is laid upon anyone who is with you in the house, his blood shall be on our head. But if you tell this business of ours, then we shall be guiltless with respect to your oath which you have made us swear."

The spies hurried off to the hills and remained in hiding for three days until the officers of the city no longer searched for them. Then they returned to the camp of Israel and gave their report. "Truly the Lord has given all the land into our hands; and moreover all the inhabitants of the land are faint-hearted because of us," they said to Joshua.

Joshua knew that the nation faced a great test. Would his people have courage when they advanced against the enemy, or would they lose heart as their fathers had done thirty-eight years before? That night he prayed for strength to be a faithful leader. The words of the Lord echoed in his ears, "Only be strong and very courageous. . . . Have I not commanded you? Be strong and of good courage; be not frightened, neither be dismayed; for the Lord your God is with you wherever you go."

The next morning the people left the acacia groves in the valley of Shittim and marched forward to the banks of the Jordan River not far from Jericho. After camping there for three days, the leaders went to each tribe and told the people to prepare to advance when they saw the priests take up the golden ark.

At a signal from Joshua the priests marched forward with

91

the ark, and the people followed in an orderly procession. There were no bridges; there were no boats. At this season of the year the river was flooded from bank to bank, and it seemed impossible for them to cross; but when the feet of the priests touched the muddy waters of the river, the waters plunging down from upstream came to a stop and formed a wall. The rest of the water flowed on downstream, leaving dry ground so that the people with their cattle and herds could pass to the other side. Then the Lord told Joshua to choose a man from each tribe for a special mission. Joshua summoned twelve men and said to them, "Pass on before the ark of the Lord your God into the midst of the Jordan, and take up each of you a stone upon his shoulder, according to the number of the tribes of the people of Israel."

### Crossing the Jordan River

The twelve men took the stones from the bed of the river and set them up as a monument at Gilgal where Israel made camp that night. Joshua told the people, "When your children ask their fathers in time to come, 'What do these stones mean?' then you shall let your children know, 'Israel passed over this Jordan on dry ground.' For the Lord your God dried up the waters of the Jordan for you until you passed over, as the Lord your God did to the Red Sea, which He dried up for us until we passed over, so that all the peoples of the earth may know that the hand of the Lord is mighty."

The Israelites had now crossed the Jordan River and entered the Promised Land. With thankful hearts they ate the Passover Feast, which reminded them of the wonderful deliverance from Egypt. The next day men were able to get grain that was grown in the land, and so the manna ceased. For forty years the food from heaven had appeared every day in the week except on the seventh day, the Sabbath. Now the Israelites were to live on the produce of the country.

Joshua walked alone outside the camp to plan the strategy of attack on the city of Jericho. Suddenly he saw a man

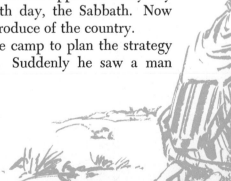

92

standing before him with a drawn sword in his hand. Thinking this might be a spy from the enemy, Joshua approached the warrior and said, "Are you for us, or for our adversaries?"

"No; but as commander of the army of the Lord I have now come," said he.

Joshua knelt on the ground and bowed his head, saying, "What does my lord bid his servant?"

"Put off your shoes from your feet," the captain of the host of the Lord said to Joshua; "for the place where you stand is holy."

Joshua removed his sandals and waited for the voice of the Lord to speak. Then the leader of Israel received this instruction, "See, I have given into your hand Jericho, with its king and mighty men of valor. You shall march around the city, all the men of war going around the city once. Thus shall you do for six days. And seven priests shall bear seven trumpets of rams' horns before the ark; and on the seventh day you shall march around the city seven times, the priests blowing the trumpets. And when they make a long blast with the ram's horn, as soon as you hear the sound of the trumpet, then all the people shall shout with a great shout; and the wall of the city will fall down flat, and the people shall go up every man straight before him."

## The Conquest of Jericho

When Joshua had heard this instruction, he rejoiced, for now he knew God's plan for taking the walled city. The leader called the priests and commanded them to start the march around Jericho with the golden ark of the covenant and with seven priests carrying rams' horns.

In the city of Jericho there was a fever of excitement. Rumors passed from merchant to merchant. The news was whispered in every house, The Israelites are coming! Although the Jordan River was flooded, the entire nation of Israel had crossed safely. The river had actually stopped flowing and the people had marched across on dry land!

93

The citizens of Jericho were afraid that they would soon be attacked. The gates of the city were closed and barred, and no one was allowed to enter or leave.

In the house of Rahab, the harlot, built in the wall of Jericho, there was excitement, too. Every morning the woman went to the window to be certain that the scarlet rope was in plain sight. As she looked out the window she could see the soldiers of Jericho with swords and spears, guarding the city wall.

One morning Rahab heard rams' horns sounding in the distance. While she watched a strange cavalcade appeared on the highway. Picked soldiers of Israel were leading the procession, and priests dressed in white came marching behind, carrying a beautiful golden chest. In the morning sunlight the ark of the covenant shone in rich splendor. Behind the ark came other soldiers in full battle array.

In breathless wonder Rahab watched the strange procession. Not a sound came from the priests carrying the ark or from the soldiers. Seven priests blew the rams' horns, and the sound echoed through the valley. Around the walled city marched the men of Israel. After they had circled the city, all was quiet. The procession disappeared in the direction of the camp. Rahab and her family wondered what was going to happen. Would the soldiers capture the city today? Would Rahab and her family be spared, as the spies had promised?

The next morning the soldiers and priests came marching again. This happened every morning for six days. By this time the soldiers of Jericho were sneering at the men of Israel, calling them cowards who were afraid to fight.

On the seventh morning Rahab and her family watched the soldiers march by once more, and the priests carrying the golden ark of the covenant moved with determined step. On this day, however, the procession did not stop when it had circled the city once. It kept on marching, marching, until it had encompassed the wall of Jericho seven times. Then the priests blew their horns. Joshua called to the vast throng of

When the walls of Jericho fell, the soldiers of Israel ran forward and destroyed the enemy without mercy.

JOHN STEEL, ARTIST          © P. P. P. A.

Israel, who had been gathered nearby, and said, "Shout; for the Lord has given you the city. And the city and all that is within it shall be devoted to the Lord for destruction; only Rahab the harlot and all who are with her in her house shall live, because she hid the messengers that we sent." Then the people gave a mighty shout that echoed through the valley and mingled with a terrible rumbling sound. When the shout died away, the rumbling grew louder and louder! The walls of Jericho shook, then crumbled and fell with a thunderous roar! The soldiers of Israel ran forward and quickly conquered the city, taking the silver and the gold for the treasury of the Lord. Every building was burned by fire except the house of Rahab. Joshua gave this command to the spies, "Go into the harlot's house, and bring out from it the woman, and all who belong to her as you swore to her."

When the two spies arrived at the house in the city wall, they found Rahab and all the members of her family waiting for the promised protectors to arrive. Rahab's family was welcomed in the camp of Israel, for the people had heard how she had saved the lives of the spies. Rahab, though of a disreputable background, believed in God, and later she married a man of Israel named Salmon. She became the great-great-grandmother of David, king of Israel.

Joshua had given strict orders that no one should take any of the loot from the city of Jericho. He had said, "Keep yourselves from the things devoted to destruction, lest when you have devoted them you take any of the devoted things and make the camp of Israel a thing for destruction, and bring trouble upon it. But all silver and gold, and vessels of bronze and iron, are sacred to the Lord; they shall go into the treasury of the Lord." Through the power of God the enemy had been conquered. Therefore the people did not deserve to keep any of the treasure for themselves.

Long before this time Moses had warned the people against secret sin. He said, "Be sure your sin will find you out." Now there was a man of the tribe of Judah named Achan who did not believe these words. He was certain he was too clever to get caught! He went into the city to destroy the enemy; but as he made his way among the smoking ruins, he saw a bag of silver and gold spilled in the street. His greedy eyes looked at the treasure, and he knelt down and began putting the gold and silver into the bag. He also found a beautiful robe and hid it under his coat. Then he hurried back to his tent in the camp of Israel and buried the loot in the ground.

## A Traitor Is Discovered

Another city, smaller than Jericho, now lay in the way of Israel's advance. Joshua said to his men, "Go up and spy out the land." The warriors went to the town of Ai, surveyed the surrounding country, and returned to their leader, saying, "Let not all the people go up, but let about two or three thousand men go up and attack Ai; do not make the whole people toil up there, for they are but few."

So about three thousand soldiers marched up to take the city; but the men of Ai came out and fought savagely, killing thirty-six Israelite soldiers before the army fled in defeat. When the men of Israel heard of the disaster that had befallen their comrades, their courage failed. Joshua mourned and called upon the Lord for help. God told Joshua that there was disobedience and dishonesty in the camp. The divine message declared, "Israel has sinned; they have transgressed My covenant which I commanded them; they have taken some of the devoted things; they have stolen, and lied, and put them among their own stuff. Therefore the people of Israel cannot stand before their enemies. . . . I will be with you no more, unless you destroy the devoted things from among you."

When Joshua found that an Israelite had disobeyed God by stealing some of the treasure from Jericho, he called the leaders of the camp together. By casting lots it was found that the guilty man was in the tribe of Judah. Finally it was discovered that Achan was the traitor in the camp. Joshua said to Achan, "My son, give glory to the Lord God of Israel, and

97

render praise to Him; and tell me now what you have done; do not hide it from me."

Achan confessed to Joshua, "Of a truth I have sinned against the Lord God of Israel, and this is what I did: when I saw among the spoil a beautiful mantle from Shinar, and two hundred shekels of silver, and a bar of gold weighing fifty shekels, then I coveted them, and took them; and behold, they are hidden in the earth inside my tent, with the silver underneath."

Messengers ran to Achan's tent and found the money hidden in a hole in the ground, as he had said. Then Achan was taken to the valley of Achor, and Joshua said, "Why did you bring trouble on us? The Lord brings trouble on you today."

Achan, the traitor, was put to death by the men of Israel, who stoned him. He had disobeyed his general in time of war, and he had broken the law of the Lord. Then the Lord said to Joshua, "Do not fear or be dismayed; take all the fighting men with you, and arise, go up to Ai; see, I have given into your hand the king of Ai, and his people, his city, and his land; and you shall do to Ai and its king as you did to Jericho and its king; only its spoil and its cattle you shall take as booty for yourselves."

Joshua, the mighty warrior, sent thirty thousand men against Ai, and instructed them to hide near the city. The next morning Joshua took command of about five thousand men, and they marched up to the gate of Ai. When the king of the city saw the small army with Joshua, he hurried out through the city gate with his soldiers and attacked the Israelites. Joshua's men fled toward the desert pretending they were beaten. A fierce battle cry echoed through the valley as the soldiers from Ai ran in pursuit. They were so sure of victory that they left the city completely undefended.

Then Joshua stretched out his javelin as a signal for the thirty thousand soldiers who were in hiding to come out and take the city. They marched through the open gates, conquered the city, and burned it. At that moment the fleeing army of

When confronted with the gold bar and the beautiful mantle, Achan confessed that he had disobeyed orders.

99

Israel turned on the soldiers of Ai; and when the enemy saw their city going up in flames, they lost heart and surrendered.

With military conquests suspended for the time, Joshua called the people together in the luxuriant valley between the two mountains, Ebal and Gerizim. Here, in harmony with the instructions previously given by Moses, a monument of stones was erected. After the monument was covered with plaster, the Ten Commandments were inscribed upon the memorial.

Six of the tribes walked up the slopes of Mount Gerizim, and the other six climbed Mount Ebal. At the signal from a trumpet there was majestic silence. Then Joshua read the list of blessings while the tribes on Gerizim responded by an Amen. Afterward he read the curses, and the multitude on Ebal gave the solemn response. Thus, in dramatic antiphonal style of response, the nation pledged to obey the law of God and to teach it to succeeding generations forever.

# Dividing the Land of Canaan

*Joshua 9 to 24*

chapter 10 &

FEAR came upon all the kings in the highlands and the lowlands of Canaan when they heard how the armies of Israel defeated their enemies. The Lord went before His people, as He had promised, and they continued to win victory after victory.

When the inhabitants of Gibeon heard what Joshua had done to Jericho and Ai, they conceived a plan to save their lives. Although their city was less than twenty miles from the camp of Israel, the ambassadors from Gibeon disguised themselves by wearing old clothes and worn-out sandals. After loading their pack animals with old sacks and patched wineskins and putting dry, crumbly bread in their saddlebags, they then set out on the short journey to Gilgal. Here the delegation met Joshua and presented their request, saying, "We have come from a far country; so now make a covenant with us."

The leaders of Israel, thinking that these ambassadors might be telling a falsehood, said, "Perhaps you live among us; then how can we make a covenant with you?"

"We are your servants," they said to Joshua.

But Joshua said, "Who are you? And where do you come from?"

Then the Gibeonites deceived the leaders of Israel, saying, "From a very far country your servants have come, because of the name of the Lord your God; for we have heard a report of Him, and all that He did in Egypt, and all that He did to the two kings of the Amorites who were beyond the Jordan, Sihon the king of Heshbon, and Og king of Bashan, who dwelt in Ashtaroth. And our elders and all the inhabitants of our country said to us, 'Take provisions in your hand for the journey, and go to meet them, and say to them, "We are your servants; come now, make a covenant with us."' Here is our bread; it was still warm when we took it from our houses as our food for the journey, on the day we set forth to come to you, but now, behold, it is dry and moldy; these wineskins were new when we filled them, and behold, they are burst; and these garments and shoes of ours are worn out from the very long journey."

When the leaders of Israel saw this evidence of a long journey, they accepted the story and made peace terms with the foreigners without seeking advice from the Lord. But three days afterward Joshua and his officers learned the truth —the people of Gibeon actually lived only a few miles away. When the camp of Israel heard how the leaders had been deceived, they grumbled. Some of the Israelites said the foreigners should be killed, but Joshua and his leaders said, "We have sworn to them by the Lord, the God of Israel, and now we may not touch them. This we will do to them, and let them live, lest wrath be upon us, because of the oath which we swore to them."

He summoned the men of Gibeon and said to them, "Why did you deceive us, saying, 'We are very far from you,' when you dwell among us? Now therefore you are cursed, and some of you shall always be slaves, hewers of wood and drawers of water for the house of my God."

They answered Joshua, "Because it was told to your servants for a certainty that the Lord your God had commanded His servant Moses to give you all the land, and to destroy all the inhabitants of the land from before you; so we feared greatly for our lives because of you, and did this thing. And now,

102

The Gibeonites pretended that they had made a long journey to the camp, and Israel's leaders were deceived.

JOHN STEEL, ARTIST          © P.P.P.A.

behold, we are in your hand: do as it seems good and right in your sight to do to us." From that day the Gibeonites became servants in the camp of Israel.

### *When the Sun Stood Still*

Not long afterward five kings of the cities of Canaan assembled their armies and marched against the people of Gibeon, because that city had made a peace treaty with Israel. The Gibeonites sent a message to Joshua at Gilgal, saying, "Do not relax your hand from your servants; come up to us quickly, and save us, and help us; for all the kings of the Amorites that dwell in the hill country are gathered against us."

Quickly mustering his army, Joshua marched all night and made a surprise attack on the enemy. The army of Israel threw the enemy into a panic and they fled, only to be destroyed by a hailstorm. All day long the army of Israel fought, and Joshua pleaded for more time to finish the battle. The Bible declares, "And the sun stood still, and the moon stayed, until the nation took vengeance on their enemies. . . . The sun stayed in the midst of heaven, and did not hasten to go down for about a whole day. There has been no day like it before or since, when the Lord hearkened to the voice of a man; for the Lord fought for Israel."

Joshua led the nation from victory to victory. Thirty-one kings, who held territory from the desert south of Beersheba to the northern highlands near Mount Hermon, were vanquished. Then "the land had rest from war."

Not all the wicked enemies had been conquered, however; but it was time to divide the Promised Land among the twelve tribes. The leaders decided that each tribe should take the responsibility of vanquishing the enemies that remained in its assigned territory.

The boundaries of land for each tribe were drawn by lot. When the tribe of Judah came for its inheritance, Caleb, the faithful spy who had stood with Joshua to give a good report of the land, made this request, "And now, behold, the Lord has

kept me alive, as He said, these forty-five years since the time that the Lord spoke this word to Moses, while Israel walked in the wilderness; and now, lo, I am this day eighty-five years old. I am still as strong to this day as I was in the day that Moses sent me; my strength now is as my strength was then, for war, and for going and coming. So now give me this hill country of which the Lord spoke on that day; for you heard on that day how the Anakim were there, with great fortified cities: it may be that the Lord will be with me, and I shall drive them out as the Lord said."

Caleb was asking for the walled cities of the giants! Although he was eighty-five years old, he was confident that God would help him conquer these fierce people.

Caleb had a beautiful daughter named Achsah. He made this offer to the valiant young warriors: "Whoever smites Kiriath-sepher, and takes it, to him will I give Achsah my daughter as wife."

Now Othniel, a brave young man, loved Achsah. When he heard this announcement by Caleb, he took a band of brave men with him, captured this city of the giants, and received Caleb's daughter as his wife.

When each tribe had received its share of the land, Joshua asked for one city that was still unassigned. It was Timnath-serah, which means, "That which is left."

Years of peace came to the people of Israel. Joshua established the sanctuary in the city of Shiloh, and the people went there to offer sacrifices and to worship the Lord.

But the day came when Joshua realized that his leadership was nearing an end, so he summoned the leaders of the tribes and said to them, "I am now old and well advanced in years, and you have seen all that the Lord your God has done to all these nations for your sake, for it is the Lord your God who has fought for you. Behold, I have allotted to you as an inheritance for your tribes those nations that remain, along with all the nations that I have already cut off, from the Jordan to the Great Sea in the west. The Lord your God will push them back

105

before you, and drive them out of your sight; and you shall possess their land, as the Lord your God promised you. Therefore be very steadfast to keep and do all that is written in the book of the law of Moses, turning aside from it neither to the right hand nor to the left, that you may not be mixed with these nations left here among you, or make mention of the names of their gods, or swear by them, or serve them, or bow down yourselves to them, but cleave to the Lord your God as you have done to this day."

Joshua added this courageous testimony concerning the Lord's care for the nation, "And now I am about to go the way of all the earth, and you know in your hearts and souls, all of you, that not one thing has failed of all the good things which the Lord your God promised concerning you; all have come to pass for you, not one of them has failed."

Then Joshua spoke to all the people assembled at Shechem. He told them how Abraham had made his first home at Shechem when he entered the Land of Promise. He reminded them of God's care and protection to their fathers during the long years in Egypt, how He had delivered them and cared for them through the wanderings in the desert. He gave thanks to the Lord for the victory they had won over their enemies. To the throng of people he said, "Choose this day whom you will serve; . . . but as for me and my house, we will serve the Lord."

The great crowd shouted, "We also will serve the Lord, for He is our God."

Joshua wrote the pledge of Israel in the book of the law which was kept in the side of the ark of the covenant. Then he set up a great stone as a monument and said, "Behold, this stone shall be a witness against us; for it has heard all the words of the Lord which He spoke to us; therefore it shall be a witness against you, lest you deal falsely with your God."

Joshua died at the age of one hundred ten years and was buried with great honor in the city that had been given to him as his possession.

Joshua directed the men to set up
a stone monument as a witness to
the people's pledge to serve God.

107

It is also interesting to note that about this time the body of Joseph, which had been embalmed in Egypt, was buried in Shechem, the city which had been given the sons of Joseph as their inheritance. The children of Israel had brought the bones of Joseph with them when they left Egypt.

# When Judges Delivered Israel

*Judges 1 to 8*

chapter 11 *

WHEN Joshua died, there was no strong leader among the tribes of Israel to take his place. The people did not complete the conquest of the land, and they soon forgot God and refused to obey the Ten Commandments. The nation had been warned against the worship of idols, for Moses had said, "You shall not bow down to their gods, nor serve them, nor do according to their works, but you shall utterly overthrow them and break their pillars in pieces. You shall serve the Lord your God, and I will bless your bread and your water; and I will take sickness away from the midst of you."

Settled in their own land, the tribes were separated from one another more than they had ever been before. Thus they lost their unity and their strength. They bowed before the god Baal and the goddess Ashtoreth, pagan gods of the Canaanites. By their failure to obey God, the nation lost His guidance and protection, and it was possible for enemies to attack them, steal their crops, and leave whole communities in terror.

The kings of Mesopotamia, Moab, and Philistia became oppressors of Israel, as well as the Canaanites. In order to save Israel, God called men to champion the truth and to deliver the people from their enemies. Leaders such as Othniel, Shamgar, Ehud, Deborah, and Barak were known as judges. The land usually enjoyed peace and security during the rule of these judges; but there were periods when there was no leader, and in those times the people forgot God and went into idolatry.

A powerful enemy, Jabin, king of Canaan, sent his army under a general named Sisera, with nine hundred chariots of iron, to attack Israel. At that time Deborah the prophetess lived in a village between Ramah and Bethel. This influential woman heard of the fierce invaders and she sent for Barak, a valiant soldier. She summoned him to gather an army of ten thousand men and camp at Mount Tabor. She said that the Lord had promised to deliver the enemy into his hands. Barak said to the prophetess, "If you will go with me, I will go; but if you will not go with me, I will not go."

"I will surely go with you," she said; "nevertheless, the road on which you are going will not lead to your glory, for the Lord will sell Sisera into the hand of a woman."

So Deborah and Barak led the army of Israel toward Mount Tabor. When Sisera heard that Israel's warriors were on the march, he came out with his nine hundred chariots to meet them. When Deborah saw the evil hordes approaching, she said to Barak, "Up! For this is the day in which the Lord has given Sisera into your hand. Does not the Lord go out before you?"

Leading his men in a fierce charge, Barak went down the mountainside to attack the enemy. There was a pitched battle between men on horses and men on the ground. The chariots dashed into the thick of the fight, but the Canaanites saw that they were defeated. Sisera, the enemy general, jumped from his chariot and ran for his life. Barak and his army pursued the beaten soldiers, who were now running from the battlefield; but in the confusion Barak did not see their general escape.

The defeated Sisera ran northward and sought refuge in the tent of Heber, a Kenite tribesman. Now, Heber was away; but Jael, his wife, met the weary general. She said to him, "Turn aside, my lord, turn aside to me; have no fear."

The general stopped at the tent, for he was tired and hungry; and the woman hid him under a robe.

"Pray, give me a little water to drink," he said to her, "for I am thirsty."

Instead of giving Sisera a glass of water, Jael gave him a bowl of milk curds. If she had given him a drink of water she could not have killed him, as she intended, because the customs of the people were such that if a cup of water were given to a visitor he was protected as long as he was a guest in the tent.

After eating the food, the tired general wanted to sleep. "Stand at the door of the tent, and if any man comes and asks you, 'Is anyone here?' say, 'No,'" he commanded the woman.

But Jael, the wife of Heber, seized a tent pin; and, taking a hammer in her hand, she stole up softly to the general when he was asleep and drove the great pin through his temples.

Soon Barak came hurrying along in pursuit of the enemy. Jael went to meet him and said, "Come, and I will show you the man whom you are seeking."

Barak slipped into the tent and found the general dead at the hand of a woman. Israel's great victory was celebrated throughout the land of Canaan, and Deborah wrote a commemoration ode concerning the battle. In the ode she gave the glory to Jael, who had killed Sisera:

"Most blessed of women be Jael,
        the wife of Heber the Kenite,
        of tent-dwelling women most blessed.
    He asked water and she gave him milk,
        she brought him curds in a lordly bowl.
    She put her hand to the tent peg
        and her right hand to the workmen's mallet;
        she struck Sisera a blow,
        she crushed his head,
        she shattered and pierced his temple.
    He sank, he fell,
        he lay still at her feet;
        at her feet he sank, he fell;
        where he sank, there he fell dead."

111

After forty years of peace and prosperity, Israel again returned to the worship of idols. God permitted another enemy to attack the nation. This time the armies of the Midianites and Amalekites overran the country. No one was safe in his house or in the field; the enemy was everywhere. Conditions became so bad that the Israelites fled to caves and dens in the mountains, or to any other place where they might hide. For seven years the invaders swarmed over the country like grasshoppers, ruining the farms and homes.

## Gideon, the Valiant Judge

In the hour of distress the people remembered the Lord and called upon Him for mercy. A prophet went through the land with a message, saying, "Thus says the Lord, the God of Israel: I led you up from Egypt, and brought you out of the house of bondage; and I delivered you from the hand of the Egyptians, and from the hand of all who oppressed you, and drove them out before you, and gave you their land; and I said to you, 'I am the Lord your God; you shall not pay reverence to the gods of the Amorites, in whose land you dwell.' But you have not given heed to My voice."

One day a young man of the tribe of Manasseh, who was loyal to God, threshed a little grain by his wine press. He was hiding from enemy soldiers, for if they found his wheat they would take it from him. While he was at work an angel said to him, "The Lord is with you, you mighty man of valor."

"Pray, sir," said Gideon thoughtfully, "if the Lord is with us, why then has all this befallen us? And where are all His wonderful deeds which our fathers recounted to us, saying, 'Did not the Lord bring us up from Egypt?' But now the Lord has cast us off, and given us into the hand of Midian."

Then Gideon received this instruction: "Go in this might of yours and deliver Israel from the hand of Midian; do not I send you?"

Gideon wanted to be certain that he was to be a conqueror, so he asked for definite proof. From his house he brought an

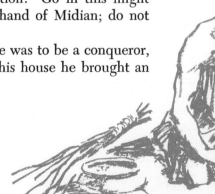

offering of meat and bread to the angel. The angel said, "Take the meat and the unleavened cakes, and put them on this rock and pour the broth over them." Gideon put the food on a flat rock and poured a pot of broth over it. Then the angel stretched forth his staff, touched the meat and cakes, and fire burst forth from the rock. As the food was consumed the angel vanished. Then Gideon knew that it was the angel of the Lord who had talked with him.

"Alas, O Lord God!" said Gideon. "For now I have seen the angel of the Lord face to face."

Then the Lord said to him, "Peace be to you; do not fear, you shall not die."

Gideon built an altar and worshiped in that place. It must have been a happy day for the young follower of the true God. Although his father had been worshiping Baal for years, Gideon was determined to wipe out the idolatry in his neighborhood. That night Gideon broke down the altar of Baal and destroyed the images. Then he offered sacrifices to the Lord of heaven.

In the morning the Baal worshipers in the town were angry when they found their altar destroyed. They shouted one to another, "Who has done this thing?"

Upon investigation they found that it was Gideon, the son of Joash, who had destroyed the altar of Baal. The men surrounded the house of Gideon's father and said to Joash, "Bring out your son, that he may die, for he has pulled down the altar of Baal and cut down the Asherah beside it."

Joash, whose conscience had troubled him for his idol worship, replied, "Will you contend for Baal? Or will you defend his cause? Whoever contends for him shall be put to death by morning. If he is a god, let him contend for himself, because his altar has been pulled down."

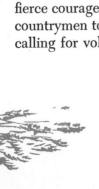

The people knew that they had sinned; therefore, they were afraid to touch Gideon. The Spirit of God gave the young judge fierce courage. He blew the trumpet and summoned his fellow countrymen to arms. He sent messengers throughout the land, calling for volunteers. Then Gideon sought further proof that

113

God would be with him in battle. To the Lord he said, "If Thou wilt deliver Israel by my hand, as Thou hast said, behold, I am laying a fleece of wool on the threshing floor; if there is dew on the fleece alone, and it is dry on all the ground, then I shall know that Thou wilt deliver Israel by my hand, as Thou hast said."

The next morning Gideon arose early and wrung the fleece, and there was a bowlful of water in it; but the ground was dry.

Gideon decided to make one more test. He said to the Lord, "Let not Thy anger burn against me, let me speak but this once; pray, let me make trial only this once with the fleece; pray, let it be dry only on the fleece, and on all the ground let there be dew."

He hurried from his tent the next morning and found a heavy dew on the ground, but the fleece was dry. Now Gideon was sure of his mission. He realized that he faced a powerful enemy, but God had promised the victory even though Israel's army was small and poorly equipped. Gideon was ready to advance by faith!

### A Battle With Pitchers and Torches

Gideon was making plans to attack the Midianites when God sent a strange message. The Lord said, "The people with you are too many for Me to give the Midianites into their hand, lest Israel vaunt themselves against Me, saying, 'My own hand has delivered me.' Now therefore proclaim in the ears of the people, saying, 'Whoever is fearful and trembling, let him return home.'"

Calling all his volunteer soldiers together, Gideon said, "Whoever is fearful and trembling, let him return home." The general tried to give his soldiers courage and faith, and he hoped that they would stay with him; but his heart sank when twenty-two thousand men picked up their swords, spears, and bags of food, and started home. Only ten thousand men were left to attack the hordes of the enemy. The Lord said to Gideon, "The people are still too many; take them down to the

The next day Gideon arose early and wrung a bowlful of water from the fleece. His prayer was answered.

JOHN STEEL, ARTIST          © P. P. P. A.

water and I will test them for you there; and he of whom I say
to you, 'This man shall go with you,' shall go with you; and
any of whom I say to you, 'This man shall not go with you,'
shall not go."

Gideon marched his men down to the riverbank and watched
them drink. Those who hurried across the stream toward the
enemy camp, lapping up water as they advanced, were put
in one group. Those who knelt by the riverbank and drank
leisurely, were put in another group. Only three hundred men
lapped the water with their tongues. God said to Gideon, "With
the three hundred men that lapped I will deliver you, and give
the Midianites into your hand; and let all the others go every
man to his home."

The three hundred picked men must have wondered what
was happening when they heard Gideon issue the order that the
group of 9,700 soldiers could return to their homes. How would
he fight the Midianites with this handful of warriors?

Gideon gave each of the three hundred men a clay pitcher,
a trumpet, and a torch—strange weapons of war! That night
Gideon and his servant crept into the enemy camp to spy on the
warriors. The Midianites were spread out in the valley below
like a horde of locusts, and their camels were as the sand on the
beach. As Gideon crept up to the side of one of the enemy tents,
he heard a man telling his comrade a dream.

"Behold, I dreamed a dream," he said, "and lo, a cake of
barley bread tumbled into the camp of Midian, and came to
the tent, and struck it so that it fell, and turned it upside down,
so that the tent lay flat."

"This," his comrade responded, "is no other than the sword
of Gideon the son of Joash, a man of Israel; into his hand God
has given Midian and all the host."

With thankful heart Gideon returned to his camp, for he
recognized this to be a sign that the Lord would give them
success. At once he gave the command to his men, "Arise;
for the Lord has given the host of Midian into your hand."

He divided his three hundred men into three groups. The

116

The soldiers broke their pitchers to
let the torches flare, and terrorized
the enemy with trumpet peals.

JOHN STEEL, ARTIST          © P. P. P. A.

men tried to look like soldiers ready to fight, although they had only torches in empty pitchers, and trumpets.

"Look at me," Gideon said to his men, "and do likewise; when I come to the outskirts of the camp, do as I do. When I blow the trumpet, I and all who are with me, then blow the trumpets also on every side of all the camp, and shout, 'For the Lord and for Gideon.'"

Stealthily the three groups of men advanced and surrounded the camp of Midian. At a signal from their commander, the three hundred men blew their trumpets and broke their pitchers. The torches gleamed brightly in the dark night. Then they shouted, "A sword for the Lord and for Gideon!" The sleeping army awoke in terror. They saw gleaming torches everywhere, and the noise of the trumpets was deafening. Believing they were far outnumbered, the soldiers of Midian fled. In the darkness and confusion they fought and killed their own comrades. A great victory was won, not by the strength of the sword, but by the power of God.

After Gideon died, "the people of Israel turned again and played the harlot after the Baals, and made Baal-berith their god. And the people of Israel did not remember the Lord their God, who had rescued them from the hand of all their enemies on every side; and they did not show kindness to the family of Jerubbaal (that is, Gideon) in return for all the good that he had done to Israel."

Forgetting the deliverance that God had given them at the hand of the faithful judge, Israel sank into idolatry and apostasy. Then the Ammonites swept down upon the tribes of Judah and Ephraim, and the Philistines attacked from the west. Once more the helpless people cried to God for help, but in this hour He did not save them. Through a prophet the Lord said, "Did I not deliver you from the Egyptians and from the Amorites, from the Ammonites and from the Philistines? The Sidonians also, and the Amalekites, and the Maonites, oppressed you; and you cried to Me, and I delivered you out of their hand. Yet you have forsaken Me and served other gods;

118

therefore I will deliver you no more. Go and cry to the gods whom you have chosen; let them deliver you in the time of your distress."

The hour of judgment had come to the tribes for their flagrant rejection of the Eternal One. They must reap the harvest from the seeds they had sown.

# Samson, a Power and a Failure

*Judges 13 to 16*

## chapter 12

THE tribe of Dan received as its inheritance the small territory stretching west from Jerusalem to the Great Sea. On the borders of this region lived a powerful and cruel enemy, the Philistines, who constantly threatened Israel. Five of the chief cities of the pagan Philistines were Gaza, Gath, Ashdod, Ekron, and Askelon. Since this area was well watered, the country had an independent supply of food. Furthermore, the Philistines possessed a monopoly on iron, knowing where to get the ore and how to forge it into weapons.

When Israel forgot God and His protection was withdrawn, the Philistines would invade the farms and homes of the people of Dan. In times of peace the Israelites traded with the Philistines, and some of them married heathen wives.

There was a faithful man named Manoah, of the tribe of Dan, who lived in the little town of Zorah. An angel told him and his wife that they would have a son who should be brought up according to the strict rules of a Nazirite. This meant that he must not drink wine nor strong drink, nor eat food that was ceremonially unclean. "No razor shall come upon his head," said the angel, "for the boy shall be a Nazirite to God from birth; and he shall begin to deliver Israel from the hand of the Philistines."

Manoah and his wife felt the serious responsibility of be-

Samson married a Philistine maid and he invited thirty young men to the joyous wedding feast at Timnah.

121

coming parents and training a son. The father offered a prayer that might well be the petition of every parent when he said, "O, Lord, I pray Thee, let the man of God whom Thou didst send come again to us, and teach us what we are to do with the boy that will be born."

When the child was born, his mother named him Samson. He grew to be a giant of a man, with tremendous strength. As a restless youth he left the farm many times to visit the village of Timnah, across the border in the land of the Philistines. There he fell in love with a maiden, and when he came home he asked his father and mother to help him in his marriage plans.

"I saw one of the daughters of the Philistines at Timnah; now get her for me as my wife," he said.

The faithful mother and father were shocked by this announcement, for they had dreamed of Samson's becoming a devoted religious leader who would deliver Israel from the Philistines. His parents urged him to marry a girl from a family of Israel, who loved and worshiped the true God; but Samson was determined to have his own way regardless of the consequences. He said to his father, "Get her for me; for she pleases me well."

Manoah and his wife went with their son to the Philistine village to make arrangements for the marriage. Suddenly a young lion plunged out of the vineyard and with a roar attacked Samson. Catching the savage beast, the strong youth tore him to pieces with his bare hands until the carcass was only broken bones.

Later when he went to visit the maiden of Timnah, Samson turned aside to look at the carcass of the lion he had killed. When he examined it closely, he found that a swarm of bees had stored honey there. He scraped out some of the honey and ate it as he went on his journey.

Soon after this Samson married the Philistine woman and invited thirty young men to a wedding feast. It was the custom for guests to entertain one another with riddles. Samson pro-

pounded a riddle, saying, "Let me now put a riddle to you; if you can tell me what it is, within the seven days of the feast, and find it out, then I will give you thirty linen garments and thirty festal garments; but if you cannot tell me what it is, then you shall give me thirty linen garments and thirty festal garments."

"Put your riddle," they said to him, "that we may hear it." So he said to them:

> "Out of the eater came something to eat.
> Out of the strong came something sweet."

For three days the young men puzzled over the riddle, but they could not guess the answer. On the fourth day they threatened Samson's wife, saying, "Entice your husband to tell us what the riddle is, lest we burn you and your father's house with fire. Have you invited us here to impoverish us?"

So Samson's wife cried on her husband's shoulder and begged him to tell her the answer. Her tears finally weakened the young bridegroom so that he gave her the secret. She immediately betrayed her husband by giving the Philistine guests the answer to the hard riddle.

On the last day of the feast, the thirty men came to Samson and said:

> "What is sweeter than honey?
> What is stronger than a lion?"

Realizing that his wife had let the secret be known, Samson said sharply:

> "If you had not plowed with my heifer,
> you would not have found out my riddle."

Boiling with anger, Samson left the feast to get the garments to pay his debt. He went to Askelon, a Philistine city, where he slew thirty men and stripped them of their clothing. Then he returned to Timnah with the garments and gave them to the young Philistines to fulfill his bargain. He was so furious, however, that he went straight to his father's house and would

123

not stop to see his wife. It was a disgrace for a woman to be deserted by her husband, and so her parents arranged for her to marry another husband.

Shortly after this, however, Samson took a present and went to make peace with his wife; but his father-in-law met him and would not let him into the house.

"I really thought that you utterly hated her; so I gave her to your companion," her father tried to explain.

Then the strong young giant was beside himself with rage. He said to himself, "This time I shall be blameless in regard to the Philistines, when I do them mischief."

It was the harvest season, and the fields of grain and the vineyards were ready to harvest. Samson went out into the hills and snared three hundred foxes. This was certainly no easy task; but his next job required more patience and perseverance. He tied two foxes together by their tails and then attached a flaming torch between the tails. In this way he turned one hundred fifty pairs of foxes loose in the grainfields of the Philistines. They ran through the fields, setting the wheat on fire. Soon the wheat fields, the vineyards, and the olive groves lay in total ruin, for the land was as dry as tinder in that season of the year.

"Who has done this?" said the Philistines.

"Samson, the son-in-law of the Timnite, because he has taken his wife and given her to his companion," it was said.

In cruel revenge the Philistines set fire to the house where Samson's wife lived and burned her and her father to death.

Then Samson said to the mob, "If this is what you do, I swear I will be avenged upon you, and after that I will quit." Then he attacked the men of Timnah, and there was a great slaughter.

All this strife and bloodshed came about because Samson dishonored his parents and refused to obey the God of heaven. He might have delivered his people with a strong program of reform and defense; but instead, he took his grievances out on the Philistines like a big bully. Sick of his mistakes, Samson went to live alone in a cave in Etam.

124

## *A Crafty Betrayal*

Samson! The name struck terror to the Philistines. They sought in every way possible to track down and kill this judge, who had done so much damage to their nation. Finally a band of Philistine warriors came up against the people of Judah and raided the town of Lehi.

"Why have you come up against us?" asked the Judeans.

"We have come up to bind Samson, to do to him as he did to us," they said.

Three thousand men of Judah went down to the cave at Etam and found Samson and said to him, "Do you not know that the Philistines are rulers over us? What then is this that you have done to us?"

And he said to them, "As they did to me, so have I done to them."

"We have come down to bind you, that we may give you into the hands of the Philistines," the Judeans told him.

"Swear to me that you will not fall upon me yourselves."

"No," they responded, "we will only bind you and give you into their hands; we will not kill you."

Samson allowed his fellow Israelites to bind him with two pieces of new rope, and take him to the Philistines at Lehi. When the Philistines saw the men of Judah bringing Samson as a prisoner, they shouted for joy and rushed out to capture him. In that moment the power of God came upon Samson, and he snapped the ropes that bound him as if they were flax burned in the fire. He picked up the whitened jawbone of an ass that lay by the roadside. With this weapon he attacked the Philistines and killed a thousand of them. Then Samson shouted triumphantly:

> "With the jawbone of an ass, heaps upon heaps.
> With the jawbone of an ass have I slain a thousand men."

Soon after this Samson went to Gaza, the capital city of Philistia, to visit a harlot. When the people of the city saw the strong young man, they whispered, "Samson has come here." They surrounded the woman's house and watched for him, saying, "Let us wait till the light of the morning; then we will kill him." But at midnight Samson went to the city gate, which was locked, and when he could not get out, he took hold of the gateposts and pulled them up, together with the bars. He put the huge city gates on his shoulders and carried them out to the top of the hill, and again he escaped from his enemies.

Even after these experiences Samson could not learn that he should stay away from the heathen people. Although he was judge over Israel, he fell in love with Delilah, a Philistine beauty, who lived in the valley of Sorek.

The Philistine chiefs came to her and said, "Entice him, and see wherein his great strength lies, and by what means we may overpower him, that we may bind him to subdue him; and we will each give you eleven hundred pieces of silver."

So Deliah said to Samson, "Please tell me wherein your great strength lies, and how you might be bound, that one could subdue you."

Samson said to her, "If they bind me with seven fresh bow-strings which have not been dried, then I shall become weak, and be like any other man."

Delilah told the Philistine chiefs what he had said, and they brought to her bowstrings and she bound him. When the chiefs came in and tried to capture Samson, he snapped the bowstrings as if they were straw touched by fire. So the source of his strength was not discovered.

Then Delilah realized that Samson had tricked her. "Behold, you have mocked me, and told me lies; please tell me how you might be bound," she cooed.

Samson had a great deal of fortitude when he would use it, and he seems to have determined not to give away the secret of his strength. So he said to her, "If they bind me with new ropes that have not been used, then I shall become weak, and be like any other man."

Delilah took new ropes and bound him with them. Then

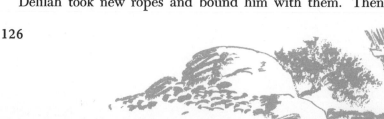

she said to him, "The Philistines are upon you, Samson!"

Philistine chiefs rushed into the room once more, but Samson snapped the ropes as if they were thread, and his enemies could not capture him.

The third time Delilah tried to obtain the secret from Samson, but the third time she failed to find the secret of his strength.

It would seem that the most foolish of men would have seen that Delilah was being used as a tool to betray him into the hands of his enemies; but Samson was so infatuated by her charms that he could not think clearly. The woman said, "How can you say, 'I love you,' when your heart is not with me? You have mocked me these three times, and you have not told me wherein your great strength lies."

Day after day Delilah coaxed Samson, and finally he told her the truth. "A razor has never come upon my head; for I have been a Nazirite to God from my mother's womb," he said to her. "If I be shaved, then my strength will leave me, and I shall become weak, and be like any other man."

Delilah knew that he had revealed the whole secret to her, and she sent for the Philistine chiefs, saying, "Come up this once, for he has told me all his mind."

Then the chiefs came with money in their hands to pay Delilah. When Samson slept on her knees she called a man and he shaved off his hair. Then she said, "The Philistines are upon you, Samson!"

Samson awoke and thought, "I will go out as at other times, and shake myself free." He did not know that his hair had been cut, that his power had vanished. The cunning enemies seized Samson and gouged out his eyes—a blind, helpless giant! Now he was a prisoner, bound with bronze shackles, and his tormentors set him to work to turn the great stone to grind grain. But the hair of his head began to grow again!

John Milton, the famous English poet, who was also blind, in one of his magnificent poems imagines Samson speaking in his hour of slavery and degradation:

127

"O glorious strength,
Put to the labor of a beast, debased
Lower than bondslave!  Promise was that I
Should Israel from Philistian yoke deliver!
Ask for this great deliverer now, and find him
Eyeless in Gaza, at the mill with slaves,
Himself in bonds under Philistian yoke.

✿     ✿     ✿     ✿

O loss of sight, of thee I most complain!
Blind among enemies!  O worse than chains.

✿     ✿     ✿     ✿

Life in captivity
Among inhuman foes."

To celebrate the capture of mighty Samson, the Philistines held a lavish feast at which they offered sacrifices to their idol, Dagon.  In their merrymaking, they said, "Our god has given Samson our enemy into our hand."

The revelers shouted for blind Samson to be brought in to the feast for all to see.  They said, "Call Samson, that he may make sport for us."  Soon a boy appeared, leading the blind, groping giant.  When Samson's enemies saw him, they laughed and jeered.  They made him stand between the pillars of the temple.  Samson said to the lad who held him by the hand, "Let me feel the pillars on which the house rests, that I may lean against them."

The hall was full of chiefs of the Philistines, for about three thousand men and women were present.  Samson bowed his head and prayed to the Lord, saying, "O Lord God, remember me, I pray Thee, and strengthen me, I pray Thee, only this once, O God, that I may be avenged upon the Philistines for one of my two eyes."

This was the man's last prayer.  With terrible strength he braced himself against the two great pillars, which supported the roof of the hall.

"Let me die with the Philistines," gasped Samson.  With all his might he leaned against the pillars, and there was a crack-

In the midst of the pagan revels, Samson leaned with all his might against
the pillars and cracked the beams.

129

JOHN STEEL, ARTIST          © P. P. P. A.

ing as the beams snapped. The roof fell with a resounding crash upon the merrymakers. "So the dead whom he slew at his death were more than those whom he had slain during his life," says the Bible.

Samson's relatives came to Gath for the body of the judge who had been strong physically but weak in moral power. They buried him in the family tomb. Samson, who could not control his own habits and desires, had attempted to govern Israel for twenty years. What a glorious chapter in the history of his people he might have written if he had been true to God! Enticed by feminine charms, he forgot that true greatness is measured not by physical strength but by self-control and obedience to God.

# Ruth, a Woman of Faith

*The Book of Ruth*

chapter 13 &

IT WAS not enough to have pagan enemies harass the country of Canaan. There was also famine that struck again and again during the days of the judges. The parched ground baked in the torrid sun, and grain shriveled in the stalk. Fruit withered and fell from the trees; the grass became brown in the pasture, worthless as food for the cattle and sheep. There had been similar blights upon the land in the days of Abraham and in the time of Jacob. The patriarchs had been forced to leave Canaan when deadly famines struck.

Elimelech, a man of the tribe of Judah, lived in Bethlehem with his wife, Naomi. They had two sons, Mahlon and Chilion. When the crops failed and the famine spread through the land, Elimelech decided to move east and south across the Jordan River to the land of Moab. This was a country with rich plateaus that received rain when Canaan was stricken with drought. In that foreign country the family was welcomed and lived for ten years. The two sons married young women of the neighborhood. One was named Orpah, the other Ruth.

Death came to mar the happiness of the home. Naomi's husband died, and soon afterward her two sons were fatally stricken. This left Naomi a lonely widow in a foreign land with only her two daughters-in-law to comfort her. Homesick for friends and loved ones of Bethlehem, the woman decided to

131

return to Bethlehem, for she heard that the famine had ended.

As Naomi started on her journey, Ruth and Orpah accompanied her. But when the woman thought of the future for the two young widows, she realized the best hope for their future was in Moab. She said, "Turn back, my daughters, why will you go with me?"

Orpah was persuaded by these words. She bade her mother-in-law good-by and returned to her own people; but Ruth had faith in the God of heaven, and she loved her mother-in-law. She said to Naomi, "Entreat me not to leave you or to return from following you; for where you go I will go, and where you lodge I will lodge; your people shall be my people, and your God my God; where you die I will die, and there will I be buried."

The two women made the journey to Bethlehem where they were greeted by Naomi's relatives and friends. When the people of Bethlehem saw how their friend of former years had been aged by sorrow and hardship, they whispered, "Is this Naomi?"

But she said to them, "Do not call me Naomi [pleasant], call me Mara [bitter], for the Almighty has dealt very bitterly with me. I went away full, and the Lord has brought me back empty."

Naomi and Ruth found a home in Bethlehem in the season of the barley harvest. Now, the laws of Israel required owners of grainfields to allow the poor to glean the stalks of grain that were left behind by the reapers. They could also have the grain that grew in the corners of the fields.

## Work in the Grainfield

Although the two women had a place to live, they needed grain to grind into flour so they might bake bread. So Ruth, knowing the law of the harvest, said to Naomi, "Let me go to the field, and glean among the ears of grain after him in whose sight I shall find favor."

Ruth went to glean in the grainfields following the regular

Ruth, the Moabitess, gleaned the stalks of grain left by the reapers, and thus got food enough for Naomi and herself.

JOE MANISCALCO, ARTIST      © P. P. P. A.

MANISCALCO

reapers. Now it happened that she came to glean in the field of Boaz, a wealthy bachelor and a relative of Naomi's husband. As she was picking up the grain that had fallen from the hands of the reapers, Boaz entered the field. He saw the beautiful woman and wondered who she could be.

"Whose maiden is this?" asked Boaz of his overseer in charge of the harvesters.

"It is the Moabite maiden, who came back with Naomi from the country of Moab," the overseer explained. "She said, 'Pray, let me glean and gather among the sheaves after the reapers.'"

The overseer had noticed that Ruth was a diligent worker, for he added, "She came, and she has continued from early morning until now, without resting even for a moment."

Then Boaz said to Ruth, "Now, listen, my daughter, do not go to glean in another field or leave this one, but keep close to my maidens. Let your eyes be upon the field which they are reaping, and go after them. Have I not charged the young men not to molest you? And when you are thirsty, go to the vessels and drink what the young men have drawn."

Ruth bowed before Boaz in grateful thanks, and she said to him, "Why have I found favor in your eyes, that you should take notice of me, when I am a foreigner?"

Boaz in reply said to her, "All that you have done for your mother-in-law since the death of your husband has been fully told me, and how you left your father and mother and your native land and came to a people that you did not know before."

Boaz could not forget the young widow's beauty and her winsome smile. At mealtime the man said to her, "Come here, and eat some bread, and dip your morsel in the wine." Ruth seated herself beside the gleaners, and Boaz gave her some of the parched grain to eat. It was a custom for the reapers to tie some of the stalks of grain in bunches and roast them over the fire. When the grain was a golden brown, they would rub the ears in their hands and eat the delicious roasted kernels that had a rich, nutlike flavor.

After dinner, when Ruth had returned to her work, Boaz gave orders to his servants, "Let her glean even among the sheaves, and do not reproach her. And also pull out some from the bundles for her, and leave it for her to glean, and do not rebuke her."

She worked in the field until evening, and then she beat out the grain she had gleaned. There was about an ephah of barley, or nearly three bushels. Ruth hurried home with her gleanings. "Where did you glean today? And where have you worked?" her mother-in-law asked her with interest. "Blessed be the man who took notice of you."

Ruth told her mother-in-law all that had happened. "The man's name with whom I worked today is Boaz."

## A Relative of the Family

"The man is a relative of ours, one of our nearest kin," Naomi said to her.

"Besides," said Ruth, the Moabitess, "he said to me, 'You shall keep close by my servants, till they have finished all my harvest.'"

"It is well, my daughter," Naomi said to her daughter-in-law, "that you go out with his maidens, lest in another field you be molested." The mother-in-law dreamed of security and happiness for Ruth and she hoped that Boaz would continue to look with favor upon the beautiful girl.

"Then Naomi her mother-in-law said to her, 'My daughter, should I not seek a home for you, that it may be well with you? Now is not Boaz our kinsman, with whose maidens you were? See, he is winnowing barley tonight at the threshing floor. Wash therefore and anoint yourself, and put on your best clothes and go down to the threshing floor; but do not make yourself known to the man until he has finished eating and drinking.'"

"And she replied, 'All that you say I will do.'"

"So she went down to the threshing floor and did just as her mother-in-law had told her."

When startled Boaz awoke and found Ruth lying at his feet, he said, "May you be blessed by the Lord, my daughter; you have made this last kindness greater than the first, in that you have not gone after young men, whether poor or rich. And now, my daughter, do not fear, I will do for you all that you ask, for all my fellow townsmen know that you are a woman of worth. And now it is true that I am a near kinsman, yet there is a kinsman nearer than I. Remain this night, and in the morning, if he will do the part of the next of kin for you, well; let him do it; but if he is not willing to do the part of next of kin for you, then, as the Lord lives, I will do the part of the next of kin for you. Lie down until the morning."

The relative of whom Boaz spoke also lived in Bethlehem, and according to the law of Israel, if a man died without leaving children, the nearest relative had the right to the property and he could also marry the widow. If the nearest relative did not wish to buy the land, the next nearest relative could do so. So Boaz went to the city gate where all business transactions were carried on. He met the man who was the nearest relative of Naomi's husband and told him about the land which should be redeemed. "I will redeem it," he said.

Then Boaz said, "The day you buy the field from the hand of Naomi, you are also buying Ruth the Moabitess, the widow of the dead, in order to restore the name of the dead to his inheritance."

"I cannot redeem it for myself," said the man to Boaz, "lest I impair my own inheritance. Take my right of redemption yourself, for I cannot redeem it."

There was an ancient custom in the land that any business transaction should be completed when one man pulled off his sandal and gave it to the other. This was the manner of sealing a bargain. Therefore, when the nearest relative said to Boaz, "Buy it for yourself," he drew off his sandal and handed it to Boaz.

Then Boaz said to the chief men of the city and to all the people, "You are witnesses this day that I have bought from the

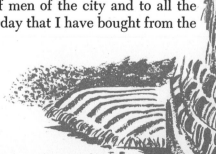

hand of Naomi all that belonged to Elimelech and all that belonged to Chilion and to Mahlon.  Also Ruth the Moabitess, the widow of Mahlon, I have bought to be my wife."

So the chief men of the city witnessed the transaction, and they said, "We are witnesses.  May the Lord take the woman, who is coming into your house, like Rachel and Leah, who together built up the house of Israel."

Naomi, the aged mother-in-law, rejoiced to see Ruth happily married.  Months later the women of the neighborhood brought Naomi wonderful news.  Ruth and Boaz had a baby son.  The women said to Naomi, the grandmother, "Blessed be the Lord, who has not left you this day without next of kin; and may his name be renowned in Israel!  He shall be to you a restorer of life and a nourisher of your old age."

Grandmother Naomi went to Ruth's home and took the child in her arms, rocking him tenderly.  She became the baby's nurse, and she watched over him so lovingly that the neighborhood women teased her, saying, "A son has been born to Naomi."  The child's name was Obed.  He became the grandfather of David, the mighty king of Israel.

In this idyllic story set in the fields of Bethlehem we have a wonderful lesson.  God has made of one blood all peoples that live in our world.  Ruth, a woman of pagan ancestry, was brought into the nation chosen of God.  Because of her faithfulness and devotion she became the great-grandmother of King David and a progenitor of Jesus Christ on the human side of his ancestry.

10—H.F. 2

# Samuel, a Devout Leader

1 Samuel 1 to 8

chapter 14 &

THE center of worship in Israel was at the sanctuary set up permanently at Shiloh. Each year many of the faithful went there to worship God and to offer sacrifices and thank offerings.

Now, Elkanah, a man from the town of Ramah, journeyed to Shiloh with the pilgrims. Every year Hannah, one of his wives, went to the tent of meeting to worship with him. She wept and was despondent because she had no children, while the other wife, Peninnah, had several children to make her husband proud. But Elkanah was thoughtful, and he told Hannah how much he loved her; however, she still longed for a son. In the morning she went to the temple to pray, and she made a vow to God that if she were given a son she would give him to the Lord all the days of his life.

Eli, who was the high priest at the tent of meeting, saw Hannah in deep emotion while she prayed, and he said, "How long will you be drunken? Put away your wine from you."

"But Hannah answered, 'No, my lord, I am a woman sorely troubled; I have drunk neither wine nor strong drink, but I have been pouring out my soul before the Lord. Do not regard your maidservant as a base woman, for all along I have been speaking out of my great anxiety and vexation.'"

Then Eli said, "Go in peace, and the God of Israel grant your petition which you have made to Him."

To fulfill her vow, Hannah brought little Samuel to the temple to be of service to Eli, the high priest.

JOE MANISCALCO, ARTIST          © P.P.P.A.

It was a happy day for Hannah when a son was born to her. She named him Samuel, which means, "Asked of God."

The years slipped by all too quickly for the mother, who remembered her vow to God. When Samuel was old enough to leave home, she took him to the house of the Lord at Shiloh and presented him to Eli, saying, "Oh, my lord! As you live, my lord, I am the woman who was standing here in your presence, praying to the Lord. For this child I prayed; and the Lord has granted me my petition which I made to Him. Therefore I have lent him to the Lord; as long as he lives, he is lent to the Lord."

All honor is due the mothers who train their children to be good citizens, who dedicate the lives of their youth to God's service and to humanity. In the midst of a thousand humdrum duties in the home, the mother has the privilege of guiding her sons and daughters on the pathway to heaven. Like Hannah, the modern mother may seek God for wisdom in guiding the youth in the home, and her prayers will be answered.

Samuel must have been homesick when his mother left him. Eli was an old man, and there was little time for play when a boy lived with the high priest. But Samuel did his work faithfully. He opened and closed the doors of the sanctuary. He kept the lamps trimmed, and he probably cleaned the floors and dusted the rooms.

Young Samuel wore a linen robe, such as the priests wore in their services; and each year when Hannah came to worship at Shiloh and to visit her son, she brought him a new coat she had made with her own hands. Other sons and daughters were given Hannah so she was not lonely in her home.

Samuel slept in the sanctuary near where the lamps burned before the golden ark. He was aroused from a sound sleep one night by a voice calling, "Samuel! Samuel!"

"Here I am!" he replied.

Then he ran to Eli, and said, "Here I am, for you called me."

"I did not call," the aged man said to the inquiring youth; "lie down again."

140

Samuel went back and lay down on his sleeping mat. Again a voice called, "Samuel!"

Once more the boy arose and went to Eli's bed. "Here I am, for you called me," Samuel responded.

"I did not call, my son," replied the priest; "lie down again."

When the voice called the third time, the boy arose and went to Eli and said, "Here I am, for you called me."

Then Eli realized that the Lord was calling the lad. The high priest instructed Samuel to lie down again, and if he should hear the voice he should say, " 'Speak, Lord, for Thy servant hears.' "

Samuel was filled with amazement at the thought that the Lord had called him. He went back and lay down on his bed. The Lord called again, "Samuel! Samuel!"

So Samuel said, "Speak, for Thy servant hears."

Then the Lord spoke these words to Samuel, "Behold, I am about to do a thing in Israel, at which the two ears of everyone that hears it will tingle. On that day I will fulfill against Eli all that I have spoken concerning his house, from beginning to end. And I tell him that I am about to punish his house forever, for the iniquity which he knew, because his sons were blaspheming God, and he did not restrain them."

Eli's two sons, Hophni and Phinehas, had grown to manhood defying their father and ridiculing the religion of Israel. Although they were worthless characters, they were appointed as priests in the sanctuary. Here they committed crimes under the cloak of piety. They robbed worshipers who offered sacrifices, and they seduced the women who assisted in keeping the sanctuary in order. Since these men were the sons of the high priest, their actions had a great influence in the nation. Their evil deeds were known everywhere, and young Samuel saw the hypocrisy and cheating that went on in God's house.

In the morning when Samuel opened the double doors of the house of the Lord, Eli called the boy to him and said, "Samuel, my son."

"Here I am," he answered.

141

"What was it that He told you? Do not hide it from me," he asked.

Then Samuel told the high priest everything that the Lord had told him, and he concealed nothing from him.

"It is the Lord; let Him do what seems good to Him," said the high priest.

## The Golden Ark Is Captured

Years passed and new wars broke out between Israel and the Philistines. In a fierce struggle at the crest of a hill near Aphek, the army of Israel lost four thousand men on the field of battle. The attack had been made without the counsel of the high priest or prayer to God for guidance. When news of the defeat reached the people, the older men said, "Why has the Lord put us to rout today before the Philistines? Let us bring the ark of the covenant of the Lord here from Shiloh, that He may come among us and save us from the power of our enemies."

The people went to Shiloh, and with the help of Eli's two evil sons took the ark of the covenant from the sanctuary. When the golden chest with the two beautiful angels on the mercy seat was brought into the camp of Israel, the soldiers gave a loud cheer, which echoed across the valley to the camp of the Philistines. The enemy heard the noise and the soldiers asked, "What does this great shouting in the camp of the Hebrews mean?"

When the Philistine soldiers learned that the ark of the Lord had arrived at the camp, they were afraid. "The gods have come into the camp," they whispered in awe.

"Woe to us!" they said, "for nothing like this has happened before. Woe to us! Who can deliver us from the power of these mighty gods? These are the gods who smote the Egyptians with every sort of plague in the wilderness. Take courage, and acquit yourselves like men, O Philistines, lest you become slaves to the Hebrews as they have been to you; acquit yourselves like men and fight."

142

In the midst of the fighting between Israel and Philistia, the ark of the covenant was captured by the pagans.

This new challenge put courage into the Philistines, and they fought grimly. There was a terrible slaughter, and among the thirty thousand men of Israel who fell that day were the two sons of Eli. In the overwhelming defeat the ark of the covenant was captured by the Philistine army.

A messenger came running to Shiloh from the battlefield. He found Eli sitting beside the city gate, waiting anxiously for news. The aged man said to the runner, "How did it go, my son?"

Hurriedly the man told his tragic story: "Israel has fled before the Philistines, and there has also been a great slaughter among the people; your two sons also, Hophni and Phinehas, are dead, and the ark of God has been captured."

This was more tragedy than the ninety-eight-year-old high priest could endure. When the messenger told how the ark of the Lord had been taken, Eli fell backward from his seat, broke his neck, and died. Eli had judged Israel forty years.

The tidings of defeat had a tragic sequel which typifies the sorrow and suffering that war brings to innocent women and children. The wife of Phinehas was about to give birth to a child when news of national defeat and the death of her husband reached her. With her loved ones gone, the country desolated, she had no desire to live. In her last moments she gasped the name of her son, "Ichabod," which means "the glory is departed."

There are moments in our experience when we feel God may have deserted us; but beyond the darkness the light of divine love still shines. We can be certain we are not alone. In this time of defeat for Israel, God used the enemy to awaken the people to their spiritual need. Suffering turned them to the Eternal One, who was ready to forgive and to offer pardon.

Meanwhile the Philistines marched back to their own country in a triumphal procession, carrying the golden ark to Ashdod. They placed it in the temple of their god, Dagon, as a trophy of victory. The next morning the Philistines found that their idol had fallen face downward upon the ground before the ark of the Lord. They lifted the idol up and restored it to its place; but the following morning the idol had fallen over again, and its head and hands were broken. The people of the city were scourged with tumors, so that the Philistines said, "The ark of the God of Israel must not remain with us; for His hand is heavy upon us and upon Dagon our god."

The lords of the Philistines assembled, and they said, "What shall we do with the ark of the God of Israel?"

"Let the ark of the God of Israel be brought around to Gath."

The ark of God was taken to the city of Gath, but a plague of tumors broke out in that city also as soon as the sacred chest arrived. Then it was moved to another town, and again the plague struck. The lords of the Philistines again held a council. They said, "Send away the ark of the God of Israel, and let it return to its own place, that it may not slay us and our people."

"If you send away the ark of the God of Israel," the priests told them, "do not send it empty, but by all means return Him a guilt offering. Then you will be healed, and it will be known to you why His hand does not turn away from you."

And the lords said, "What is the guilt offering that we shall return to Him?"

"Five golden tumors and five golden mice, according to the number of the lords of the Philistines; for the same plague was upon all of you and upon your lords. So you must make images of your tumors and images of your mice that ravage the land, and give glory to the God of Israel; perhaps He will lighten His hand from off you and your gods and your land," they answered.

Among the pagan peoples it was the custom to make images of silver or gold of that which caused a plague or illness. At the same time it was thought necessary to make an image of the part of the body affected by the disease. So in this case, the Philistines sent a "guilt offering" with the ark of the

145

covenant when they returned it to Israel. They made five golden mice and five tumors. The disease may have been the bubonic plague, as some Bible commentators point out, for rodents were associated with the deadly disease, and its symptoms were horrible boils in the groin, under the armpits, and on the neck.

The ark had been in the land of the Philistines for seven months, but men quickly prepared a special peace offering and put it with the ark. They placed the golden chest on a cart drawn by two cows whose calves had been shut up in the barn. The cows left their calves and pulled the cart straight to the town of Beth-shemesh, in Israel. Five Philistine chiefs followed the cart to the boundary of their country to see that it would arrive safely in Israel.

The people of Beth-shemesh were harvesting their grain at the time. When they saw the cart bearing the ark of the Lord, they stopped their work. The cart came to a halt in the field of a man named Joshua. The men of Israel made an altar and offered sacrifices to God. When the Philistine chiefs, from a distance, saw that the ark had arrived safely, they returned to their own country, glad to be rid of the sacred chest which had brought so much trouble to them.

The golden ark was taken to the house of Abinadab, and Eleazar, his son, had charge of it.

## The People Ask for a King

Samuel was the judge in Israel for many years. He called for the nation to obey God, saying, "If you are returning to the Lord with all your heart, then put away the foreign gods and the Ashtaroth from among you, and direct your heart to the Lord, and serve Him only, and He will deliver you out of the hand of the Philistines." The good man made an annual tour from city to city, hearing complaints, passing judgments, giving counsel, and teaching the people the way of God. When he grew old, he made the serious mistake of establishing his two wicked sons, Joel and Abijah, as judges over Israel. He

146

should have learned a lesson from the evil conduct of the sons of Eli, but he loved his sons and was blind to their sins. Like many other great men, he could see right and wrong in others, but he had a blind spot as far as his own sons were concerned. Now Samuel's sons were greedy men, who took bribes from the people and perverted justice. When the people could not stand the evil any longer, the leaders came to see Samuel at Ramah, and they said to him, "Behold, you are old and your sons do not walk in your ways; now appoint for us a king to govern us like all the nations."

This request troubled Samuel. He knew that it was not in God's plan that the nation should have a king. He realized, too, that when the people longed for a royal monarch they were forgetting the Lord. Disappointed with the leaders, Samuel sought the will of the Eternal One. The Lord said to Samuel, "Hearken to the voice of the people in all that they say to you; for they have not rejected you, but they have rejected Me from being king over them. According to all the deeds which they have done to Me, from the day I brought them up out of Egypt even to this day, forsaking Me and serving other gods, so they are also doing to you. Now then, hearken to their voice; only, you shall solemnly warn them, and show them the ways of the king who shall reign over them."

Samuel, the wise judge, stood before the men of Israel, and in ringing words he warned them that they would lose their freedom by choosing a king to rule over them. He said, "These will be the ways of the king who will reign over you: he will take your sons and appoint them to his chariots and to be his horsemen, and to run before his chariots; and he will appoint for himself commanders of thousands and commanders of fifties, and some to plow his ground and to reap his harvest, and to make his implements of war and the equipment of his chariots. He will take your daughters to be perfumers and cooks and bakers. He will take the best of your fields and vineyards and olive orchards and give them to his servants. He will take the tenth of your grain and of your vineyards and give it to

his officers and to his servants. He will take your menservants and maidservants, and the best of your cattle and your asses, and put them to his work. He will take the tenth of your flocks, and you shall be his slaves."

The people refused to accept Samuel's counsel. They said, "No! but we will have a king over us, that we also may be like all the nations, and that our king may govern us and go out before us and fight our battles."

The Lord said to Samuel, "Hearken to their voice, and make them a king."

The nation was at a turning point in its history. It had been ruled by Moses, Joshua, and the judges, who trusted in the Lord. From time to time God had sent His instruction directly to the leaders. Now the twelve tribes desired to be like the nations around them. If the judges had always been humble, God-directed men, who were honest and upright, the nation might well have been satisfied with the government. The people did not realize that they were placing more power and wealth in the hands of a leader, and that these monarchs would seek personal prowess and glory. When men disregard divine counsel and go their own way in opposition to God's will, they may carry out their selfish schemes and through bitter experience learn the folly of their way. Human pride and self-centered knowledge are dangerous guides for an individual or a nation.

# Israel's First King

*1 Samuel 9 to 15*

chapter 15 &

GIVE us a king to govern us. Give us a king to govern us."
The words of the leaders of the twelve tribes of Israel
continued to ring in the ears of Samuel, long after
the throng had left his house at Ramah. The prophet did not
hurry to settle the issue, for he wanted the Lord to guide in
the selection of a king. One day the prophet received a message from God saying, "Tomorrow about this time I will send
to you a man from the land of Benjamin, and you shall anoint
him to be prince over My people Israel. He shall save My
people from the hand of the Philistines; for I have seen the
affliction of My people, because their cry has come to Me."

Of course, Samuel was anxious to know whom the Lord had
chosen to be king. After a restless night, the prophet arose
early and went to the gate of the city to watch for the man who
would be ruler of Israel.

Now Saul, the son of a powerful and wealthy chief named
Kish, had been searching for some jackasses that had strayed
from his father's farm at Gibeah, about halfway between Ramah
and Jerusalem. For three days the young man and his servant
had been hiking through the hill country in search of the
animals. The servant suggested that they stop at the town of
Ramah to seek the advice of the prophet.

Saul was not too ambitious, for on numerous occasions he

would slip away from his family and acquaintances to day-dream or to hide his despondency. On this trip in search of the jackasses, he was ready to turn back. "Come, let us go back," he said to his servant who was with him, "lest my father cease to care about the asses and become anxious about us."

"Behold, there is a man of God in this city," the servant answered, "and he is a man that is held in honor; all that he says comes true. Let us go there; perhaps he can tell us about the journey on which we have set out."

Saul said to his servant, "But if we go, what can we bring the man? For the bread in our sacks is gone, and there is no present to bring to the man of God. What have we?"

"Here, I have with me the fourth part of a shekel of silver," said the servant, "and I will give it to the man of God, to tell us our way."

"Well said," agreed Saul; "come, let us go."

As the two men approached the city, they met some girls carrying empty pitchers who were on their way to get water from the town well. When Saul asked them where he might find the man of God, the girls replied that the prophet was in the city and that he was going to a religious service that would be followed by a feast. As Saul and his servant hurried into the city, the prophet saw them. When Samuel beheld the tall, handsome youth in the prime of life, he heard the Lord say, "Here is the man of whom I spoke to you! He it is who shall rule over My people." Saul approached Samuel, the prophet or seer of Israel, and asked, "Tell me where is the house of the seer?"

"I am the seer; go up before me to the high place, for today you shall eat with me, and in the morning I will let you go and will tell you all that is on your mind."

The bashful young man could scarcely believe the words of the prophet. The farmer's son had left home in search of lost animals, never dreaming that he would end up going to a feast as the guest of the prophet of Israel. "Am I not a Benjaminite, from the least of the tribes of Israel?" said Saul humbly,

150

Samuel presented Saul, a head taller than most of the people, to the throng. "God save the king," they shouted.

"and is not my family the humblest of all the families of the tribe of Benjamin? Why then have you spoken to me in this way?"

Samuel did not attempt to explain, for if he did they would be late at the assembly. Therefore, he hurried the son of Kish to the hall where there were about thirty guests, and he placed the young man at the head of the table.

Samuel said to the cook, "Bring the portion I gave you, of which I said to you, 'Put it aside.'"

"So the cook took up the leg and the upper portion and set them before Saul; and Samuel said, 'See, what was kept is set before you. Eat; because it was kept for you until the hour appointed, that you might eat with the guests.'"

After the feast Saul went to the house of Samuel and slept in a bed on the roof top.

At daybreak the next morning, Samuel called Saul and helped him prepare for the homeward journey. The prophet accompanied the young man beyond the city wall, and after the servant had been sent on ahead, Samuel took a flask of oil and poured it upon Saul's head and kissed him. Then Samuel explained by saying, "Has not the Lord anointed you to be prince over His people Israel? And you shall reign over the people of the Lord and you will save them from the hand of their enemies round about." The prophet also told Saul that the lost animals had been found and returned to his father's farm.

As a part of his farewell to Saul, the prophet told him he would receive the power of God in his life. "The Spirit of the Lord will come mightily upon you, and you shall prophesy with them and be turned into another man," promised Samuel.

When God comes into the life of an individual, that person is truly "turned into another man." This happens again and again in our world, as men and women are converted; yet many do not believe in salvation from sin. Saul received courage and wisdom for his important responsibility, and if he had remained faithful he would have been a great leader for Israel.

Saul went on his way with a strange thrill in his heart. He could scarcely believe that he had been anointed king over Israel. As he journeyed toward his home he resolved he would keep the matter a close secret until the proper time arrived.

## "God Save the King"

Soon the day came when Samuel, the judge, called the leaders of the nation together to choose publicly the new king. The choice of the Lord was to be manifest in the casting of lots. The prophet asked the tribes of Israel to pass before him one by one, and the tribe of Benjamin was chosen. Then the families of the tribe of Benjamin passed in review, and Saul's family was picked by lot. Finally, a man of the family of Kish was selected, and, behold, it was Saul! When the young man was brought before the people, they saw that he was tall and strong. In fact, he was so tall that most of the men came only to his shoulders. Samuel spoke to the people, saying, "Do you see him whom the Lord has chosen? There is none like him among all the people."

"Long live the king!" shouted all the people.

Samuel outlined the rights and duties of the kingship before all the people. Then he recorded the business of choosing a king in a book and laid it with the other records in the house of God. The prophet dismissed the crowd, and the people went home; but some of the brave men showed their devotion by immediately following Saul. Others, however, were jealous· and despised the new king. They whispered among themselves, "How can this man save us?"

About a month after the coronation of Saul, the young king had his first test in leadership. The savage people of Ammon threatened the children of Israel who lived at Jabesh on the east side of the Jordan River. Nahash, the savage king of the Ammonites, declared he would make peace, but only on this condition: "I will make a treaty with you, that I gouge out all your right eyes, and thus put disgrace upon all Israel."

"Give us seven days respite," said the leaders of Jabesh.

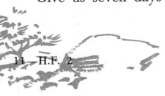

153

Then they sent messengers through the land, calling for help. When King Saul heard the brutal threat, he killed a yoke of oxen and cut their bodies into pieces and sent the bloody pieces to all the tribes of Israel by messengers who said, "Whoever does not come out after Saul and Samuel, so shall it be done to his oxen!"

The people rallied quickly, and 330,000 men met King Saul at Bezek, about thirteen miles north of Shechem. After dividing his warriors into three companies, Saul marched them eastward until they crossed the Jordan River and faced the enemy. From morning until midday the armies fought, and the Ammonites were defeated and scattered by the warriors of Israel.

Now Israel was proud of Saul, and the warriors celebrated the victory. Remembering the words that had been spoken against the new king, some of the soldiers hurried to Samuel, saying, "Who is it that said, 'Shall Saul reign over us?' Bring the men that we may put them to death."

But King Saul said, "Not a man shall be put to death this day, for today the Lord has wrought deliverance in Israel." Instead of taking the glory to himself, Saul gave thanks to God for the victory over the enemy.

And Samuel, who had witnessed the battle, called the people together at Gilgal, the historic town where the children of Israel made their first camp after entering the land of Canaan. The prophet stood before the people and said, "Behold, I have hearkened to your voice in all that you have said to me, and have made a king over you. And now, behold, the king walks before you; and I am old and gray, and behold, my sons are with you; and I have walked before you from my youth until this day."

The people held a celebration and offered thank offerings to the Lord for His blessings. The prophet placed this benediction upon the assembled thousands, "Only fear the Lord, and serve Him faithfully with all your heart; for consider what great things He has done for you."

## Saul Disobeys God's Command

In the hour of victory King Saul should have led his army against the other enemies that threatened Israel, for by this move he might have liberated all his people. However, the king was satisfied too easily, and he disbanded the main body of his army, keeping only a royal guard of two thousand soldiers with him at Michmash. He placed another thousand warriors under the command of his son, Jonathan, who faced the warlike Philistines at Gibeah.

The Israelites had been cruelly oppressed by the Philistines during the days of the judges. The enemy had taken all the swords and spears from the men of Israel and had left no metal workers in the country to make more weapons. The farmers were forced to go to the land of the Philistines to sharpen their plows and hoes. Therefore the soldiers of King Saul were at a great disadvantage in battle. Yet in spite of this disgraceful plight, the king made no effort to arm his men with swords and spears; so they were forced to fight with bows and slings, with axes and hoes.

In the second year of Saul's reign Jonathan grew impatient because his father would not attack the enemy. The bold Philistines came with 30,000 chariots, 6,000 horsemen, and soldiers "like the sand of the seashore in multitude, challenging the men of Israel to fight. Saul's army acted cowardly; the warriors slipped away from the camp and hid in caves and among the rocks of the hills. The days went by and the king made no move to go into action against the enemy.

When Samuel arrived at Gilgal, he asked Saul, "What have you done?"

"When I saw that the people were scattering from me," he began simply, "and that you did not come within the days appointed, and that the Philistines had mustered at Michmash, I said, 'Now the Philistines will come down upon me at Gilgal, and I have not entreated the favor of the Lord;' so I forced myself, and offered the burnt offering."

155

Samuel said to Saul, "You have done foolishly; you have not kept the commandment of the Lord your God, which He commanded you; for now the Lord would have established your kingdom over Israel forever. But now your kingdom shall not continue; the Lord has sought out a man after His own heart; and the Lord has appointed him to be prince over His people, because you have not kept what the Lord commanded you."

When Jonathan saw the Philistines encamped at Michmash, a rocky hill across the valley from the crags where the Israelites were hiding, he went into action. Trusting in the power of God to help him deliver the nation, he said to the faithful youth who carried his armor, "Come, let us go over to the Philistine garrison on yonder side." Jonathan added these words of courage, "It may be that the Lord will work for us; for nothing can hinder the Lord from saving by many or by few."

Without telling anyone else of his plan, Jonathan took his armor-bearer and made his way down the mountainside, across the valley, and up the steep cliffs to where the Philistine fortress stood. When the enemy guards saw the two soldiers from Israel climbing up the rocks, they said, "Look, Hebrews are coming out of the holes where they have hid themselves." The guards then challenged Jonathan and his armor-bearer, saying, "Come up to us, and we will show you a thing."

Jonathan accepted the challenge as a sign that God was with him. He and his armor-bearer moved out of sight of the Philistines and made their way forward stealthily along a steep and difficult path. Suddenly they reached the summit, overpowered the guards, and killed about twenty Philistines.

Terror took hold of the enemy forces, and, to make matters worse for them, an earthquake shook the mountain. The Philistines were in panic and began a hasty retreat. When King Saul heard the noise and saw the enemy in tumult, he commanded his officers to check on who was absent from the camp. It was found that Jonathan and his armor-bearer were missing. Then Saul called for an attack on the enemy, and many of the soldiers who had deserted came out of hiding to join in the

156

battle. Soon the Philistines were routed and driven back to their own country.

After this, Saul selected the bravest men he could find for his army, and he appointed his cousin, Abner, to be his general. The armies of Moab, Ammon, and Edom were defeated; but there was another enemy that had long troubled Israel, the Amalekites. When the prophet Samuel saw how successful King Saul was in battle, he sent him a message calling for Israel to make war against this wicked nation. The aged prophet said, "The Lord sent me to anoint you king over His people Israel; now therefore hearken to the words of the Lord. Thus says the Lord of hosts, 'I will punish what Amalek did to Israel in opposing them on the way, when they came up out of Egypt. Now go and smite Amalek, and utterly destroy all that they have; do not spare them, but kill both man and woman, infant and suckling, ox and sheep, camel and ass.'" Samuel referred to the attacks the tribe of Amalek had made on the children of Israel when they journeyed through the desert. God had promised that this nation would someday be destroyed for its bloody warfare. Samuel believed that the time had arrived for the enemy to be exterminated.

As Saul advanced with an army of 210,000 men against the Amalekites, he sent a warning to the Kenites to flee and save themselves, for they had once shown kindness to Israel. In a brilliant victory Saul destroyed most of the tribe of Amalek; but he spared Agag, the king, and the soldiers of Israel were allowed to keep the best of the sheep, lambs, oxen, and calves. Selfish King Saul was determined to keep this booty in spite of God's command to destroy everything.

Early in the morning Samuel met Saul and his army at Carmel. The king said proudly to the prophet, "Blessed be you to the Lord; I have performed the commandment of the Lord."

"What then is this bleating of the sheep in my ears, and the lowing of the oxen which I hear?" asked Samuel.

"They have brought them from the Amalekites; for the people spared the best of the sheep and of the oxen, to sacrifice

157

to the Lord your God; and the rest we have utterly destroyed," said Saul. Poor, weak Saul! He had been faced with the test of obedience to God, and he had failed miserably. He tried to blame his soldiers for his own disobedience.

"Stop! I will tell you what the Lord said to me this night," said Samuel to Saul.

"Say on," replied the king.

"The Lord anointed you king over Israel. And the Lord sent you on a mission, and said, 'Go, utterly destroy the sinners, the Amalekites, and fight against them until they are consumed.' Why then did you not obey the voice of the Lord? Why did you swoop on the spoil, and do what was evil in the sight of the Lord?"

King Saul attempted to excuse himself by saying that he had kept the best of the sheep and cattle to make a sacrifice to the Lord. But Samuel swept away this excuse built upon false piety, by saying:

"Has the Lord as great delight in burnt offerings and sacrifices,
    as in obeying the voice of the Lord?
Behold, to obey is better than sacrifice,
    and to hearken than the fat of rams."

Then Saul said to Samuel, "I have sinned; for I have transgressed the commandment of the Lord and your words, because I feared the people and obeyed their voice. Now therefore, I pray, pardon my sin, and return with me, that I may worship the Lord."

But Samuel said to Saul, "I will not return with you; for you have rejected the word of the Lord, and the Lord has rejected you from being king over Israel."

Then the valiant old prophet sent for Agag, the cruel king of the Amalekites, whom Saul had spared. Samuel took the sword and destroyed this wicked enemy with his own hands. Saul was rejected as king of Israel because he had disobeyed. He had asked for forgiveness, not because he was sorry for what he had done; but he was afraid of the penalty. Too many

When Samuel heard and saw the sheep and cattle he knew that King Saul had disobeyed the divine command.

159

times men expect an easy repentance will absolve them from the penalty of sin. They forget that forgiveness does not imply that penalties will not be exacted. Saul failed because he did not believe that "to obey is better than sacrifice." Samuel and Saul parted, and only once did the prophet and the dishonored king ever meet again.

# David Rises to Power

*1 Samuel 16 to 20*

chapter 16 ✤

W HEN the prophet Samuel returned to his house at
Ramah, he grieved because Saul had failed to obey
God. The aged seer loved the young ruler, and he
had dreamed that this youth whom he had anointed would
lead Israel on to victory; but now there was no possibility of
success. Soon the Lord spoke to Samuel, "How long will you
grieve over Saul, seeing I have rejected him from being king
over Israel? Fill your horn with oil, and go; I will send you to
Jesse the Bethlehemite, for I have provided for Myself a king
among his sons."

The prophet was afraid and said, "How can I go? If Saul
hears it, he will kill me."

Then the Lord told Samuel to journey to Bethlehem with
an offering. When he arrived in the town he was to make a
sacrifice at a special ceremony and invite Jesse of the tribe of
Judah to attend.

The prophet arrived in Bethlehem, and the chief men of
the town saw him. Trembling with fear, they said to Samuel,
"Do you come peaceably?"

"Peaceably; I have come to sacrifice to the Lord," said
Samuel. So the men of the town gathered at the altar to
worship God, and Jesse and his sons were present.

Now, Jesse was the son of Obed, the son of Ruth, the gleaner who married Boaz. Jesse was a sheep rancher, and he had eight sons who helped him tend the flocks.

After the sacrifice had been offered, the prophet desired to inspect the sons of Jesse. Beginning with Eliab, the eldest, Samuel studied the young men carefully. The prophet was pleased with the appearance of Eliab, for he was strong and handsome. Samuel would have anointed him king of Israel at once, but the Lord said, "Do not look on his appearance or on the height of his stature, because I have rejected him; for the Lord sees not as man sees; man looks on the outward appearance, but the Lord looks on the heart."

One by one the sons came before Samuel until seven had been carefully observed, but none was accepted. Now the prophet was perplexed. Had he misunderstood God's message? Turning to Jesse, Samuel asked, "Are all your sons here?"

"There remains yet the youngest," he said, "but behold, he is keeping the sheep."

"Send and fetch him," said Samuel, breathing more easily, "for we will not sit down till he comes here."

David, the ruddy shepherd boy, was brought in from the field and presented to Samuel. When the prophet saw the keen eyes and beautiful countenance of the youth, he heard God say, "Arise, anoint him; for this is he."

### The Young Musician

In the meantime, Saul grew sad and despondent. He was beginning to crack mentally, for he had no faith to sustain him. In fact, he showed so many signs of madness that his servants proposed that a talented harpist be found whose soft music might soothe the king's troubled mind. Saul liked the suggestion and said, "Provide for me a man who can play well, and bring him to me."

Thereupon one of the young men said, "Behold, I have seen a son of Jesse the Bethlehemite, who is skillful in playing, a man of valor, a man of war, prudent in speech, and a man of good presence; and the Lord is with him."

162

David, the ruddy shepherd boy, was called from sheepherding, and he was anointed to be king by Samuel.

JOE MANISCALCO, ARTIST     © P. P. P. A.

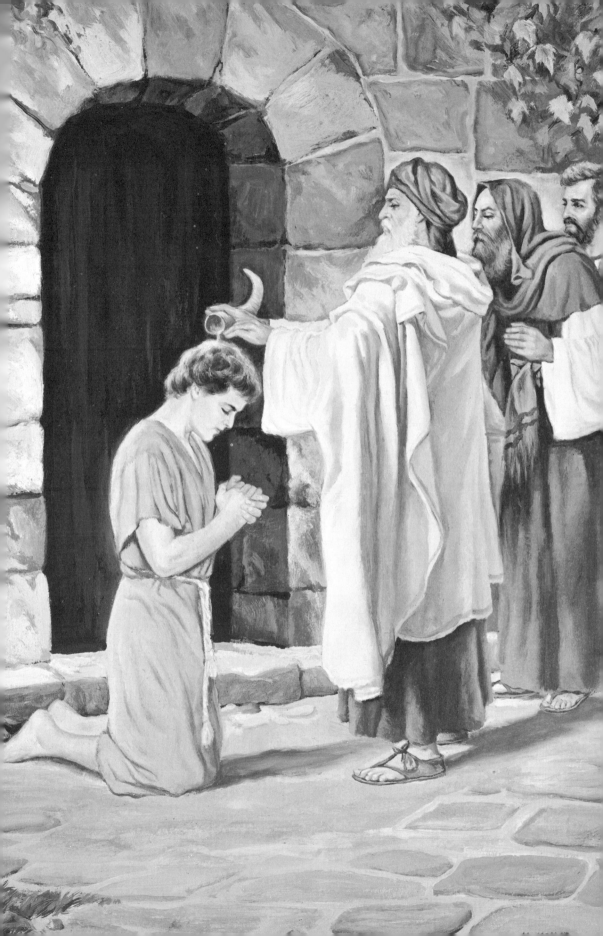

Saul sent royal messengers to Jesse requesting that David be allowed to come and play before the king. So the father sent the shepherd boy with presents for the monarch. David played beautiful melodies on his harp, many of which he had composed while he herded sheep in the hills. Perhaps he sang the poem that later became the Shepherd Psalm:

"The Lord is my Shepherd, I shall not want;
    He makes me lie down in green pastures.
He leads me beside still waters;
    He restores my soul.
He leads me in paths of righteousness
    for His name's sake.
Even though I walk through the valley of the shadow of death,
    I fear no evil;
for Thou art with me;
    Thy rod and Thy staff,
    they comfort me.
Thou preparest a table before me
    in the presence of my enemies;
Thou anointest my head with oil,
    my cup overflows.
Surely goodness and mercy shall follow me
    all the days of my life;
and I shall dwell in the house of the Lord
    forever."

Although the honor of being the next king of the nation had been conferred upon David, the youth humbly waited in the presence of Saul. Because of his humility and his desire to learn, David grew in favor with God and men. Many young persons in David's position would have refused to be a musician in Saul's court. They would have said that they were already anointed king, so why should they serve a man who was half crazy? But David had learned to be patient and to trust in the Lord. His years of sheepherding on the hills of Bethlehem had not been spent in vain!

Saul was refreshed by the music, and his heart was at peace once more. He liked David and made him his armor-bearer, a high honor for a servant of the monarch. To the youth's father Saul sent this request, "Let David remain in my service, for he has found favor in my sight."

Now, the Philistines continued to make attacks on the men of Israel. The enemy camped on one mountain, while Israel's army was stationed on another across the valley from the enemy. Every day Goliath, a mighty champion from the camp of the Philistines, marched down into the valley of Elah and ridiculed the Israelites. A giant about ten feet tall, he wore a helmet and a coat of mail made of bronze, and his spear and sword were of great weight. Every morning and evening for forty days he stood before the soldiers of Israel, insulting them and throwing out the challenge, "Why have you come out to draw up for battle? Am I not a Philistine, and are you not servants of Saul? Choose a man for yourselves, and let him come down to me. If he is able to fight with me and kill me, then we will be your servants; but if I prevail against him and kill him, then you shall be our servants and serve us." Then he would add, "I defy the ranks of Israel this day; give me a man, that we may fight together."

When Saul and all Israel heard the words of the Philistine, they were terrified and their hearts failed within them. They said, "Have you seen this man who has come up? Surely he has come up to defy Israel; and the man who kills him, the king will enrich with great riches, and will give him his daughter, and make his father's house free in Israel."

In the meantime David had returned home to help his father care for the sheep so that three of his older brothers could join the army of Saul. One day Jesse said to David, "Take for your brothers an ephah of this parched grain, and these ten loaves, and carry them quickly to the camp of your brothers; also take these ten cheeses to the commander of their thousand. See how your brothers fare, and bring some token from them."

Young David was anxious to visit the army of Israel to see how the soldiers fought the enemy; but when he arrived at the camp he found the men in panic because of Goliath. Upon

165

hearing that no man was willing to challenge the giant, David asked, "What shall be done for the man who kills this Philistine, and takes away the reproach from Israel?"

Eliab, the eldest brother of David, was angry and said, "Why have you come down? And with whom have you left those few sheep in the wilderness? I know your presumption, and the evil of your heart; for you have come down to see the battle."

Saul heard of this and sent for the young shepherd. When he was questioned, David encouraged King Saul concerning Goliath, for the youth said, "Let no man's heart fail because of him; your servant will go and fight with this Philistine."

"You are not able to go against this Philistine to fight with him," said Saul to David; "for you are but a youth, and he has been a man of war from his youth."

"Your servant used to keep sheep for his father; and when there came a lion, or a bear, and took a lamb from the flock, I went after him and smote him and delivered it out of his mouth," David replied modestly; "and if he arose against me, I caught him by his beard, and smote him and killed him. Your servant has killed both lions and bears; and this uncircumcised Philistine shall be one of them, seeing he has defied the armies of the living God." Then David added these words of sheer faith, "The Lord who delivered me from the paw of the lion and from the paw of the bear, will deliver me from the hand of this Philistine."

King Saul was satisfied that David was a valiant fighter. Therefore he commanded his servants to dress David in the heavy armor of the king, but the young man felt uncomfortable in such equipment, and he said, "I cannot go with these; for I am not used to them."

Then David took his sling, which he was expert in using, and he went to the brook, where he chose five smooth stones. He put these in his leather bag and started toward the giant. Goliath approached the boy cautiously, for he thought he might be walking into a trap. When he saw young David carry-

ing a sling, he shouted angrily, "Am I a dog, that you come to
me with sticks?" Then he cursed the shepherd and jeered at
him, "Come to me, and I will give your flesh to the birds of
the air and to the beasts of the field."

Then David said to Goliath:

"You come to me with a sword and with a spear and with a javelin;
  but I come to you in the name of the Lord of hosts,
  the God of the armies of Israel, whom you have defied.
  This day the Lord will deliver you into my hand,
  and I will strike you down, and cut off your head;
  and I will give the dead bodies of the host of the Philistines
  this day to the birds of the air and to the wild beasts of the earth;
  that all the earth may know that there is a God in Israel,
  and that all this assembly may know
  that the Lord saves not with sword and spear;
  for the battle is the Lord's and He will give you into our hand."

Goliath advanced toward David, towering above the youth
in his might. Pushing back his helmet, the giant raged in
scorn; but in that moment David acted. Quickly he slipped a
stone in his sling and let it fly with all the strength and skill that
he possessed. The stone went straight to its mark, striking
Goliath in the forehead! The giant reeled and crashed to the
ground like a mighty tree in a windstorm. Then David ran forward, grabbed the sword of the giant, and cut off his head.
When the Philistines saw their champion lying dead on the
battlefield, they fled in terror. The armies of Israel pursued
the enemy and defeated them, and David became the hero of
his people.

### Saul Threatens David

As David returned from his victorious fight with Goliath,
he was met by Abner, the general of Israel's armies, and he took
the hero to Saul. Not recognizing David, the king asked,
"Whose son are you, young man?"

David answered, "I am the son of your servant Jesse the
Bethlehemite."

In his half-crazed condition, jealous Saul threw his javelin at David in an attempt to destroy him.

JOE MANISCALCO, ARTIST                    © P. P. P. A.

The son of Jesse was not permitted to return to his home at Bethlehem when he could be a valuable leader in the army. David was given command of a thousand soldiers, and he played on his harp to lift the king from despondency.

King Saul soon became jealous of David, however, when he saw that the people loved this young hero. When the king and the shepherd returned from the battle, the women welcomed them with songs of joy as they played on their tamborets:

> "Saul has slain his thousands,
> And David his ten thousands."

As David's prestige increased, the king became furious. We read that "David had success in all his undertakings; for the Lord was with him." But the love of praise flowed in Saul's veins, and he hated David's popularity. One day while the youth was playing for Saul, the angry monarch seized his spear and hurled it at the harp player, saying, "I will pin David to the wall." But the young man escaped from the mad king, for the Lord was with him.

While living at Saul's court, David became acquainted with Jonathan, Saul's son. The young men became true friends, and soon their affection for one another was stronger than that between brothers. Grieved because his father hated David, Jonathan determined to shield his new-found friend from his father's wrath.

While in the royal court, David was offered Saul's daughter as his wife. The king said, "Here is my elder daughter Merab; I will give her to you for a wife." But in his heart the crafty ruler was plotting David's death, for he thought to himself, "Let not my hand be upon him, but let the hand of the Philistines be upon him."

Young David realized he was in a perilous situation, for the king was seeking by marriage to spy on David's activities. The youth modestly answered, "Who am I, and who are my kinsfolk, my father's family in Israel, that I should be son-in-law to the king?"

King Saul kept urging David to wed Merab, but when the
hero refused he was invited to take the younger sister Michal
as his wife. Now David had known this beautiful girl long
enough to find that she was honest and trustworthy. She would
be a faithful wife in spite of the king's evil plotting.

The couple were married after David and his men had
slaughtered two hundred Philistines. In all the fighting, the
son of Jesse was protected from death, and this enraged Saul
all the more.

One day Jonathan slipped into David's presence and said,
"Saul my father seeks to kill you; therefore take heed to yourself in the morning, stay in a secret place and hide yourself;
and I will go out and stand beside my father in the field where
you are, and I will speak to my father about you; and if I
learn anything I will tell you." Jonathan did his best to change
his father's mind, and finally the king said, "As the Lord lives,
he shall not be put to death."

Saul's mood soon changed and he was more determined than ever to destroy his son-in-law. Again the crazed king threw his spear at David in an attempt to kill him, but once more the youth escaped and fled to his own house. Saul sent spies to David's home with instructions to kill him, but Michal made a plan to save her husband. "If you do not save your life tonight, tomorrow you will be killed." So in the darkness Michal let David down from a second-story window, and he sought refuge in Samuel's house at Ramah.

Soon after this, King Saul sent an assuring message to David, stating that he would make peace; but David did not have faith in the king's word. David met Jonathan secretly and said to him, "What have I done? What is my guilt? And what is my sin before your father, that he seeks my life?"

Jonathan tried to convince his friend that the king would not kill him, but David was skeptical. He said, "As the Lord lives and as your soul lives, there is but a step between me and death."

A sacred festival was to be held the following day, and David and Jonathan were expected to be present. David was afraid to appear at the king's table, however, because of Saul's treachery. Therefore the two friends decided that Jonathan should go to the feast and David would hide in a field near the royal banquet hall. If Saul asked where David was, Jonathan would say that he had gone to Bethlehem to visit his family. If the king said, "Good," and seemed to be pleased, David would know that it was safe for him to return to the court. If Saul was angry, however, they would know that the old jealousy gnawed at his heart.

Jonathan went to the king's hall, and on the first day of the feast his father did not ask about David. However, on the second day, when he saw the seat still vacant, the king said, "Why has not the son of Jesse come to the meal, either yesterday or today?"

Jonathan explained to his father, saying, "David earnestly asked leave of me to go to Bethlehem; he said, 'Let me go;

170

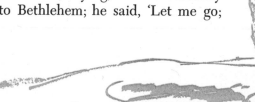

for our family holds a sacrifice in the city, and my brother has commanded me to be there. So now, if I have found favor in your eyes, let me get away, and see my brothers.' For this reason he has not come to the king's table."

When Saul heard these words, he was angry, and he picked up his spear and threw it at his own son. Dodging out of the way, Jonathan escaped, and on the third morning he went to the field, accompanied by a small boy.

Jonathan said to the lad, "Run and find the arrows which I shoot."

As the boy ran, Jonathan shot an arrow beyond him and shouted, "Is not the arrow beyond you? Hurry, make haste, stay not."

Quickly the boy gathered up the arrows and brought them back to Jonathan, who commanded him to carry the hunting equipment back to town. The boy went on his way, not knowing that the shooting of the arrows had been a signal for David to flee from Saul. But before the shepherd of Bethlehem departed, he came out of his hiding place behind a heap of stones and said good-by to his friend. Afterward Jonathan returned to the king's court, but David became a fugitive from King Saul.

171

# The Strong and the Disobedient

1 Samuel 21 to 31

chapter 17 &

WHERE should David go? What should he do? He was an outcast, a man hunted by the king's soldiers. Scarcely realizing where he was going, the fugitive made his way along the road leading to the city of Nob. It was in that town that the sanctuary had been set up after the golden ark was taken by the Philistines.

Making his way to the sanctuary, David met Ahimelech, the high priest. The man of God trembled when he saw David, for he recognized that this was the brave warrior who had killed the giant Goliath. The priest remembered, too, that the giant's sword, a trophy of the great victory that had been won over the enemy, hung on the wall of the sanctuary. Without revealing to the high priest that he was trying to escape from King Saul, David sought food from the priest.

"I have no common bread at hand," said Ahimelech, "but there is holy bread." The priest gave David the hallowed bread from the golden table in the holy place. Since the fugitive was without weapons, he asked the aged priest, "And have you not here a spear or a sword at hand?"

"The sword of Goliath the Philistine, whom you killed in the valley of Elah, behold, it is here wrapped in a cloth behind the ephod," said the priest. "If you will take that, take it, for there is none but that here."

David was hunted by the king's men. With Goliath's great sword, the fugitive went to the cave of Adullam.

JOE MANISCALCO, ARTIST       © P. P. P. A.

"There is none like that; give it to me," said David, his eyes glistening at the sight of the huge weapon.

Ahimelech had no idea that he was helping an enemy of the king. He knew David was Saul's armor-bearer; therefore, he thought he was pleasing the monarch when he gave this young warrior food and a sword and helped him on his journey. Now, Doeg, the royal shepherd, happened to be at the sanctuary, and he heard what the priest said. By hurrying to tell the king what had happened at Nob, he sealed the doom of the priests of Nob.

David pushed into the mountain regions of Judah and finally reached the cave of Adullam; and soon his father and brothers visited him. They were afraid that Saul would try to kill them because they were related to David. The brave warrior arranged for his family to live with the king of Moab in the land where his great-grandmother Ruth was born.

### A Gallant Leader

Now that David was an outlaw, other men began flocking to him for protection. They offered him their allegiance, for they knew that Saul was a wicked king. Soon the cave of Adullam was the headquarters for about four hundred men who were loyal to their leader.

Word that David was hiding in a cave reached Saul, and he made plans to surround it. But David heard of the king's plan and led his band of men to new hiding places where they could not be trapped by the royal army.

When the tyrant Saul heard that Ahimelech, the high priest, had given food and a sword to David, he insanely commanded that all the priests of Nob should be killed. The aged priest of the Lord tried to explain to the monarch that he was innocent, but the wicked king would not listen to reason. All the priests were massacred except Abiathar, a son of Ahimelech, who escaped to David and told him what had happened. David remembered how he had deceived the high priest, and he was sorry for his terrible mistake. He said to Abiathar, "I

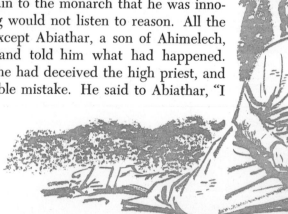

knew on that day, when Doeg the Edomite was there, that he would surely tell Saul. I have occasioned the death of all the persons of your father's house. Stay with me, fear not; for he that seeks my life seeks your life; with me you shall be in safe-keeping."

Still hunted by King Saul, David found no place of security. He heard that the Philistines had attacked the Israelites at Keilah, so he led his warriors against the enemy and saved the town from ruin. However, since the king of Israel was in hot pursuit, David hurried his men into the tortuous desert regions of Ziph, where they were safe. In this lonely desert Jonathan found his friend and cheered him with words of courage. He said, "Fear not; for the hand of Saul my father shall not find you; you shall be king over Israel, and I shall be next to you; Saul my father also knows this." The character of Jonathan was unfolding in all its magnanimity. He loved his friend so much that he was willing to give up his claim to the throne of Israel in order that David might be king.

When Saul heard that David was in the desert of Engedi, he led his army of three thousand men in search of him. As the warriors were climbing the mountains, King Saul entered a cave to rest. Now, who should be hiding in that cave but David and his soldiers! Of course David's men urged him to kill his enemy, but the young leader refused. He said he would not destroy the man whom the Lord had anointed king. David did, however, steal up to Saul while he rested and cut off a part of the king's robe.

After Saul had departed from the cave, David called to him saying, "Why do you listen to the words of men who say, 'Behold, David seeks your hurt'? Lo, this day your eyes have seen how the Lord gave you today into my hand in the cave; and some bade me kill you, but I spared you."

Saul looked at his robe and saw that a piece had been cut from it. Then David said, "May the Lord judge between me and you, may the Lord avenge me upon you; but my hand shall not be against you."

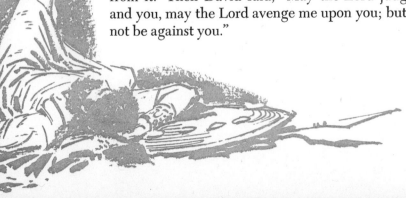

When David had finished speaking, Saul said, "Is this your voice, my son David?"

Then Saul lifted up his voice and wept. He said to David, "You are more righteous than I; for you have repaid me good, whereas I have repaid you evil."

Then Saul and David made peace; and the king returned to his home, while.David went down to the desert of Paran. Now, a rancher named Nabal and his wife Abigail lived at Carmel. He was busy at the time shearing his sheep and goats. David and his men had helped protect the flocks of Nabal from bandits who roamed in the region. Since David knew that the sheepshearing season was one of hospitality, he sent ten of his men to call on Nabal. "Go up to Carmel, and go to Nabal," said the gallant leader, "and greet him in my name. And thus you shall salute him: 'Peace be to you, and peace be to your house, and peace be to all that you have. I hear that you have shearers; now your shepherds have been with us, and we did them no harm, and they missed nothing, all the time they were in Carmel. Ask your young men, and they will tell you. Therefore let my young men find favor in your eyes; for we come on a feast day. Pray, give whatever you have at hand to your servants and to your son David.' "

Nabal was a selfish churl, a fool and a braggart. When the young men requested gifts, the rancher said, "Who is David? Who is the son of Jesse? There are many servants nowadays who are breaking away from their masters. Shall I take my bread and my water and my meat that I have killed for my shearers, and give it to men who come from I do not know where?"

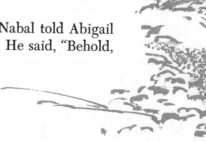

When David heard of the insult to his men, he angrily commanded, "Every man gird on his sword!" Impulsive and bloodthirsty, David moved quickly with some four hundred men. He was determined to teach this rancher a much-deserved lesson.

In the meantime one of the servants of Nabal told Abigail about David and how he had been treated. He said, "Behold,

176

David sent messengers out of the wilderness to salute our master; and he railed at them. Yet the men were very good to us, and we suffered no harm, and we did not miss anything when we were in the fields, as long as we went with them; they were a wall to us both by night and by day, all the while we were with them keeping the sheep. Now therefore know this and consider what you should do; for evil is determined against our master and against all his house, and he is so ill-natured that one cannot speak to him."

When the charming and shrewd woman heard this, she went into action. She directed the loading of two hundred loaves of bread, wine, meal, grain, raisins, and figs on pack animals, and sent them ahead by servants as gifts for David. Then Abigail rode to meet the band of warriors. When she saw David, she dismounted from her animal and bowed before him, saying, "Upon me alone, my lord, be the guilt; pray let your handmaid speak in your ears, and hear the words of your handmaid. Let not my lord regard this ill-natured fellow, Nabal; for as his name is, so is he; Nabal is his name, and folly is with him; but I your handmaid did not see the young men of my lord, whom you sent. Now then, my lord, as the Lord lives, and as your soul lives, seeing the Lord has restrained you from bloodguilt, and from taking vengeance with your own hand, now then let your enemies and those who seek to do evil to my lord be as Nabal. And now let this present which your servant has brought to my lord be given to the young men who follow my lord. Pray forgive the trespass of your hand-maid; for the Lord will certainly make my lord a sure house, because my lord is fighting the battles of the Lord; and evil shall not be found in you so long as you live. If men rise up to pursue you and to seek your life, the life of my lord shall be bound in the bundle of the living in the care of the Lord your God; and the lives of your enemies He shall sling out as from the hollow of a sling. And when the Lord has done to my lord according to all the good that He has spoken concerning you, and has appointed you prince over Israel, my lord

shall have no cause of grief, or pangs of conscience, for having shed blood without cause or for my lord taking vengeance himself. And when the Lord has dealt well with my lord, then remember your handmaid."

David was touched by the kind words, and he replied, "Blessed be the Lord, the God of Israel, who sent you this day to meet me! Blessed be your discretion, and blessed be you, who have kept me this day from bloodguilt and from avenging myself with my own hand! For as surely as the Lord the God of Israel lives, who has restrained me from hurting you, unless you had made haste and come to meet me, truly by morning there had not been left to Nabal so much as one male."

The gallant warrior told Abigail to go home in peace. That night Nabal feasted and drank, and while in a drunken orgy suffered a stroke. About ten days later the rancher died.

When David heard of Nabal's death he sent his sympathy to Abigail, and later he married her. About this time he also took another wife, Ahinoam of Jezreel; while back at home Michal was lost to him, for Saul gave her to be the wife of Palti.

David now had a band of "mighty men" daring in battle and completely loyal to their leader. Once while David was far from his home, his men heard him say, "O that someone would give me water to drink from the well of Bethlehem which is by the gate!"

Three of his men slipped away from the camp, went through the enemy lines, and got a pitcher of water from that well. When they brought the water to David and he realized the grave danger they had faced to get it, he would not drink it, but poured it on the ground as an offering to the Lord.

King Saul and the entire nation mourned when Samuel the prophet died, for he had been a mighty influence for truth in Israel. From the day that his mother, Hannah, had brought him to the tent of meeting, he had obeyed the Lord and served Him faithfully. He had been a good judge, urging the people to do right.

When Abigail bowed before David and apologized for her husband's boorish way, David was touched.

179

## Saul's Final Battle

The king felt alone and forsaken as he faced the fierce armies of the Philistines encamped on the plain of Jezreel, the place where Gideon had once fought victoriously with his three hundred men. Saul wished he could talk with Samuel so he might know how to save the nation; but the prophet was dead, and the Lord would not communicate with the rejected ruler.

Saul remembered that there were witches in the land, people who claimed to make the dead speak. The Lord had commanded that all witches and spirit mediums should be destroyed, and King Saul had tried to do this. Now, however, he desired to find one who, he hoped, might help him talk to Samuel.

The king's servants reported there was a woman living at Endor who could reveal secrets. The witch could not bring the dead who sleep in their graves back to life, but she could deceive Saul by her trickery.

Disguised as common soldiers, the king and two of his guards made their way by night to the witch's hiding place in a cave. The woman was afraid when she saw the three visitors, but the king immediately promised her safety. The woman asked, "Whom shall I bring up for you?"

"Bring up Samuel for me," requested Saul.

When a ghostlike figure appeared, the woman screamed and said, "Why have you deceived me? You are Saul."

"Have no fear," said the king. "What do you see?"

The woman declared she had seen an old man coming up out of the earth. It was not Samuel, but an evil spirit, and it brought a warning of defeat and death to Saul. The king fell to the ground weak and frightened, and his servants were afraid that he would die. The woman prepared some food, and after the king had rested and eaten, he was able to return to his army.

The misconduct of Saul in consulting a spirit medium of

180

In desperation Saul went to the witch of Endor to find out, if possible, whether Israel would be victorious.

JOE MANISCALCO, ARTIST    © P.P.P.A.

that age is cited in the Bible as one reason why he was rejected as king of Israel. We read, "Saul died for his unfaithfulness; he was unfaithful to the Lord in that he did not keep the command of the Lord, and also consulted a medium, seeking guidance, and did not seek guidance from the Lord. Therefore the Lord slew him, and turned the kingdom over to David the son of Jesse."

Most forms of ancient sorcery were based upon the belief that man could communicate with the dead. Modern spiritism is likewise based upon the idea that the living can call the dead from the grave. This is not in harmony with Bible teaching, however, for we are told, "The living know that they will die, but the dead know nothing, and they have no more reward; but the memory of them is lost. Their love and their hate and their envy have already perished, and they have no more forever any share in all that is done under the sun." Of the one who dies we are told, "When his breath departs he returns to his earth; on that very day his plans perish."

Modern spiritism is not founded upon divine truth. Instead it is but ancient sorcery and witchcraft in twentieth-century disguise. The apostle Paul warned that "in later times some will depart from the faith by giving heed to deceitful spirits and doctrines of demons."

The same apostle also reveals how the evil forces will make their presence and power known, for these spirit manifestations are "the activity of Satan" who comes "with all power and with pretended signs and wonders, and with all wicked deception for those who are to perish, because they refused to love the truth and so be saved."

The lure to know the future draws many persons into spiritism, and they are deceived by false messages even as King Saul was deluded. We have the word of God with its sure prophecies to tell us of the great events ahead. The Bible is a searchlight on the pathway before us, and if by faith we trust our heavenly Father, He will guide us safely through hours of darkness and trial to His eternal home of peace.

182

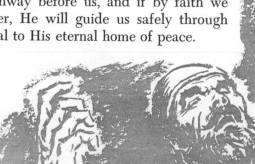

The message from the woman of Endor did not turn Saul
to God. While there was denunciation of sin in the words
there was no hope of salvation. The king faced the battle without hope in God, and he failed to inspire courage in the
hearts of his soldiers.

The next morning the armies of Israel and the hordes of
the Philistines clashed on the plains of Shunem. The princes
of the Philistines pushed forward so fiercely that the men of
Israel could not stop them.

Finally the soldiers of King Saul broke and ran, and the
Philistines overtook Saul and his sons. Jonathan and his two
brothers were killed, and the king was wounded. When Saul
saw that the enemy would capture him, he fell on his own
sword and died a suicide!

David and his warriors were camped at Ziklag when a mes-
senger from the king's army came to tell David the news.
When the man bowed before David, the brave warrior said,
"Where do you come from?"

"I have escaped from the camp of Israel," he replied.

"How did it go? Tell me," said David.

"The people," said the messenger, "have fled from the battle,
and many of the people also have fallen and are dead; and
Saul and his son Jonathan are also dead."

Then David took hold of his garments and tore them as a
sign of mourning, and all the men who were with him did
likewise. Memories of his deep friendship with Jonathan came
to David's mind. Taking his harp, the man who had comforted Saul with beautiful music now sang a beautiful lament
for the loss of the king and of Jonathan. The elegy in its complete form is as follows:

> "Thy glory, O Israel, is slain upon thy high places!
>     How are the mighty fallen!
> Tell it not in Gath,
>     publish it not in the streets of Ashkelon;
>   lest the daughters of the Philistines rejoice,
>     lest the daughters of the uncircumcised exult.

183

"Ye mountains of Gilboa,
    Let there be no dew or rain upon you,
    Nor upsurging of the deep!
For there the shield of the mighty was defiled,
    The shield of Saul, not anointed with oil.

"From the blood of the slain,
    from the fat of the mighty,
the bow of Jonathan turned not back,
    and the sword of Saul returned not empty.

"Saul and Jonathan, beloved and lovely!
In life and in death they were not divided;
they were swifter than eagles,
they were stronger than lions.

"Ye daughters of Israel, weep over Saul,
who clothed you daintily in scarlet,
who put ornaments of gold upon your apparel.
How are the mighty fallen in the midst of the battle!

"Jonathan lies slain upon thy high places.
I am distressed for you, my brother Jonathan;
very pleasant have you been to me;
your love to me was wonderful, passing the love of women.

"How are the mighty fallen,
and the weapons of war perished!"

# The Triumph and Tragedy of David

*2 Samuel 1 to 19:8*

chapter 18 ❧

T HE hour had come for David to take the leadership of his weak and disunited country. He knew that God had chosen him to be ruler of Israel after Saul, but he was not certain how he should win the people to him.

Instructed by the Lord to go to Hebron, a city once taken by Joshua during the conquest of the land, David led six hundred warriors with their families and possessions to the chief city of Judah. As the procession entered Hebron, the men of the city welcomed David as heir to the throne. Since he came from the tribe of Judah, the tribesmen were proud to have him rule over them.

David, the newly appointed king, was told that the men of Jabesh-gilead had brought the bodies of Saul and Jonathan from the battlefield and given them honorable burial. The new ruler commended them for their courage and loyalty, for he said, "May you be blessed by the Lord, because you showed this loyalty to Saul your lord, and buried him! Now may the Lord show steadfast love and faithfulness to you! And I will do good to you because you have done this thing. Now therefore let your hands be strong, and be valiant; for Saul your lord is dead, and the house of Judah has anointed me king over them."

Now David's kingship had scarcely been announced when

185

Abner, commander of Saul's army, made a proclamation that Ish-bosheth, Saul's weak and incompetent son, was king. This rival ruler made his headquarters at Mahanaim, a town on the east side of Jordan. For seven and a half years David ruled over the people of Judah at Hebron. Ish-bosheth ruled as a rival king for over two years, and then quarreling broke out among Saul's men, and Abner was killed. Soon afterward Ish-bosheth was murdered by his own guards. With the death of the rival king, all of the tribes of Israel came to David in Hebron and offered him their allegiance.

What memories must have flooded through David's mind on his coronation day! He remembered the long years of hardship and danger he had suffered since the time he had been called from sheepherding to be anointed by Samuel. Now, at thirty years of age, David stood before the vast throng of his people. Priests, soldiers, and leaders from all of the twelve tribes were present as the son of Jesse, in royal robes, knelt before the vast assembly and the crown was placed on his head.

It was time to choose a capital city near the geographical center of the kingdom. After studying the situation, David selected the mountain city of Jerusalem, a stronghold of the Jebusites which the armies of Israel had never conquered. The king led his soldiers against the fortress, and they captured it. Thus Jerusalem became the City of David, and here the king built his palace. In centuries to come this city was destined to become a focal point of three great religions— Jewish, Moslem, and Christian.

From his wealthy kingdom on the Mediterranean Sea, King Hiram of Tyre sent congratulations to his friend David. The ruler of the city by the sea offered masons, carpenters, and architects to assist David in erecting a magnificent palace. As the work began, gifts of choice wood from the cedars of Lebanon and other building materials were sent by King Hiram.

Soon the Philistines heard of the rising power of Israel's new king, and the enemy decided to strike. Once more the Philistines came against Israel in the valley of Rephaim, only a short distance from Jerusalem. David asked the Lord what he should do in this emergency. "Shall I go up against the Philistines? Wilt Thou give them into my hand?" he prayed.

The Lord gave the king instructions to go into battle, and the promise was given that Israel would have the victory. The king led his valiant soldiers against the enemy and defeated them, but this did not discourage the Philistines. Once more they came up against Israel, and again David sought divine counsel. This time he was told, "You shall not go up; go around to their rear, and come upon them opposite the balsam trees. And when you hear the sound of marching in the tops of the balsam trees, then bestir yourself; for then the Lord has gone out before you to smite the army of the Philistines."

David did as the Lord commanded, and the enemy was defeated and driven out of the land of Israel. Never again during the reign of David did the Philistines trouble the people of Israel.

### Uzzah Touches the Ark

As peace came to the country, the king was determined to bring the golden ark to Jerusalem. It had remained in the house of Abinadab since the day the Philistines had sent it back to Israel on an oxcart. The king summoned thirty thousand prominent men from the twelve tribes to join him in the royal procession. They marched to the house of Abinadab at Kirjath-jearim, nine miles from Jerusalem. The ark was placed on a new cart drawn by oxen, and the people followed, singing songs and playing musical instruments.

As the cart was moving along the rough road nearing the threshing floor of Nacon, one of the oxen stumbled, and the ark tottered and wobbled so much it looked as if it might fall off the cart. Uzzah, who was walking beside the cart, reached out to steady the ark. "And the anger of the Lord was kindled against Uzzah; and God smote him there because he put forth his hand to the ark; and he died there beside the ark of God."

Long before this God had given instructions that no one

187

except the priests should carry or touch the sacred ark. It was supposed to be carried with poles passed through rings attached to the ark, and thus balanced on the shoulders of Levites who carried it safely without bodily contact. If David had followed the Lord's command, this divine judgment would not have fallen on Uzzah. The people were afraid because of the sudden death of this man. The king was displeased and worried at the turn of events, so he left the golden ark in the house of a farmer, Obed-edom, and the procession returned to Jerusalem.

Three months later the king called his leaders together. With priests to perform the sacred work of carrying the ark, the procession marched to Jerusalem, where a special service of thanksgiving was planned. The golden ark was placed in the tent which David had prepared, and the people blessed the name of the Lord. Then the king gave each visitor a loaf of bread, a piece of meat, and a cake of raisins, and every man departed for his home.

As the king looked at his sumptuous palace and contrasted it with the tent which housed the golden ark of the covenant as well as the other sacred furniture, he was unhappy. One day David called the prophet Nathan to the court and said, "See now, I dwell in a house of cedar, but the ark of God dwells in a tent."

"Go, do all that is in your heart," said the prophet; "for the Lord is with you."

But that night the prophet received a divine message to stop plans for a temple. The prophet returned to the king's court and said, "Thus says the Lord of hosts, I took you from the pasture, from following the sheep, that you should be prince over My people Israel; and I have been with you wherever you went, and have cut off all your enemies from before you; and I will make for you a great name, like the name of the great ones of the earth. And I will appoint a place for My people Israel, and will plant them, that they may dwell in their own place, and be disturbed no more; and

When Uzzah touched the ark to steady it, he fell dead—a judgment for disobeying the divine command.

189

JOE MANISCALCO, ARTIST　　　© P. P. P. A.

violent men shall afflict them no more, as formerly, from the time that I appointed judges over My people Israel; and I will give you rest from all your enemies. Moreover the Lord declares to you that the Lord will make you a house. When your days are fulfilled and you lie down with your fathers, I will raise up your son after you, who shall come forth from your body, and I will establish his kingdom. He shall build a house for My name, and I will establish the throne of his kingdom forever."

David was submissive to the divine will, for he prayed to the Lord, saying, "Who am I, O Lord God, and what is my house that Thou hast brought me thus far? And yet this was a small thing in Thy eyes, O Lord God; Thou hast spoken also of Thy servant's house for a great while to come, and hast shown me future generations, O Lord God! . . . Therefore Thou art great, O Lord God; for there is none like Thee, and there is no God besides Thee, according to all that we have heard with our ears."

The memory of his close friendship with Jonathan lingered in King David's mind. Neither did he forget that he had made a pledge to Jonathan to show kindness to the house of Saul, as a token of his enduring love. One day David asked, "Is there still anyone left of the house of Saul, that I may show him kindness for Jonathan's sake?"

Royal servants soon found a servant named Ziba who had been in Saul's palace. When he was brought before David, he said, "There is still a son of Jonathan; he is crippled in his feet."

And the king said, "Where is he?"

Ziba told David that Mephibosheth, the son of Jonathan, lived at Lo-debar. The king sent for him at once; but the crippled man who came to the royal court was fearful, since it was customary in the East for a new dynasty to wipe out all possible claimants to the throne from the old regime.

"Do not fear," said David to him; "for I will show you kindness for the sake of your father Jonathan, and I will restore to

190

you all the land of Saul your father; and you shall eat at my table always."

Such kindness was more than Mephibosheth could have ever expected. He dwelt in the king's palace and ate at David's table like one of his sons.

## *David and Bath-sheba*

For many years David served Israel faithfully, and the borders of the nation stretched from Egypt to the Euphrates River. After he had built his palace at Jerusalem, however, the king committed a heinous sin. Luxurious living and the laxity of the court had weakened the king's character. Life always offers opportunities to sin when the door of evil is left unguarded.

It was springtime in Israel, and the armies had marched to war against the Ammonites; but David remained at his palace in Jerusalem. Spring is a time of love, and the fever took possession of the king. As the ancient writer tells the story we have this picture:

"It happened, late one afternoon, when David arose from his couch and was walking upon the roof of the king's house, that he saw from the roof a woman bathing; and the woman was very beautiful. And David sent and inquired about the woman. And one said, 'Is not this Bath-sheba, the daughter of Eliam, the wife of Uriah the Hittite?' So David sent messengers, and took her; and she came to him, and he lay with her. (Now she was purifying herself from her uncleanness.) Then she returned to her house. And the woman conceived; and she sent and told David, 'I am with child.' "

The king was trapped by his sin, and he decided to move swiftly in an attempt to cover up his iniquity. To his general Joab, David sent this message, "Send me Uriah the Hittite."

When the faithful soldier stood before the king's throne, David asked him about news from the battlefront. Then he commanded Uriah to go to his house and comfort his wife Bath-sheba. The conscientious soldier left the palace, but he

191

did not go home. When David heard this he called Uriah and asked, "Why did you not go down to your house?"

"The ark and Israel and Judah dwell in booths," answered Uriah; "and my lord Joab and the servants of my lord are camping in the open field; shall I then go to my house, to eat and to drink, and to lie with my wife? As you live, and as your soul lives, I will not do this thing."

That night the king made a party for Uriah and the soldier became drunk; but he adamantly refused to go home. The next morning David sent Uriah back to the army with a letter to the general. The instructions were, "Set Uriah in the forefront of the hardest fighting, and then draw back from him, that he may be struck down, and die."

The battle raged, the army withdrew, and faithful Uriah died as David had desired. When the message reached the king he must have breathed easier, for now—after a respectable period of mourning—he could marry Bath-sheba, the widow. Soon the day came when his dream was fulfilled and the woman became his wife and the mother of his son.

David thought that his clever manipulation had hidden the sin for all time; but the Bible records that "the thing that David had done displeased the Lord."

The day came when the Lord gave Nathan, the prophet, a message for David. The prophet stood before the throne and revealed the king's terrible sin by relating a parable.

"There were two men in a certain city, the one rich and the other poor," began Nathan, looking straight at King David. "The rich man had very many flocks and herds; but the poor man had nothing but one little ewe lamb, which he had bought. And he brought it up, and it grew up with him and with his children; it used to eat of his morsel, and drink from his cup, and lie in his bosom, and it was like a daughter to him. Now there came a traveler to the rich man, and he was unwilling to take one of his own flock or herd to prepare for the wayfarer who had come to him, but he took the poor man's lamb, and prepared it for the man who had come to him."

192

As David walked on the roof of his house, he saw Bathsheba taking a bath, and sent for her and took her.

JOE MANISCALCO, ARTIST     © P. P. P. A.

The king was furious when he heard the prophet's story of pathos and power, and he said, "As the Lord lives, the man who has done this deserves to die; and he shall restore the lamb fourfold, because he did this thing, and because he had no pity."

The prophet looked at the king of Israel and said, "You are the man." Then he went on to reveal David's sin by telling him that God said, "You have smitten Uriah the Hittite with the sword, and have taken his wife to be your wife, and have slain him with the sword of the Ammonites. Now therefore the sword shall never depart from your house, because you have despised Me, and have taken the wife of Uriah the Hittite to be your wife."

Then the prophet continued, "Thus says the Lord, 'Behold, I will raise up evil against you out of your own house; and I will take your wives before your eyes, and give them to your neighbor, and he shall lie with your wives in the sight of this sun. For you did it secretly; but I will do this thing before all Israel, and before the sun.' "

With humble, sorrowful heart David said, "I have sinned against the Lord."

"The Lord also has put away your sin; you shall not die," the prophet replied.

The spiritual quality of the king is revealed in this tragic moment. He might have defied the prophet and pronounced himself above the law, as was the custom of Oriental kings. No, David recognized that he had sinned against God, and he repented. He was a humbled man, conscious of his sin and of its far-reaching result. Nathan the prophet showed how sin affected innocent lives when he said, "Because by this deed you have utterly scorned the Lord, the child that is born to you shall die."

When the young child became ill, the king fasted and prayed that God might spare its life; but after a week of ceaseless vigil, the baby died. Upon receiving the news that the child was dead, David accepted the will of God. He said, "While the

child was still alive, I fasted and wept; for I said, 'Who knows whether the Lord will be gracious to me, that the child may live?' But now he is dead; why should I fast? Can I bring him back again? I shall go to him, but he will not return to me."

The king's repentance from sin is reflected in some of his magnificent psalms. He knew the agony of a guilty conscience and the blessing of heaven's forgiveness when he wrote:

> "Blessed is he whose transgression is forgiven,
> whose sin is covered.
> Blessed is the man to whom the Lord imputes no iniquity,
> and in whose spirit there is no deceit.
> When I declared not my sin, my body wasted away
> through my groaning all day long.
> For day and night Thy hand was heavy upon me;
> my strength was dried up as by the heat of summer."

Or again we feel the emotion of the man as he claims the pardon of a merciful God:

> "I acknowledged my sin to Thee,
> and I did not hide my iniquity;
> I said, 'I will confess my transgressions to the Lord;'
> then Thou didst forgive the guilt of my sin.
> Therefore let everyone who is godly offer prayer to Thee;
> at a time of distress, in the rush of great waters,
> they shall not reach him.
> Thou art a hiding place for me,
> Thou preservest me from trouble;
> Thou dost encompass me with deliverance."

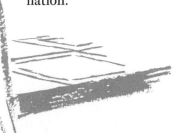

David was forgiven for adultery and murder—two of the crimes considered among the worst in society. We can take courage from God's dealing with him that if we sincerely confess our sins and turn from them our heavenly Father will "abundantly pardon."

The day came when another child was born to Bath-sheba —a son, whom the proud father named Solomon. This child was to become a comfort to his father and the hope of the nation.

## A Rebellious Son

Trouble arose in David's family, and there was strife between the king and his sons, and among the sons themselves. David had been indulgent toward his children and he had failed to require obedience from them. When they did wrong he was afraid to punish them, probably because he realized his own weakness and remembered his failures.

Two of David's sons, Absalom and Amnon, rose to power in the court at Jerusalem, where they had been pampered with wealth and pleasure. In his teens Amnon had seduced Tamar, his half sister, and after his lust had been satisfied, he hated the lovely girl. When the scandal broke in the family, Absalom hated Amnon and waited for the king to punish the evil brother. But David made no move to discipline Amnon.

After two years the hotheaded Absalom decided to take matters into his own hands and revenge his sister. He invited the king's sons to a feast at Baalhazor; and when Amnon was drunk Absalom gave orders for his servants to strike and kill his brother. The other sons of David fled from the scene, and Absalom sought protection of Talmai the son of Ammihud, king of Geshur.

Wild, exaggerated rumors reached the palace that all of David's sons had been slain by Absalom. The king mourned the murder in the family, but he took no action to punish the criminal. Finally, after intercession by Joab, Absalom was allowed to return to Jerusalem, but David refused to see him or permit him at court.

Thus began a breach that widened into rebellion and split the house of David. Clever Absalom finally won his way into the king's presence and wormed his way into favor with the masses of the people. He was a handsome prince, proud of his thick, beautiful hair. Indeed, it was so heavy, we are told he trimmed off more than three pounds of hair when he went to the barber each year.

Proud Absalom rode about Jerusalem in a chariot drawn by

196

Proud Absalom rode through the streets of Jerusalem, while fifty men ran ahead to clear the way for him.

JOE MANISCALCO, ARTIST       © P. P. P. A.

fine horses, while fifty men ran before him to clear the streets. Soon the prince became a popular hero, followed by many people. He was clever and crafty, too, for he would rise up early in the morning and go to the city gate where the men entered who desired to see the king. Absalom would stop the travelers, listen to their stories, and pretend to sympathize with them in their trouble. Then he would say slyly, "Oh that I were judge in the land! Then every man with a suit or cause might come to me, and I would give him justice." Whenever a man would bow before him, the prince would put out his hand and take hold of him and kiss him. In this way Absalom won the hearts of many people in Israel.

## Open Revolt in the Nation

Now the aging king, listless and irresolute, did not know that his son was trying to take the throne from him. However, the day came when Absalom decided to act. He sent messengers to the leaders of the twelve tribes, calling on them to revolt against King David. Then the prince went to his father and under the guise of being very religious, planned to overthrow the kingdom. He said to David, "Pray let me go and pay my vow, which I have vowed to the Lord, in Hebron."

"Go in peace," said the king.

Now Absalom went to Hebron for the purpose of gathering his army. The next thing David knew, a messenger hurried to the palace saying, "The hearts of the men of Israel have gone after Absalom."

When David heard the fearful news, he was panic-stricken and said, "Arise, and let us flee; or else there will be no escape for us from Absalom; go in haste, lest he overtake us quickly, and bring down evil upon us, and smite the city with the edge of the sword."

Ittai, a loyal friend from the Philistines, joined David, bringing six hundred warriors with him. In disgrace the king left Jerusalem with a few faithful followers—driven from his throne by a rebellious son who had never known discipline. As

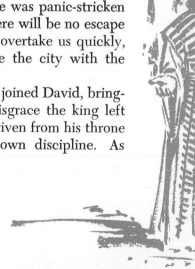

198

David climbed the road leading over Mount Olivet, he wept. His head was covered as a sign of mourning, and he walked barefoot to show his humility. Through the night the king's company fled eastward, making their way down the rocky, desolate slopes to the Jordan River. Ziba, Mephibosheth's servant, brought food for the fugitives and mules for the king to ride on.

The priests attempted to take the ark of the covenant from the besieged city, but the king sent them back with the sacred piece of furniture. Hushai, a trusted counselor of King David, joined the royal party as it left the city; but the king sent this friend back to the palace to act as a spy and defeat Absalom's counselors. When Absalom captured Jerusalem without a struggle, Hushai pretended to support the rebel cause. This pleased the prince, and he listened to Hushai's advice. Absalom had planned to send an army at once in pursuit of his father, but Hushai determined to delay action so that the king would have time to gather his warriors and prepare to fight.

"You know that your father and his men are mighty men," said cunning Hushai to Absalom, "and that they are enraged, like a bear robbed of her cubs in the field. Besides, your father is expert in war; he will not spend the night with the people. Behold, even now he has hidden himself in one of the pits, or in some other place. And when some of the people fall at the first attack, whoever hears it will say, 'There has been a slaughter among the people who follow Absalom. Then even the valiant man, whose heart is like the heart of a lion, will utterly melt with fear; for all Israel knows that your father is a mighty man, and that those who are with him are valiant men. But my counsel is that all Israel be gathered to you, from Dan to Beersheba, as the sand by the sea for multitude, and that you go to battle in person. So we shall come upon him in some place where he is to be found, and we shall light upon him as the dew falls on the ground; and of him and all the men with him not one will be left. If he withdraws into a city, then all Israel will bring ropes to that city, and we

199

shall drag it into the valley, until not even a pebble is to be found there."

Absalom liked this counsel and said, "The counsel of Hushai the Archite is better than the counsel of Ahithophel." Then Hushai sent a secret message to David, telling him to cross the Jordan River with his loyal followers and seek safety in a walled city.

Ahithophel had been the chief counselor of Absalom in his rebellion and evil course against his father David. Now that young Absalom refused to strike at once, according to Ahithophel's advice, the man was angry, frustrated, and desperate. The counselor went out from Absalom to his own city, put his business in order, and hanged himself. Ahithophel was a traitor to his country, and he met a tragic death. He had felt that Tamar had been treated unjustly; but no matter how great the injustice he had no grounds for rebelling against the king, "the Lord's anointed." The man's suicide was not the result of remorse, but it came from fear of the consequences of failure. He knew he could never again stand before his king!

Meanwhile, David planned his strategy with Joab, his general, to divide the small loyal army into three groups in order to fight Absalom's forces. We can imagine the heartache of David, who loved Absalom in spite of his rebellion. When a battle was about to be fought, David said, "I myself will also go out with you."

Then the men said, "You shall not go out. For if we flee, they will not care about us. If half of us die, they will not care about us. But you are worth ten thousand of us; therefore it is better that you send us help from the city." So the king stood at the gate as his army marched to battle, and he said to his officers, "Deal gently for my sake with the young man Absalom."

### Tragedy in Victory

The fight took place in the woods, and David's warriors won an overwhelming victory. Absalom was riding through the

David deeply mourned the loss of Absalom, and Joab reproved him for not welcoming the nation's victors.

14—H.F. 2

forest on a mule when he met some of David's men. The prince probably turned to flee, and as he rode under a giant oak tree his head caught in the thick branches and the mule galloped off, leaving Absalom hanging in mid-air. When a servant told Joab of Absalom's plight, the stalwart general hurried to the oak tree and thrust three spears through the heart of the rebel prince. The pretender to the throne was dead.

The trumpet was blown, the signal of victory, and the soldiers stopped fighting on the field of battle. When they came to their general they saw the body of Absalom, and they cast it into a deep pit. Afterward a heap of stones was raised over the grave of the traitor.

Joab knew that news of the victory and of Absalom's death must be sent to King David, who sat at the gate in the town of Mahanaim. Ahimaaz wanted to run with the message, but Joab told a Cushite follower who had seen all that had happened to go and tell the king of the battle. Ahimaaz was unhappy to be left behind, so Joab gave him permission to run to the king.

Ahimaaz was a swift runner, and he passed the Cushite; but when he came to the king he had no message. He bowed before King David and said, "All is well."

"Is it well with the young man Absalom?" asked the king anxiously.

"When Joab sent your servant, I saw a great tumult, but I do not know what it was," explained Ahimaaz. He had been a fast runner, but he had no news.

"Turn aside, and stand here," said the king.

So Ahimaaz turned aside and stood still. At that moment the Cushite entered the king's presence. The messenger said, "Good tidings for my lord the king! For the Lord has delivered you this day from the power of all who rose up against you."

Then the king asked the messenger, "Is it well with the young man Absalom?"

The Cushite broke the news as gently as he could, in true Oriental dignity, for he said, "May the enemies of my lord the

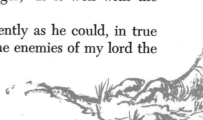

king, and all who rise up against you for evil, be like that young man."

Then the king was deeply moved and went up to his room and wept. "O my son Absalom, my son, my son Absalom! Would I had died instead of you, O Absalom, my son, my son!" cried David.

When Joab, the general of the army, heard that the king would not welcome back his victorious soldiers who had risked their lives to preserve the king, he was indignant. The private grief of David was endangering the public good of Israel. Then Joab went to David and said pointedly, "You have today covered with shame the faces of all your servants, who have this day saved your life, and the lives of your sons and your daughters, and the lives of your wives and your concubines, because you love those who hate you and hate those who love you. For you have made it clear today that commanders and servants are nothing to you; for today I perceive that if Absalom were alive and all of us were dead today, then you would be pleased. Now therefore arise, go out and speak kindly to your servants; for I swear by the Lord, if you do not go, not a man will stay with you this night; and this will be worse for you than all the evil that has come upon you from your youth until now."

The king came to his senses and realized the reproof was needed. He arose and went to the gate to cheer the warriors as they marched in review before him. A wave of patriotic fervor swept over the waiting crowds, and they whispered one to another, "Behold, the king is sitting in the gate." The people rejoiced because peace and order had been restored to Israel.

# The Kingdom Passes to Solomon

*2 Samuel 19:9 to 24; 1 Kings 1 to 13*

chapter 19 &

TO UNIFY the nation after the rebellion of Absalom took time and patience on the part of King David. When he returned to his throne in Jerusalem, he was more determined than ever to build a strong, unified Israel as the heritage of the kings who would rule after him. Men, such as Shimei and Ziba, bowed before the king and asked to be forgiven for the wrongs they had committed during the revolution. Shimei said, "Let not my lord hold me guilty or remember how your servant did wrong on the day my lord the king left Jerusalem; let not the king bear it in mind. For your servant knows that I have sinned; therefore, behold, I have come this day, the first of all the house of Joseph to come down to meet my lord the king."

David showed mercy to his enemies by giving his oath that they should not be put to death. This magnanimous action helped to quell the counterrevolution so that peace was soon restored throughout the kingdom.

In planning a program to build the defenses of Israel, David determined to increase the size of his army and require military service of all able-bodied men. To do this required taking a census of the people, an act that brought divine reproof to David. Building military strength was a wise procedure from the human viewpoint, but it revealed David's lack of faith in

Shimei and Ziba, who had done wrong
in the rebellion, bowed before the king
and sought his forgiveness.

205

the Lord. The king was a father to his people, and he mani-
fested his love toward them in many kindnesses. Although
David failed to keep the commandments of the Lord on several
occasions, yet he longed to walk humbly with his God. He
composed one of the psalms (Psalm 18; 2 Samuel 22) when
the Lord delivered him from his enemies:

"The Lord is my rock, and my fortress, and my deliverer,
  my God, my rock, in whom I take refuge,
  my shield and the horn of my salvation,
      my stronghold and my refuge,
      my savior; Thou savest me from violence.
I call upon the Lord, who is worthy to be praised,
      and I am saved from my enemies.

      ❀  ❀  ❀  ❀

"Thou hast given me the shield of Thy salvation,
      and Thy help made me great.
Thou didst give a wide place for my steps under me,
      and my feet did not slip;
I pursued my enemies and destroyed them,
      and did not turn back until they were consumed.
I consumed them; I thrust them through, so that they did not rise;
      they fell under my feet.
For Thou didst gird me with strength for the battle;
      Thou didst make my assailants sink under me.

      ❀  ❀  ❀  ❀

"For this I will extol thee, O Lord, among the nations,
      and sing praises to Thy name.
  Great triumphs He gives to His king,
      and shows steadfast love to His anointed,
      to David, and his descendants forever."

King David was about seventy years old when he chose his
son Solomon to be his successor. But new treachery was foment-
ing in the court, for Adonijah, another of David's sons, was determined to rule on the throne. Once more we find that David
had failed as a father, for the record states he had never
questioned his son's actions or disciplined him for his evil
deeds. Handsome Adonijah made a feast and invited all his

206

brothers except Solomon to attend. Now Nathan the prophet and Zadok the priest were excluded from the feast, but they heard of the treacherous plot. They hurried to the palace, where the king was on his sickbed, and told Bath-sheba of the evil purpose of Adonijah to usurp the throne. Nathan said, "Have you not heard that Adonijah the son of Haggith has become king and David our lord does not know it? Now therefore come, let me give you counsel, that you may save your own life and the life of your son Solomon. Go in at once to King David, and say to him, 'Did you not, my lord the king, swear to your maidservant, saying, "Solomon your son shall reign after me, and he shall sit upon my throne"? Why then is Adonijah king?' Then while you are still speaking with the king, I also will come in after you and confirm your words."

The tired king accepted the counsel of Nathan and Bath-sheba, for he said, "As the Lord lives, who has redeemed my soul out of every adversity, as I swore to you by the Lord, the God of Israel, saying, 'Solomon your son shall reign after me, and he shall sit upon my throne in my stead;' even so will I do this day."

Then Nathan and Zadok took Solomon to the town of Gihon. The priest anointed Solomon, the trumpets were blown, and the people shouted, "Long live King Solomon!" Soon the people of Jerusalem heard that Solomon had been proclaimed king, and they followed him, playing upon flutes and singing so loudly that it seemed they would shake the earth.

The brothers of Solomon were enjoying Adonijah's feast when they heard the tumult and they asked, "What does this uproar in the city mean?"

While the guests were wondering what had happened, a messenger entered and Adonijah said, "Come in, for you are a worthy man and bring good news."

The messenger replied, "No, for our lord King David has made Solomon king."

Then he went on to explain that the noise was a celebration in honor of the new king, who at that very moment was riding

207

through the streets of Jerusalem on the mule of King David. When the guests heard this, they left hurriedly, and Adonijah quickly repented of his rash conduct. He went to the sanctuary and took hold of the horns of the altar as a means of protecting himself from the vengeance of the new king. Adonijah promised complete loyalty to the anointed ruler, and Solomon granted clemency to his brother, saying, "If he prove to be a worthy man, not one of his hairs shall fall to the earth; but if wickedness is found in him, he shall die."

On his deathbed David solemnly charged the young king to keep the religious faith of his fathers. "I am about to go the way of all the earth," said David to Solomon. "Be strong, and show yourself a man, and keep the charge of the Lord your God, walking in His ways and keeping His statutes, His commandments, His ordinances, and His testimonies, as it is written in the law of Moses, that you may prosper in all that you do and wherever you turn; that the Lord may establish His word which He spoke concerning me, saying, 'If your sons take heed to their way, to walk before Me in faithfulness with all their heart and with all their soul, there shall not fail you a man on the throne of Israel.' "

Sincere were the words of the dying king. He knew from stern reality how much one could suffer when he disregarded the commands of God. He had been impetuous at times, quick to anger and to shed blood. His heart had turned toward the Eternal One with the sincere longing to be at peace. This mighty man had been a poet, the gifted composer of many of the psalms. These glorious spiritual treasures range through all phases of human experience, from the depths of guilt to the heights of praise. David could say:

"The angel of the Lord encamps around those who fear Him,
  and delivers them.

O taste and see that the Lord is good!
  Happy is the man who takes refuge in Him!"

Solomon entered Gihon amid the blowing of trumpets and the shouts of the crowd, "Long live King Solomon!"

209

"Wait for the Lord;
    be strong, and let your heart take courage;
    yea, wait for the Lord!"

"Blessed is the man who makes the Lord his trust,
  who does not turn to the proud,
    to those who go astray after false gods!"

"God is our refuge and strength,
    a very present help in trouble.
Therefore we will not fear though the earth should change,
    though the mountains shake in the heart of the sea;
though its waters roar and foam,
    though the mountains tremble with its tumult."

    "Cast your burden on the Lord,
      and He will sustain you;
    He will never permit
      the righteous to be moved."

    "In Thee, O Lord, do I take refuge;
      let me never be put to shame!
    In Thy righteousness deliver me and rescue me;
      incline Thy ear to me, and save me!
    Be Thou to me a rock of refuge,
      a strong fortress, to save me,
      for Thou art my rock and my fortress."

"Bless the Lord, O my soul,
    and forget not all His benefits,
who forgives all your iniquity,
    who heals all your diseases,
who redeems your life from the Pit,
    who crowns you with steadfast love and mercy,
who satisfies you with good as long as you live
    so that your youth is renewed like the eagle's."

"Out of my distress I called on the Lord;
    the Lord answered me and set me free.

With the Lord on my side I do not fear.
What can man do to me?
The Lord is on my side to help me;
I shall look in triumph on those who hate me.
It is better to take refuge in the Lord
than to put confidence in man.
It is better to take refuge in the Lord
than to put confidence in princes."
Psalms 34:7, 8; 27:14; 40:4; 46:1-3; 55:22; 71:1-3; 103:2-5; 118:5-9.

David had dreamed of building a magnificent temple where the Lord would dwell with His people; but because he had been a man of war and there had been strife during his reign, God told him that this privilege must be left to Solomon. Blueprints for the house of God had been made; and building materials, silver, gold, brass, and precious stones, had been collected by David in order to make his son's task easier. King David died after ruling Israel for forty years, and he was buried in Jerusalem.

## The Young King's Dream

Solomon, the son of David and Bath-sheba, loved the Lord and followed the good counsel of his father. Feeling the need for spiritual guidance, the young king went to Gibeon to offer sacrifices. One night God appeared to him in a dream and said, "Ask what I shall give you."

Solomon said, "Thou hast shown great and steadfast love to Thy servant David my father, because he walked before Thee in faithfulness, in righteousness, and in uprightness of heart toward Thee; and Thou hast kept for him this great and steadfast love, and hast given him a son to sit on his throne this day. And now, O Lord my God, Thou hast made Thy servant king in place of David my father, although I am but a little child; I do not know how to go out or come in. And Thy servant is in the midst of Thy people whom Thou hast chosen, a great people, that cannot be numbered or counted for multitude. Give Thy servant therefore an understanding mind to govern

211

Thy people, that I may discern between good and evil; for who is able to govern this Thy great people?"

The Lord was so pleased with the king's humble request that He not only gave Solomon wisdom, but He also blessed him with great riches and power. During his lifetime the king wrote three thousand proverbs and composed over a thousand songs. He knew many wonderful facts about trees, flowers, beasts, birds, and creeping things. Potentates came to him from other nations to learn of his great wisdom.

Among the royal visitors to the king of Israel was the queen of Sheba. When she saw his palace and his great wealth, and heard his wise sayings, she said, "The report was true which I heard in my own land of your affairs and of your wisdom, but I did not believe the reports until I came and my own eyes had seen it; and, behold, the half was not told me; your wisdom and prosperity surpass the report which I heard."

Gifts were exchanged between the visiting queen and King Solomon, for the record says that he gave her "all that she desired."

When the time came to build the temple, Hiram, king of Tyre, supplied Solomon with cedar and other choice woods required in the building. Thousands of men were sent into the mountains of Lebanon to cut down trees, while other thousands cut and squared massive stones and polished them for the building. King Hiram also sent Solomon skilled craftsmen who would carve wood and engrave in silver, gold, and brass. Weavers spent years making rich and beautiful tapestries. While the house of God was being erected, not a hammer, ax, nor any iron tool was heard in it. All the stone was prepared at the quarry, and the wood and metal were made ready before they were brought into the temple.

After seven years of continual labor the house of God was finished. Built upon a hill, with its entrance facing east, this shrine was to be the center for the worship of God. The king set the time for the dedication service, and he invited the people from all over the nation to witness the glorious event. The

golden ark and the other furniture that had been in the sanctuary tent were brought to the temple. Never had there been such lavish sacrifices, for 22,000 oxen and 120,000 sheep were slaughtered for a peace offering. Trumpets were blown as the priests entered the holy place for the first time. The cloud of glory, representing the presence of the Lord, filled the temple with such splendor that the priests could not perform their service.

Then the king blessed all the people, saying, "Blessed be the Lord, the God of Israel, who with His hand has fulfilled what He promised with His mouth to David my father, saying, 'Since the day that I brought My people Israel out of Egypt, I chose no city in all the tribes of Israel in which to build a house, that My name might be there; but I chose David to be over My people Israel.' Now it was in the heart of David my father to build a house for the name of the Lord, the God of Israel. But the Lord said to David my father, 'Whereas it was in your heart to build a house for My name, you did well that it was in your heart; nevertheless you shall not build the house, but your son who shall be born to you shall build the house for My name.' Now the Lord has fulfilled His promise which He made; for I have risen in the place of David my father, and sit on the throne of Israel, as the Lord promised, and I have built the house for the name of the Lord, the God of Israel. And there I have provided a place for the ark, in which is the covenant of the Lord which He made with our fathers, when He brought them out of the land of Egypt."

As he stood before the altar he stretched forth his hands toward heaven and prayed, "O Lord, God of Israel, there is no God like Thee, in heaven above or on earth beneath, keeping covenant and showing steadfast love to Thy servants who walk before Thee with all their heart; who hast kept with Thy servant David my father what Thou didst declare to him; yea, Thou didst speak with Thy mouth, and with Thy hand hast fulfilled it this day."

213

For seven days the great assembly joined in the dedication celebration with sacrifices and feasting, and on the eighth day Solomon sent the people to their homes. The record states that they were "joyful and glad of heart for all the goodness that the Lord had shown to David His servant and to Israel His people."

Among the building projects of Solomon were a lavish palace for himself and an exotic home for one of his wives, the daughter of Pharaoh. He erected stables for forty thousand horses. The ruins of these vast stables have been unearthed by modern archaeology. The king built fleets of ships that sailed from ports on the Red Sea and the Mediterranean Sea. They voyaged afar and returned with gold, silver, ivory, apes, and peacocks. The record states that the king made silver in Jerusalem as common as stone and cedars as plentiful as the sycamore trees that grew on the foothills.

## The King's Apostasy

During the years that David and Solomon reigned, Israel grew strong among the nations. It was the golden age of expansion and wealth, as well as the period of spiritual greatness. Yet in spite of riches and fame, the reign of Solomon did not end in glory. Luxury and wealth were too much for even this wise man. He had seven hundred wives, princesses, and three hundred concubines, many of them from heathen nations, who turned his heart from serving the Lord. After a glorious beginning, in which he walked with God, Solomon lost his way and wandered in the darkness of apostasy. The king thought only of pagan pleasures and luxurious living; but they failed to give him true happiness. He confesses this in his writings, when he says, "I made great works; I built houses and planted vineyards for myself; I made myself gardens and parks, and planted in them all kinds of fruit trees. I made myself pools from which to water the forest of growing trees. I bought male and female slaves, and had slaves who were born in my house; I had also great possessions of herds and

In his old age Solomon looked back upon his days of luxury, fame, and riches, and he said, "All is vanity."

flocks, more than any who had been before me in Jerusalem. I also gathered for myself silver and gold and the treasure of kings and provinces; I got singers, both men and women, and many concubines, man's delight. So I became great and surpassed all who were before me in Jerusalem; also my wisdom remained with me. And whatever my eyes desired I did not keep from them; I kept my heart from no pleasure, for my heart found pleasure in all my toil, and this was my reward for all my toil. Then I considered all that my hands had done and the toil I had spent in doing it, and behold, all was vanity and a striving after wind, and there was nothing to be gained under the sun. So I turned to consider wisdom and madness and folly; for what can the man do who comes after the king? Only what he has already done. Then I saw that wisdom excels folly as light excels darkness. The wise man has his eyes in his head, but the fool walks in darkness; and yet I perceived that one fate comes to all of them. Then I said to myself, 'What befalls the fool will befall me also; why then have I been so very wise?' And I said to myself that this also is vanity. For of the wise man as of the fool there is no enduring remembrance, seeing that in the days to come all will have been long forgotten. How the wise man dies just like the fool! So I hated life, because what is done under the sun was grievous to me; for all is vanity and a striving after wind. I hated all my toil in which I had toiled under the sun, seeing that I must leave it to the man who will come after me." Ecclesiastes 2:4-18.

Enemies arose against Israel, and there was internal strife among the twelve tribes. The Lord reproved Solomon for his conduct, saying, "Since this has been your mind and you have not kept My covenant and My statutes which I have commanded you, I will surely tear the kingdom from you and will give it to your servant. Yet for the sake of David your father I will not do it in your days, but I will tear it out of the hand of your son. However I will not tear away all the kingdom; but I will give one tribe to your son, for the sake of

David My servant and for the sake of Jerusalem which I have chosen."

By this message Solomon knew that the nation would never be strong and united again. The king reigned over Israel forty years, and when he died he was buried in Jerusalem. Rehoboam, the son of Solomon, took the throne of his father.

During Solomon's reign the people had been forced to pay heavy taxes. When Rehoboam became king, the chief men of the tribes begged him to lighten their burdens. However, the young king refused to listen to counsel, and he said to the people, "Whereas my father laid upon you a heavy yoke, I will add to your yoke. My father chastised you with whips, but I will chastise you with scorpions."

The rash threats of the new king caused the ten northern tribes, known as Israel, to rebel and form their own government. Two tribes, Benjamin and Judah, remained loyal to Rehoboam; but the ten tribes selected Jeroboam as their king, and he made his capital at Shechem. He was "a mighty man of valor" who had seen the need for just leadership, and he had urged Rehoboam to deal wisely with the nation.

Rehoboam attempted to reunite the tribes, first by diplomacy and then by armed force; but a message from God warned him, "You shall not go up or fight against your kinsmen the people of Israel. Return every man to his home, for this thing is from Me." So the army of Judah did not march northward against its own people in a civil war.

## Darkness and Decline

Split asunder by jealousy and strife, the nation began to decline. The small kingdom of Judah, with its capital at Jerusalem, stood for almost four hundred years; but at last it fell before the overpowering attacks of Babylon. During these four centuries the throne of David was occupied by some good kings, under whose reign the nation was blessed. But there were many wicked rulers who led their people into pagan idolatry and the grossest of evil practices.

217

15—H.F. 2

Through the dark pages of history, when trial, disappointment, and eventual captivity came to God's people, there is
revealed the long-suffering and mercy of the heavenly Father,
who continued to call after His children. The faithful worshipers of the true God were to learn that:

> "It is He who made the earth by His power,
>     who established the world by His wisdom,
>     and by His understanding stretched out the heavens."
> Jeremiah 10:12.

In the kingdom of Israel to the north there was political
weakness and the loss of true religious faith from the time of
Jeroboam to the day that Israel fell to her enemies, almost
two hundred and fifty years later. Rebellion against God
reached its height in the time of King Ahab, some sixty years
after Solomon's death. Ahab married Jezebel, daughter of
the king of Sidon, and she led the nation into the worship
of the idol Baal. Of Ahab the record declares that he "did
more to provoke the Lord, the God of Israel, to anger than
all the kings of Israel who were before him." But all was not
lost. A man of God was soon to appear who would cause the
wicked king and queen to cringe in terror because of their
evil deeds. He would bring reform and the revival of true
religion in an age of darkness.

# Elijah, Crusader for God

*1 Kings 17 to 22; 2 Kings 1, 2*

chapter 20 ✋

IN THE midst of King Ahab's dissolute reign, a valiant fighter for truth suddenly appeared in the royal court. This stranger from the mountains of Gilead, east of the Jordan River, was a man of faith and prayer. He knew nothing of court luxury or pagan voluptuousness; but he hated evil and denounced sin. This prophet from the hill country was Elijah the Tishbite, a faithful crusader for the true God.

Without courtly manners or elegant clothing, the man of God stood before Ahab and said, "As the Lord the God of Israel lives, before whom I stand, there shall be neither dew nor rain these years, except by my word." Then, without waiting for an answer, he turned on his heel and left the palace.

The king was stunned by this strange threat; and since he could not alter the judgments of heaven, he determined to kill the prophet who foretold them. But the Lord was with Elijah and gave him this instruction: "Depart from here and turn eastward, and hide yourself by the brook Cherith, that is east of the Jordan. You shall drink from the brook, and I have commanded the ravens to feed you there." While Ahab sent his soldiers to search for the prophet, Queen Jezebel conferred with the priests of Baal, hoping they would put a curse on the prophet of God.

Elijah lived in hiding beside the brook Cherith. Every

morning and evening the voracious ravens brought him bread and meat. As long as there was water in the brook, Elijah could stay in this safe retreat; but a day came when the severe drought dried up the trickling stream. Then Elijah was told to go to Zarephath, a town in Sidon, outside the kingdom of Israel. As the prophet came to the city gate, he saw a widow gathering sticks to make a fire. "Bring me a little water in a vessel, that I may drink," he called to the woman.

As she went to get a jar of water, he made a second request: "Bring me a morsel of bread in your hand."

"As the Lord your God lives, I have nothing baked, only a handful of meal in a jar, and a little oil in a cruse; and now, I am gathering a couple of sticks, that I may go in and prepare it for myself and my son, that we may eat it, and die," she replied in a monotone, revealing her defeated view of life.

"Fear not; go and do as you have said; but first make me a little cake of it and bring it to me," said Elijah, "and afterward make for yourself and your son. For thus says the Lord the God of Israel, 'The jar of meal shall not be spent, and the cruse of oil shall not fail, until the day that the Lord sends rain upon the earth.'"

This woman of Zarephath was not from the tribes of Israel; but she had learned of the true God. She had faith in Elijah's words and welcomed the prophet into her poverty-stricken home. Day after day her family had food to eat, for there was always meal in the jar and enough oil to mix with it to make cakes for her family.

One day the widow's young son became sick and died. The mother came to Elijah in her grief, thinking that this evil had come upon her because of her sins. She said, "What have you against me, O man of God? You have come to me to bring my sin to remembrance, and to cause the death of my son!"

"Give me your son," the prophet replied. He carried the dead child upstairs to his room and laid him upon his own bed. Then he stretched himself over the body three times

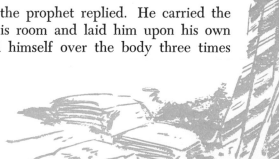

and prayed, "O Lord my God, let this child's soul come into him again." Elijah's prayer was answered, for the child arose at once, and the man of God took him downstairs to his happy mother.

The scorching sun baked the earth, and all grass and plants shriveled in the dust. During the third year of the drought and famine, Elijah received instruction from heaven to seek an interview with King Ahab and tell him that rain would fall on the parched earth. When wicked Ahab saw Elijah, he shouted angrily, "Is it you, you troubler of Israel?"

A man with God's message to sinners is always a disturber of worldly peace. Of a modern minister it was said, "He always makes me feel uncomfortable." Our smugness and complacency must be disturbed. Our conscience must trouble us until we are right with God.

"I have not troubled Israel," replied the crusading prophet; "but you have, and your father's house, because you have forsaken the commandments of the Lord and followed the Baals. Now therefore send and gather all Israel to me at Mount Carmel, and the four hundred and fifty prophets of Baal and the four hundred prophets of Asherah, who eat at Jezebel's table."

## The Test on Mount Carmel

The king sent messengers throughout the land calling the people of Israel and the false prophets to assemble on Mount Carmel. When they arrived, Elijah stood before them, a solitary figure without any associates or stalwart followers. He gave this challenge to the crowd: "How long will you go limping with two different opinions? If the Lord is God, follow Him; but if Baal, then follow him."

The people were silent; they knew they had forgotten the God of heaven and disobeyed His commands. They could no longer avoid a decision—to serve God or to grovel before pagan idols. Then Elijah said, "I, even I only, am left a prophet of the Lord; but Baal's prophets are four hundred and fifty men.

Let two bulls be given to us; and let them choose one bull for themselves, and cut it in pieces and lay it on the wood, but put no fire to it; and I will prepare the other bull and lay it on the wood, and put no fire to it. And you call on the name of your god and I will call on the name of the Lord; and the God who answers by fire, he is God."

Then all the people answered and said, "It is well spoken."

It was decided that the priests of Baal should be the first to build an altar and place their sacrifice upon it. From early morning until noon they called on their god Baal, shouting, "O Baal, answer us!" But nothing happened. Elijah watched the heathen priests, and he mocked them, saying, "Cry aloud, for he is a god; either he is musing, or he has gone aside, or he is on a journey, or perhaps he is asleep and must be awakened."

Finally the priests of Baal worked themselves into a frenzy of excitement. They shrieked and slashed themselves with swords and lances until blood gushed out upon their bodies; but there was no answer from their idol.

In the late afternoon, at the regular hour for sacrifice in the sanctuary of the Lord, Elijah was ready to make his test. Calling all the people to come near, he rebuilt the sacred altar that had been broken down and long forgotten. He also made a ditch around the altar. After placing the sacrifice on the wood, the prophet had twelve jars of water poured over the sacrifice, and the water ran down and filled the trench around the altar. He was going to prove to the watchers that no trickery or fraud was involved in this test. Then Elijah prayed earnestly to the Lord, saying, "O Lord, God of Abraham, Isaac, and Israel, let it be known this day that Thou art God in Israel, and that I am Thy servant, and that I have done all these things at Thy word. Answer me, O Lord, answer me, that this people may know that Thou, O Lord, art God, and that Thou hast turned their hearts back."

Suddenly fire flashed from heaven and consumed the sacrifice and the wood. It destroyed the stones and licked up the

Suddenly fire flashed from heaven and consumed the sacrifice, the wood, and the stones. God's truth triumphed!

water in the trench. The God of heaven had answered Elijah's prayer in a dramatic manner. When the people saw this tremendous power, they fell on their faces and said, "The Lord, He is God; the Lord, He is God."

The priests of Baal, realizing that they were defeated, started to run away; but Elijah shouted for the people to catch the false prophets and bring them to the brook Kishon. These evil men were slain because they had deliberately and maliciously led the people to do wickedly.

This vindication of faith in the Eternal One led to national reformation. The people confessed their sins and turned to the God of their fathers. Elijah said to King Ahab, "Go up, eat and drink; for there is a sound of the rushing of rain." This was a daring statement inspired by God, for as yet there was no sign of rain.

While the king was eating and drinking, the prophet took his servant, and together they climbed to the mountaintop. Elijah sat down, weary and exhausted by the day of test, while his servant went to scan the horizon over the blue Mediterranean Sea. The prophet, a man of great faith, humbly bowed his head and prayed for his people. Again and again Elijah sent the man to look out over the water, but it was not until the seventh time that he came running to the prophet and said, "Behold, a little cloud like a man's hand is rising out of the sea."

Without a moment of hesitation Elijah went into action. To his servant he gave orders, "Go up, say to Ahab, 'Prepare your chariot and go down, lest the rain stop you.'"

Soon the sky was dark with clouds, a fierce wind struck the mountainside, and with it came a downpour of rain! The storm struck with such fury the king could not find his way along the road. In that emergency Elijah came to Ahab's rescue. Tucking up his prophet's robes, he ran ahead of the royal chariot until they came to the gates of Jezreel, the capital city.

When King Ahab reached the palace and told Queen Jezebel

how Elijah had killed her priests of Baal, she sent a messenger to the prophet who lay sleeping on the ground near the city gates. The queen threatened Elijah, saying, "So may the gods do to me, and more also, if I do not make your life as the life of one of them by this time tomorrow."

Fear overcame the man of God who had been so courageous on Mount Carmel. The prophet who had dealt singlehanded with four hundred priests of Baal was now a coward before one woman. Elijah arose quickly and started down the road on the run toward the town of Beersheba, a hundred miles away. Tired, hungry, and despondent, the prophet finally slumped down under a tree. Exhausted and discouraged, he wished he were dead.

The despondent prophet could not run away from God's love. After the fugitive had been refreshed by sleep, an angel of the Lord gave him food. Elijah slept again and afterward ate another hearty meal. On the strength of that food, he arose and traveled for forty days. At last he came to Mount Horeb, in the desert far to the south, where Moses had once lived. The defeated prophet found a cave in the mountainside and crawled into it, for his mind and heart had gone into hiding.

"What are you doing here, Elijah?" asked the Lord.

"I have been very jealous for the Lord, the God of hosts," Elijah answered, bypassing the real question; "for the people of Israel have forsaken Thy covenant, thrown down Thy altars, and slain Thy prophets with the sword; and I, even I only, am left; and they seek my life, to take it away."

God did not argue with His prophet. He commanded, "Go forth, and stand upon the mount before the Lord."

There was a mighty wind that sent landslides down the mountain, and afterward there was an earthquake followed by fire; but God was in none of these. Then there was "a still small voice," that humbled Elijah and caused him to cover his head and stand at the mouth of the cave. Then the Lord said, "Go, return on your way to the wilderness of Damascus; and when you arrive, you shall anoint Hazael to be king over Syria;

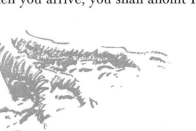

225

and Jehu the son of Nimshi you shall anoint to be king over Israel; and Elisha the son of Shaphat of Abel-meholah you shall anoint to be prophet in your place. And him who escapes from the sword of Hazael shall Jehu slay; and him who escapes from the sword of Jehu shall Elisha slay. Yet I will leave seven thousand in Israel, all the knees that have not bowed to Baal, and every mouth that has not kissed him."

## The Call of Elisha

On his way back to the capital city, Elijah met a young farmer, Elisha, plowing in the field. In harmony with the divine instructions given him, the prophet threw his cloak over the farm boy—a sign that he was called to God's service. Young Elisha accepted the invitation to go with the prophet, ministering to his need and receiving his instruction. After Elisha's parents had invited friends and neighbors to a farewell feast in honor of their son, the prophet Elijah and his new assistant started on their journey.

Elijah and his novitiate visited the schools of the prophets, centers of learning that had been established in the time of Samuel to educate young men to be teachers and leaders of the people. There was opportunity for the study of the law and other Hebrew writings. The students performed manual labor to support themselves while they studied the wonders of nature and the words of inspired writers. Elijah and Elisha visited at least three of the schools, for the record tells of their going to Bethel, Gilgal, and Jericho.

Enemies from the north threatened Israel at this time, for Ben-hadad, king of Syria, attacked the armies of King Ahab. The Eternal One was with His people, and the enemies were driven back in defeat. The selfish, despotic nature of King Ahab was revealed in his dealings with an Israelite farmer. Next to the king's palace was a vineyard, owned by Naboth, the Jezreelite. The land had passed from generation to generation, and the laws stated plainly that no one could take it from the rightful owner. Ahab wanted the land for a palace garden.

226

The prophet Elijah placed his mantle around Elisha, a sign that the man was called to the service of God.

"Give me your vineyard," said Ahab to Naboth, "that I may have it for a vegetable garden, because it is near my house; and I will give you a better vineyard for it; or, if it seems good to you, I will give you its value in money."

"The Lord forbid that I should give you the inheritance of my fathers," replied the farmer.

Then the king went into his palace and sulked as if he were a spoiled child. He refused to eat or speak to anyone.

"Why is your spirit so vexed that you eat no food?" asked Jezebel, when she found her husband in bed as if he were sick.

When King Ahab related what had happened, the crafty queen said, "Do you now govern Israel? Arise, and eat bread, and let your heart be cheerful; I will give you the vineyard of Naboth the Jezreelite."

Jezebel sent a letter to the city officials calling them to proclaim a fast day, a time of national emergency, and to charge Naboth with rebellion against God and treason to the king. False charges were made against helpless Naboth, and he was stoned to death. Then the unscrupulous Jezebel said to Ahab, "Arise, take possession of the vineyard of Naboth the Jezreelite, which he refused to give you for money; for Naboth is not alive, but dead."

Suddenly Elijah appeared on the scene. The king cringed and said, "Have you found me, O my enemy?"

"I have found you," said Elijah, "because you have sold yourself to do what is evil in the sight of the Lord. Behold, I will bring evil upon you; I will utterly sweep you away, and will cut off from Ahab every male, bond or free, in Israel; and I will make your house like the house of Jeroboam the son of Nebat, and like the house of Baasha the son of Ahijah, for the anger to which you have provoked Me, and because you have made Israel to sin. And of Jezebel the Lord also said, 'The dogs shall eat Jezebel within the bounds of Jezreel.' Anyone belonging to Ahab who dies in the city the dogs shall eat; and anyone of his who dies in the open country the birds of the air shall eat."

Ahab bartered away his soul for the price of a vineyard! We need not stand on a high mountain to view the kingdoms of earth to compromise with evil. We often sell our souls for the amusements of the hour, the glory of fleeting notoriety, or by refusing to speak out in defense of right.

King Ahab went to battle once more against Syria, and in this conflict the monarch was struck by an arrow as he was riding in his chariot. He died and his body was taken to Samaria for burial. His chariot was washed by the pool of Samaria, and the dogs licked up his blood, even as Elijah had prophesied.

## The Ascension of Elijah

One day while Elisha was traveling with Elijah from Gilgal to Bethel, the young man was made to realize that his master was soon to leave him. When they stopped at Bethel, Elijah said, "Elisha, tarry here, I pray you; for the Lord has sent me to Jericho."

"As the Lord lives, and as you yourself live, I will not leave you," the young man replied. He had been called to service by the aged prophet, and he would not part from his master as long as he could be at his side.

So the two went on to Jericho, where students from the school of the prophets met them. They said to Elisha, "Do you know that today the Lord will take away your master from over you?"

"Yes, I know it; hold your peace," he said.

Elijah said that he was going on to the Jordan River, and he suggested that Elisha could remain at Jericho; but the young man was adamant in his purpose to stay with the prophet. Fifty of the students followed at a distance to see what might happen. They saw Elijah strike the water of the river with his cloak and the waters divide, so that the two men could walk across on dry ground.

As soon as they had passed over, Elijah said to Elisha, "Ask what I shall do for you, before I am taken from you."

229

"I pray you, let me inherit a double share of your spirit," pleaded Elisha.

"You have asked a hard thing," Elijah answered; "yet, if you see me as I am being taken from you, it shall be so for you; but if you do not see me, it shall not be so."

As they were talking, a chariot of fire and glory, drawn by horses of fire, suddenly came between the two men, and Elijah was caught up to heaven by a whirlwind.

As Elisha looked, he cried out, "My father, my father! the chariots of Israel and its horsemen!" Elisha saw his beloved master no more, and in sorrow he tore his garments as in mourning. Then as he looked down he saw Elijah's cloak lying on the ground. The young man picked it up and hurried back to the Jordan River. When Elisha struck the waters, behold, they parted as they had for the mighty prophet. Thus Elisha knew by this symbolic experience that he was to take the place of Elijah and that God was bestowing power on him to do a great work for Israel.

Every age needs a flame and a fury such as Elijah, a man of God who will call sin by its right name. In the sophistication of our generation we do not bow to idols of wood and stone; we simply worship fame, riches, science, lands, pleasure, and our ego. Millions need to face the challenge, "If the Lord is God, follow Him; but if Baal, then follow him." We must possess deep and sincere convictions as to what is right and wrong. We have allowed our thinking to become warped and confused by tricks of reasoning. Our faith in spiritual values has ebbed, and we walk alone in darkness.

Elijah called Israel back to God's law and obedience to divine truths. Our generation needs a voice, inspired by heaven, that will call men and women to keep the Ten Commandments. The growing contempt for authority, the breaking of local, national, or international law, are acute symptoms of humanity's rebellion against God. Delinquency, violence, crime—all are basically the result of rejecting the Eternal One and despising His love.

Today we need the positive proof of what Christianity can do by revealing its power in our business, in matters of racial prejudice, in solving home problems, in facing the delicate razoredge diplomacy of the atomic age. The proof of Christianity begins in individual lives; there is no other way. When the heart is surrendered to Jesus Christ, all is changed. The power of God, such as was seen in Elijah, produces new ideals, new traits of character, and a glorious hope for the future. This is the message a modern Elijah must give our world, or we are hopelessly doomed!

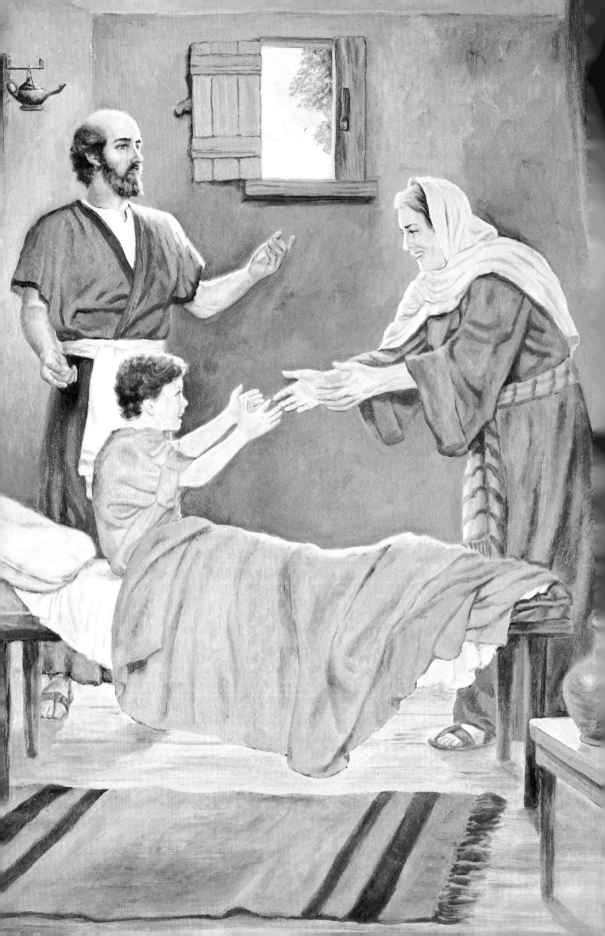

# Elisha, a Man of Peace and Power

*2 Kings 3 to 13*

## chapter 21

APOSTASY and rebellion had scourged the kingdom of Israel until the weary people yearned for a time of peace when the ravages of paganism and the wounds of strife could be healed. The young prophet Elisha was a man of faith like his master Elijah, but he was humble in spirit and less dramatic in his unflinching stand for right. In later years when men talked of the mighty prophet who destroyed the prophets of Baal on Mount Carmel, they also spoke of Elisha, who had "poured water on the hands of Elijah."

After Elijah had ascended to heaven, young Elisha made his way back to Jericho, where the sons of the prophets recognized that the Spirit of the Lord rested upon him. While the prophet stayed in Jericho, the civic leaders sought his advice concerning the bad water supply of the town. They said, "Behold, the situation of this city is pleasant, as my lord sees; but the water is bad, and the land is unfruitful."

"Bring me a new bowl," said Elisha, "and put salt in it."

Going to the spring where the town got its water, the prophet threw salt into it, and from that day the water was wholesome to drink. This was Elisha—a man ready to do acts of kindness for those who were in need, to seek God for special blessings or a miracle in times of distress.

Traveling northward to Bethel, the prophet encountered a

When the mother saw her son alive and well, she was overjoyed. Then Elisha said to her, "Take up your son."

233

group of young fellows, juvenile delinquents of his day, who ridiculed the idea that Elijah had been taken to heaven. With jeers and taunts the ruffians shouted, "Go up, you baldhead! Go up, you baldhead!"

Suddenly two bears came out of the woods and attacked the gang of forty-two boys, mangling them. It was a tragic, yet dramatic, lesson to the nation on how youth should be taught to respect religion and the representatives of God.

As Elisha traveled through towns and villages, the people believed that he was a man of God. One day the widow of a student in the school of the prophets came to Elisha and said, "Your servant my husband is dead; and you know that your servant feared the Lord, but the creditor has come to take my two children to be his slaves."

"What shall I do for you?" Elisha asked. "Tell me; what have you in the house?"

"Your maidservant has nothing in the house, except a jar of oil," she answered.

"Go outside," said he, "borrow vessels of all your neighbors, empty vessels and not too few. Then go in, and shut the door upon yourself and your sons, and pour into all these vessels; and when one is full, set it aside." Elisha taught the widow a precious lesson—that God can take what little we possess and make of it sufficient to supply all our needs.

The woman followed Elisha's instructions and shut the door upon herself and her sons. She began to pour oil into the vessels while her sons kept bringing pots and pans to her. As soon as she had one filled she said, "Bring me another vessel." Finally, when there was not another pot or pan in her house, the oil stopped.

Then the widow hurried back to Elisha and told him what had happened.

"Go, sell the oil and pay your debts, and you and your sons can live on the rest."

Some time later Elisha went to Shunem, a village in the hills north of Mount Carmel. As he walked down the street, a

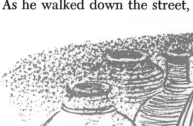

prominent woman recognized him and invited him to her home for dinner. She was so impressed by the character of the prophet that she said to her husband, "Behold now, I perceive that this is a holy man of God, who is continually passing our way. Let us make a small roof chamber with walls, and put there for him a bed, a table, a chair, and a lamp, so that whenever he comes to us, he can go in there."

## God's Providence in Daily Affairs

Elisha appreciated the family's kindness in giving him the guest room. Realizing the man and his wife had no children, the prophet gave God's promise to the woman, a promise that she would be blessed with a son. It was a happy day in that family when the baby was born. The child grew to be a strong lad, and one day he went with his father to the harvest field where the reapers were cutting grain. The hot rays of the sun beat upon the boy until he cried, "Oh, my head, my head!"

Realizing that his son was suffering a sunstroke, the father summoned a servant and said, "Carry him to his mother." When the sick boy had been carried to his mother, he sat on her lap until noon, and then he died. The sorrowing mother longed to see Elisha in her hour of bereavement, but he was not in the town. When she found that he had gone to Mount Carmel, she hurried to find him. When she told Elisha what had happened to her only son, the man of God sent his servant, Gehazi, to restore the child to life. At his master's command, the servant placed Elisha's staff on the dead boy's face; but there was no sound or response from the child.

When Elisha arrived at the house with the mother, he went to the room where the dead child lay. Closing the door, he prayed earnestly to the Lord. Then he stretched himself upon the child and placed his face against the child's face and put his hands upon the boy's hands. The child's flesh grew warm, but he did not move. Elisha walked back and forth through the house, and then he stretched himself again upon the child.

235

Suddenly the boy sneezed seven times and opened his eyes.

Elisha's servant brought the mother to the room, and when she saw her son alive and well she rejoiced. "Take up your son," said Elisha. The mother thanked God and bowed before the prophet in gratitude for his kindness to her family.

### Faith in a Time of Famine

The golden thread of human helpfulness runs through the fabric of Elisha's life. There was a famine in the land at the time that Elisha went to visit the school of the prophets at Gilgal. Food was scarce, and it was the custom for students to go out into the fields to find vegetables to make a stew. One of the men gathered some wild gourds and cut them up into the pot in which they were cooking the food. When the men sat down to eat, they noticed the peculiar taste of the food and cried out, "O man of God, there is death in the pot!"

Elisha said, "Then bring meal." When they brought meal, he threw it into the pot and told the people to eat the stew, for there was no danger of poisoning.

One day a man brought Elisha twenty loaves of barley bread and some fresh vegetables. Remembering his hungry students, the prophet said, "Give them to the men, that they may eat, for thus says the Lord, 'They shall eat and have some left.'" Although it seemed that twenty small loaves of bread would not go far among more than a hundred men, yet with God's blessing on the food, all of the group had plenty to eat, and there was some left over. Again and again Elisha's faith was rewarded. He believed that God would care for His people if they would trust in Him.

When the quarters became cramped at one of the schools of the prophets, the students decided to go to the bank of the Jordan River and cut down trees to build another house. Elisha went with the men, and while they were felling the trees, the iron axhead that one of the students was using dropped into the water.

"Alas, my master! It was borrowed," called the student.

"Where did it fall?" asked the man of God.

When the student showed Elisha the spot where the ax had fallen into the water, the prophet cut off a stick and threw it in the stream, and the iron axhead floated on the surface.

"Take it up," said Elisha.

The prophet brought God home to his people even in the little things of everyday life. How often in our daily tasks we may ask God to help us! Heaven's resources are unlimited, and in every time of need we may seek divine assistance.

### Naaman Comes to Elisha

Syria made war against Israel during the reign of King Ahab. Enemy raiders captured many of the people who lived near the city of Samaria. Among the prisoners taken to Damascus, capital of Syria, was a girl who had seen Elisha and knew of his wonderful deeds.

This girl, whose name is not recorded, became a serving maid to the wife of Naaman, commander of the Syrian army. The general was a great military man, highly esteemed by his king; but he was not happy, for he was doomed by the dread disease, leprosy. The captive maid, loyal to Naaman's wife, was grieved because her master had this incurable disease. One day she said to her mistress, "Would that my lord were with the prophet who is in Samaria! He would cure him of his leprosy." When Naaman heard these words, hope flamed in his heart. He decided to ask the king of Syria for permission to go to Israel in search of the man who might cure him.

"Go now," urged the king, "and I will send a letter to the king of Israel." Naaman set out with chariots, horsemen, and soldiers, and he carried ten talents of silver, six thousand shekels of gold, and ten beautiful robes—gifts for anyone who could rid him of his fearful malady.

Naaman expected the king of Israel to give him help; but when the visitor arrived in Samaria and presented the letter from the Syrian king to the ruler of Israel, he received an un-

237

expected reaction. The king of Israel read, "When this letter reaches you, know that I have sent to you Naaman my servant, that you may cure him of his leprosy."

The suspicious monarch threw the letter on the floor, tore his robes, and shouted in dismay, "Am I God, to kill and to make alive, that this man sends word to me to cure a man of his leprosy? Only consider, and see how he is seeking a quarrel with me."

Discouraged by the strange actions of the king, Naaman felt like turning around and heading at once for his home in Syria. However, news of Naaman's request and rebuff reached Elisha, and he sent a message to the king saying, "Why have you rent your clothes? Let him come now to me, that he may know that there is a prophet in Israel."

When Naaman and his men arrived at the house of Elisha, they expected the prophet to come out and welcome the foreign military commander. Instead, he sent Gehazi, his servant, who said, "Go and wash in the Jordan seven times, and your flesh shall be restored, and you shall be clean."

The Syrian general became very angry at this seeming insult, and he said, "Behold, I thought that he would surely come out to me, and stand, and call on the name of the Lord his God, and wave his hand over the place, and cure the leper. Are not Abana, and Pharpar, the rivers of Damascus, better than all the waters of Israel? Could I not wash in them, and be clean?"

Naaman drove away from Elisha's house in a rage. When he was calm enough to listen, one of his wise servants made this humble suggestion: "My father, if the prophet had commanded you to do some great thing, would you not have done it? How much rather, then, when he says to you, 'Wash, and be clean'?"

The Syrian paused to consider these words. Since he was going to die of leprosy unless he could be healed, why should he not follow the prophet's simple instructions?

Driving eastward until he came to the Jordan River, Naaman got down from his chariot, took off his robe, and plunged into the water. He dipped himself seven times, as Elisha had com-

As the servant girl from Israel saw Namaan's wife grieving, she told her mistress about the miracles of Elisha.

239

manded. There were ugly white patches of skin and raw leprous sores on his body; but when he arose from the water the seventh time, his skin was like the skin of a child. He was cured!

There were thousands of lepers in Israel who longed to be healed, but they were unwilling to join their efforts with a burning faith. When Naaman put his faith into action, he was healed! Millions of human beings long for healing in these modern times. In spite of the wonders of science, men and women are sick physically; their hearts long for security, for surcease from sorrow, for an answer to daily frustrations. The divine Physician brings comfort and healing to those who come to Him, seeking His will to be carried out in their lives.

After the general came out of the water, he hurried to see Elisha. This time he went into the house and spoke jubilantly to the prophet, "Behold, I know that there is no God in all the earth but in Israel; so accept now a present from your servant."

"As the Lord lives, whom I serve, I will receive none," said Elisha.

### Enticed by Wealth

Although Naaman urged Elisha to accept rich presents, the prophet would take nothing. Now, Gehazi, Elisha's servant, listened to all that was said, and he coveted the silver and gold. He compared the beautiful robes with his own shabby, patched clothing. This man had never seen such wealth before, and it dazzled his eyes and stifled his conscience. Therefore, after Naaman had started northward toward his home, Gehazi hurried after him. When the Syrian officer saw the man running along the road, he stopped his chariots and went back to meet Elisha's servant. "Is all well?" he asked.

"All is well," said Gehazi. "My master has sent me to say, 'There have just now come to me from the hill country of Ephraim two young men of the sons of the prophets; pray, give them a talent of silver and two festal garments.'"

Of course, Gehazi had fabricated his story; but Naaman

240

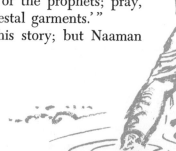

was so happy to make a gift in appreciation of his healing that he gave the servant more than he had requested. "Be pleased to accept two talents," said Naaman, heaping the treasures upon the man.

Returning to his house, Gehazi hid the gifts, and then reported to Elisha. The prophet said, "Where have you been, Gehazi?"

"Your servant went nowhere," lied Gehazi.

"Did I not go with you in spirit when the man turned from his chariot to meet you?" said the prophet. "Was it a time to accept money and garments, olive orchards and vineyards, sheep and oxen, menservants and maidservants? Therefore the leprosy of Naaman shall cleave to you, and to your descendants forever."

So Gehazi left Elisha's presence a leper as white as snow!

What a wonderful day it was when Naaman arrived home restored to full health. His wife rejoiced when she saw that her husband was free from the fearful disease. How happy the Israelite maid must have been to know that her prayers for her master had been answered. Not only had he returned well and strong, but he now worshiped the true God.

### Elisha Captures an Army

Once when the Syrian army invaded Israel, the enemy king counseled secretly with his officers on the strategy of defeating the Israelites. Time after time the Syrian army would attempt to surround Israel's forces, only to find that they had escaped. The king thought that there was surely a traitor in his army who was giving military secrets to the enemy. Therefore he called his officers together and asked, "Will you not show me who of us is for the king of Israel?"

"None, my lord, O king; but Elisha, the prophet who is in Israel, tells the king of Israel the words that you speak in your bedchamber," said one of his servants.

"Go and see where he is," commanded the king, "that I may send and seize him."

241

"Behold, he is in Dothan," a servant reported.

Immediately the king of Syria sent a large force of warriors with horses and chariots to surround that city. Under cover of darkness they laid siege to the city, and the next morning when Elisha and his servant awoke they saw the enemy army.

"Alas, my master! What shall we do?" cried Elisha's servant.

"Fear not, for those who are with us are more than those who are with them," said the prophet. Then Elisha turned to God in supplication, "O Lord, I pray Thee, open his eyes that he may see."

The astonished servant then saw the mountains around about the city full of horses and chariots of fire. The Lord had sent His angels to protect His servants in time of great danger.

If we have eyes of faith we will realize that God's agencies are at our side, strong to defend us against any enemy attack. The psalmist has said, "The angel of the Lord encamps around those who fear Him, and delivers them." Psalm 34:7. An abiding faith reaches out through the fog of evil that sometimes envelopes us and we can find the hand of our Saviour and abide in His sheltering love.

When the Syrian army advanced to capture Elisha, the prophet prayed, "Strike this people, I pray Thee, with blindness." The helpless soldiers became blind and hopelessly lost. They wandered about the town, not knowing where they were. Elisha came to them and said, "This is not the way, and this is not the city; follow me, and I will bring you to the man whom you seek."

By trusting completely in the power of the Lord, Elisha was able to capture the enemy army and lead it to Samaria to the king of Israel. The prophet then asked God to open the eyes of the captured men. When the king of Israel saw the enemy helpless before him, he asked eagerly of the prophet, "My father, shall I slay them? Shall I slay them?"

"You shall not slay them," replied Elisha, manifesting his mercy and kindness. "Would you slay those whom you have

242

taken captive with your sword and with your bow? Set bread and water before them, that they may eat and drink and go to their master."

Then the king made a great feast for the Syrian army, and when they had eaten, Elisha sent the warriors home. They gave a full report to the king as to how they had been graciously treated—a report that helped establish friendly relations and peace between the two countries for many years.

## The Reforms of Jehu

The weakness of a father is often transmitted to his son. This was the case of Ahaziah, son of Ahab, who became king of Israel when his father died. The young man should have re-membered how God vindicated His truth through Elijah on Mount Carmel, but the new king rebelled and turned defiantly to Baal worship. After reigning two years Ahaziah died with-out leaving a son, and his brother Jehoram was next in the royal succession. Jehoram ruled twelve years before he was wounded in battle at Ramothgilead while fighting the Syrians. His guards hurried him to the palace at Jezreel, while Jehu, son of Nimshi, was left in charge of the army.

About this time Elisha was given instruction to send one of the sons of the prophets to anoint Jehu to be king of Israel. The national leaders were in counsel when the messenger arrived. "I have an errand to you, O commander," said the representative of Elisha.

"To which of us all?" asked Jehu.

"To you, O commander."

Jehu left his counselors and accompanied the messenger to a private room, where he was anointed king. Then Elisha's messenger gave Jehu this commission: "Thus says the Lord the God of Israel, I anoint you king over the people of the Lord, over Israel. And you shall strike down the house of Ahab your master, that I may avenge on Jezebel the blood of My servants the prophets, and the blood of all the servants of the Lord."

After Jehu had been proclaimed king by the army, he

243

ELISHA, A MAN OF PEACE AND POWER

hurried to Jezreel to fulfill the commission. He destroyed all of
the royal family, including Jezebel. The evil woman had heard
that King Jehu was coming to the city and she knew her doom
was inevitable. When the king's chariot rolled down the
street, she looked out of the upstairs window. Jehu saw her
and commanded her servants to throw her down. The wicked
woman fell to the pavement, where the horses and chariots
trampled her to death. Later Jehu, remembering that Jezebel
was a king's daughter, commanded that she be given a decent
burial. But when servants went to take the body away, they
found that ravenous dogs had devoured her, and only her
skull, feet, and the palms of her hands remained. Thus the
terrible curse that Elijah had pronounced upon Ahab's family
had come to pass, and "Jehu wiped out Baal from Israel."

### A Lack of Faith

During the sunset years of Elisha's life he was loved and
venerated by the ten tribes of Israel. Although King Jehu had
started reforms during his twenty-eight years on the throne,
the nation was at times careless and indifferent to God's love
and mercy. Jehoahaz, the son of Jehu, was king for seventeen
years—a period of unrelieved gloom for Israel, since the kingdom was helpless in the clutches of Syria.

It was during the reign of King Joash, son of Jehoahaz, that
aged Elisha became seriously ill. The youthful monarch, failing
to treasure his heritage of faith in God, had turned to idolatry.
Nevertheless he realized that his nation was in a crisis, facing
enemies that could not be conquered with human help alone.
Therefore he visited the prophet, and with tears in his eyes he
said, "My father, my father! The chariots of Israel and its
horsemen!" These were the words Elisha had spoken when
Elijah was taken to heaven. The king admitted to the prophet
that the nation was helpless to face the Syrians, and he pleaded
for divine help in the crisis.

"Take a bow and arrows," Elisha commanded. The young
ruler obeyed, and the prophet said, "Draw the bow."

The servants obeyed King Jehu's command and threw the wicked Jezebel
from the window to the street below.

245

JOHN STEEL, ARTIST          © P. P. P. A.

As the king drew the bow, Elisha laid his hands upon the strong hands of Joash. The aged seer instructed the king to open the window toward the east and then shoot the arrow. "The Lord's arrow of victory, the arrow of victory over Syria!" cried Elisha, as the missile went on its way. "Take the arrows," continued the prophet. "Strike the ground with them."

The king struck the ground three times and then stopped. It was symbolic of the weakness in the king's character; he never did anything thoroughly. In dismay, Elisha said, "You should have struck five or six times; then you would have struck down Syria until you had made an end of it, but now you will strike down Syria only three times."

Soon after this episode the aged man of God went to his rest, and all Israel mourned his passing. Elisha was one of the mighty prophets of the Old Testament; an instrument of God to combat the evils of a dissolute age. None of us can know what Providence has in store for us; but we can be certain that faithfulness in little things—as exemplified in Elisha's life—will prepare us for greater responsibilities.

# In the Darkness, Hope!

*The Books of Jonah, Amos, Hosea*

chapter *22* ❧

ELISHA was able to leave behind him the promise of brighter days, with the hope of peace and prosperity for for the kingdom. King Joash, encouraged by the prophet's counsel to strike against Syria, was able to win back the cities that had previously been lost; while Jeroboam II restored and strengthened the frontiers of the land of Israel from the Pass of Hamath on the north to the Dead Sea on the south. In the eighth century B.C., Assyria looked greedily toward the coastlands of the Mediterranean and began overthrowing enemies that blocked her march of conquest. During the reign of Jeroboam II there lived a prophet, a well-known Bible character, who experienced a strange adventure.

Jonah, son of Amittai, came from the town of Gath-hepher, about fifteen miles southwest of the Sea of Galilee, not far from Nazareth. He was the only prophet of the age who was called to be a missionary in a foreign land to warn its citizens of the imminent destruction of their magnificent city if they did not repent of their wickedness.

Jonah received these instructions from the Lord: "Arise, go to Nineveh, that great city, and cry against it; for their wickedness has come up before Me."

Nineveh, the capital of Assyria, was located on the east bank of the Tigris River, far to the northeast of Israel. The Assyrian kings had struck terror to many an Israelite, for their fierce warriors were ruthless fighters. Jonah had heard of the city of 120,000 inhabitants, surrounded by a wall one hundred feet high and many miles in length. As the prophet pondered the divine instructions he became panic-stricken and decided to run away from God. Not realizing that he could not escape from the divine Presence, he went to the seacoast city of Joppa, found a boat sailing for Tarshish (a point in southern Spain), paid his fare, and went on board.

## The Storm and the Great Fish

After the ship had sailed from the harbor, the prophet descended into the hold and fell asleep. Soon a terrific storm struck the boat, bringing howling winds and sending waves crashing over the sides of the vessel. Even the experienced mariners were frightened, and each man called on his pagan gods for help. In desperation the crew cast the cargo overboard to lighten the ship when they saw that the vessel would be swamped by the fury of the storm.

The captain went down into the ship and found Jonah sound asleep. "What do you mean, you sleeper? Arise, call upon your god! Perhaps the god will give a thought to us, that we do not perish."

As the storm increased in intensity, the sailors began to feel that there was someone on board who had offended the gods. Therefore, they said one to another, "Come, let us cast lots, that we may know on whose account this evil has come upon us."

So they cast lots, and the lot fell upon Jonah. Looking curiously at the ship's passenger, they said, "Tell us, on whose account this evil has come upon us? What is your occupation? And whence do you come? What is your country? And of what people are you?"

Jonah told the men that he was a Hebrew who had run away from his God-given duty. He explained that he worshiped the Creator of the heavens and the earth. When the men heard

248

The sailors took Jonah up and tossed him overboard into the roaring sea where a "great fish" swallowed him.

this, they were terrified to think how he must have offended his God, and they said, "What is this that you have done!"

After talking together, the sailors asked Jonah, "What shall we do to you, that the sea may quiet down for us?"

"Take me up and throw me into the sea; then the sea will quiet down for you; for I know it is because of me that this great tempest has come upon you," said Jonah. In that moment he had a "kinship" with the pagan "foreigners." He realized that they were human beings like himself, and he was ready to make the sacrifice to save their lives.

The sailors refused to throw Jonah overboard, and they rowed the boat harder in an attempt to reach land. But the heavy waves beat against the ship and the tempest increased. Finally they cried unto the Lord in their terror and said, "We beseech Thee, O Lord, let us not perish for this man's life, and lay not on us innocent blood; for Thou, O Lord, hast done as it pleased Thee."

So they took up Jonah and tossed him overboard into the roaring sea! When they had done this, the storm abated and the waves grew calm.

### A Great Fish Swallows Jonah

Jonah was under the waves, and suddenly he saw "a great fish" swimming toward him. He cried out in fear and terror; but the huge mouth of the fish opened, and Jonah felt himself being sucked into the giant mouth! Down he went into the belly of the fish. "The Lord appointed a great fish to swallow up Jonah," says the Bible.

For three days and three nights the disobedient man tossed about in the stomach of the great fish. He cried to the Lord, saying:

> "I called to the Lord, out of my distress,
>     and He answered me;
> out of the belly of Sheol I cried,
>     and Thou didst hear my voice.
> For Thou didst cast me into the deep,
>     into the heart of the seas,

   and the flood was round about me;
  all Thy waves and Thy billows passed over me."
"When my soul fainted within me,
  I remembered the Lord;
and my prayer came to Thee,
  into Thy holy temple.
Those who pay regard to vain idols
  forsake their true loyalty.
But I with the voice of thanksgiving
  will sacrifice to Thee;
what I have vowed I will pay.
  Deliverance belongs to the Lord!"

Jonah knew what was happening, and he prayed to God, promising that if he was rescued he would obey the divine command to go to Nineveh. After three days the fish threw Jonah up on dry land, and the prophet returned to his home, thankful that his life had been spared.

Soon the message of the Lord came to Jonah a second time, saying, "Arise, go to Nineveh, that great city, and proclaim to it the message that I tell you."

This time Jonah did not hesitate, but started at once for Nineveh. When he arrived at the capital of Assyria, he went through the city streets shouting, "Yet forty days, and Nineveh shall be overthrown!"

The people of Nineveh were wicked, but when they heard this warning they believed God's message. The king made a proclamation that every person should fast and repent of his sins and call upon the Lord of heaven. When the Lord saw that the Assyrians repented of their evil, He determined not to destroy Nineveh.

When Jonah found that the city was to be spared, he was disappointed, for he had a morbid desire to see the metropolis demolished by the wrath of God. He decided that life wasn't worth living, and he prayed, "Therefore now, O Lord, take my life from me, I beseech Thee, for it is better for me to die than to live."

But the Lord asked, "Do you do well to be angry?"

Without answering the Lord's question, Jonah left the city, built a booth to shelter himself from the heat, and sat down to sulk. The sun was very warm, and the Lord made a wild gourd vine to grow and shelter the angry prophet. Then, to teach Jonah a lesson, the Lord permitted a worm to cut the vine so that it withered. The hot winds blew, the sun beat on Jonah, and again he wished he were dead.

The Lord said, "You pity the plant, for which you did not labor, nor did you make it grow, which came into being in a night, and perished in a night. And should not I pity Nineveh, that great city, in which there are more than a hundred and twenty thousand persons who do not know their right hand from their left, and also much cattle?" The heavenly Father was pleading with Jonah to recognize the common human relation of all men, the universal need for love and mercy.

How slow we are to learn that the words of John Donne are true: "No man is an island, entire of itself; every man is a piece of the continent, a part of the main; if a clod be washed away by the sea, Europe is the less, as well as if a promontory were, as well as if a manner of thy friends or of thine own were; any man's death diminishes me, because I am involved in mankind; and therefore never send to know for whom the bell tolls; it tolls for thee." The brotherhood of all men is more than an ideal; it must be a working blueprint for our generation. If we fail to help our fellow men in their suffering, degradation, or ignorance, we shall destroy ourselves. This was the lesson God gave Israel through the runaway, but repentant, Jonah.

During the latter part of the reign of Jeroboam II a generation had grown up that had not known defeat, and the prosperity of Israel was at its height. War profiteers made fortunes, which they squandered in riotous living. They built summer homes and winter homes of ivory furnished with luxurious ivory furniture. With the rise of materialism there came a decline in religious life. The nation, outwardly religious, turned to gross idol worship, superstition, and licentiousness. Those who

worshiped the true God thought more of sacrifices, feast days, ritual, and ceremonies than they did of a humble and contrite heart. In the midst of a dissolute and decadent generation, a voice was heard in Israel crying for reform. Amos, a shepherd and fruitgrower from the village of Tekoa, in the Judean hills some six miles from Jerusalem, left his flocks and went north to thrust himself into the rotten social order of Samaria. From a humble, God-fearing home, came the young prophet, fervent in spirit, dynamic in action. In the words of the shepherd-prophet we learn how he was called to his thankless mission. He says, "The Lord took me from following the flock, and the Lord said to me, 'Go, prophesy to My people Israel.' "

## The Message of Amos

In the capital city of Israel, this man of God saw crime and lawlessness. Justice was crushed by bribery and fraud; the poor and the weak were exploited by the rich. Although the people went through the forms of religion, yet idolatry was rampant, and every form of vice and immorality was practiced. With divine inspiration Amos directed his message to Israel—a message that may be summarized in eleven words: "God is soon to destroy His people because of their sins." Because their prosperity rested on a foundation of injustice and inhumanity, the prophet pronounced an oracle of doom against rebellious Israel: "For three transgressions of Israel, and for four, I will not revoke the punishment; because they sell the righteous for silver, and the needy for a pair of shoes—they that trample the head of the poor into the dust of the earth, and turn aside the way of the afflicted; a man and his father go in to the same maiden, so that My holy name is profaned; they lay themselves down beside every altar upon garments taken in pledge; and in the house of their God they drink the wine of those who have been fined."

The youthful prophet courageously attacked those with calloused conscience; they would be brought to judgment for their sins. Listen to his strong, lucid words: "Woe to those who

lie upon beds of ivory, and stretch themselves upon their couches, and eat lambs from the flock, and calves from the midst of the stall; who sing idle songs to the sound of the harp, and like David invent for themselves instruments of music; who drink wine in bowls, and anoint themselves with the finest oils, but are not grieved over the ruin of Joseph! Therefore they shall now be the first of those to go into exile, and the the revelry of those who stretch themselves shall pass away."

Amos warned that the Assyrians would descend upon Israel, and his solemn words echo to us more than twenty-five hundred years later: "For behold, I will raise up against you a nation, O house of Israel, . . . and they shall oppress you from the entrance of Hamath to the brook of Arabah." But God would not allow tragedy to strike without giving His people prophecies of warning. In words never to be forgotten, we have the reason for divine prophecy: "Surely the Lord God does nothing, without revealing His secret to His servants the prophets."

After the prophet had delivered numerous messages in the city of Samaria, he went to Bethel—a center of religious worship, probably at the time of an annual sacred festival. He called on those who professed religion to repent of their hypocrisy and disobedience. Amaziah, the priest at Bethel, was incensed by the words of Amos. Here was one of the dramatic encounters of the Bible. As the priest faced Amos, he saw only a dangerous man. Quickly he preferred charges of treason against him in a message to the king. These were the words of accusation: "Amos has conspired against you in the midst of the house of Israel; the land is not able to bear all his words."

Then the frightened priest turned on the vigorous prophet and ordered him to get out of the kingdom of Israel. "O seer, go, flee away to the land of Judah, and eat bread there, and prophesy there; but never again prophesy at Bethel, for it is the king's sanctuary, and it is a temple of the kingdom."

The evil priest was certain that any place was better for Amos than in Bethel! He felt that he must get rid of this voice

Amos, a shepherd from Tekoa, saw the
crime and lawlessness in Israel, and
he called the nation to repentance.

JOE MANISCALCO, ARTIST          © P. P. P. A.

of conscience, for the message struck at his guilty heart like a sword.

Amos humbly replied, "I am no prophet, nor a prophet's son; but I am a herdsman, and a dresser of sycamore trees, and the Lord took me from following the flock, and the Lord said to me, 'Go, prophesy to My people Israel.' "

While God declared through Amos that "the end has come upon My people," and "I will never again pass by them;" yet the messages of Amos do not end on a note of darkness and doom. Indeed, this man of the outdoors pleaded with the people to repent, and "prepare to meet your God, O Israel!" The prophet gives the divine promise, "I will restore the fortunes of My people Israel, and they shall rebuild the ruined cities and inhabit them; they shall plant vineyards and drink their wine, and they shall make gardens and eat their fruit. I will plant them upon their land, and they shall never again be plucked up out of the land which I have given them."

## The Voice of Hosea

Shortly after the ministry of Amos, a new voice spoke to Israel concerning the righteousness of God and His love for man. In the few years that had intervened the ten tribes had been torn by strife and civil war. The plundering Assyrians were poised for another invasion of fast-declining Israel. Jeroboam II was followed by his son Zechariah, who ruled only six months. Then came Shallum, and after him Menaham, a monarch who indulged in "all the sins of Jeroboam." Two weak rulers, Pekahiah and Pekah, were next in the line of Israel's royal succession; but they were noted only for their corrupt leadership.

It was in the days of these kings that Hosea condemned the social evils, the crimes, and the selfish indulgence of the ten tribes. He married a woman named Gomer, and after she had borne him three children she proved unfaithful in her love. Hosea gave names to his children that paralleled the conditions of the times; they were "walking sermons," drama-

256

Hosea's wife Gomer bore him three children, but she proved unfaithful and left her husband and little ones.

tizing the approaching doom of the nation. His first-born son was called Jezreel, for the Lord said, "Call his name Jezreel; for yet a little while, and I will punish the house of Jehu for the blood of Jezreel, and I will put an end to the kingdom of the house of Israel. And on that day, I will break the bow of Israel in the valley of Jezreel."

The prophet named his daughter Lo-ruhamah, which means "Not pitied," for God said, "I will no more have pity on the house of Israel, to forgive them at all. But I will have pity on the house of Judah, and I will deliver them by the Lord their God; I will not deliver them by bow, nor by sword, nor by war, nor by horses, nor by horsemen."

The third child, a boy, was called Lo-ammi, which means "Not My people," for the Lord had rejected Israel. Then the specter of marital unhappiness arose in Hosea's life. Gomer forsook her home and family for adulterous company with other men. As the result of his experience, the prophet found a symbolic meaning in them for Israel. Hosea saw that the kingdom was as faithless to God as his wife had been in her false love and the desertion of her family. The prophet declared, "They have left their God to play the harlot."

Striking against current social evils, the prophet said:

"Hear the word of the Lord, O people of Israel;
 for the Lord has a controversy with the inhabitants of the land.
There is no faithfulness or kindness,
    and no knowledge of God in the land;
 there is swearing, lying, killing, stealing, and committing adultery;
    they break all bounds and murder follows murder."

"My people are destroyed for lack of knowledge;
    because you have rejected knowledge,
    I reject you from being a priest to Me.
And since you have forgotten the law of your God,
    I also will forget your children."

While the destiny of Israel hung in the balance, God appealed for the love of His wayward children:

"How can I give you up, O Ephraim!
    How can I hand you over, O Israel!"

"I will not execute My fierce anger,
    I will not again destroy Ephraim;
for I am God and not man,
    the Holy One in your midst,
    and I will not come to destroy."

The nation continued to celebrate its round of feast days while it tottered on the verge of annihilation. Hosea proclaimed this warning:

"The days of punishment have come,
    the days of recompense have come;
    Israel shall know it.
The prophet is a fool,
    the man of the spirit is mad,
because of your great iniquity and great hatred."
"You have plowed iniquity,
    you have reaped injustice,
    you have eaten the fruit of lies.
Because you have trusted in your chariots
    and in the multitude of your warriors,
therefore the tumult of war shall arise among your people,
    and all your fortresses shall be destroyed,
    as Shalman destroyed Beth-arbel on the day of battle;
    mothers were dashed in pieces with their children.
Thus it shall be done to you, O house of Israel,
    because of your great wickedness."

The final message of the prophet reveals the wonderful love of the heavenly Father, who heals and restores those who come to Him with all their heart.

"Return, O Israel, to the Lord your God,
    for you have stumbled because of your iniquity.
Take with you words
    and return to the Lord;
say to Him,
    'Take away all iniquity;
accept that which is good
    and we will render
    the fruit of our lips.'"

259

"I will heal their faithlessness;
    I will love them freely,
      for My anger has turned from them."

"Whoever is wise, let him understand these things;
    whoever is discerning, let him know them;
for the ways of the Lord are right,
    and the upright walk in them,
      but transgressors stumble in them."

Deep personal emotion is displayed throughout the writings of Hosea, for the prophet had suffered deeply in his own experience, and he was sensitive to the tragedy of the times with their lack of spiritual peace and power. Through all of his bitter trials, he did not lose hope in God, the Redeemer and Restorer of His people.

# Kings and Prophets of Judah

*2 Chronicles 10 to 32; the Book of Isaiah*

chapter 23 &

WE TURN from the tragic downfall of the northern kingdom of Israel to follow the history of the smaller kingdom, Judah, through its vicissitudes. The southern kingdom consisted of two tribes, Judah and Benjamin; and although small in territory and population, it was strong because Solomon's temple, with its center of worship, was at Jerusalem, the capital city. Then, too, when Israel fell into gross idolatry, many of the devout priests and Levites, as well as truth-loving families, moved south to live where the worship of God was continued.

The first strong ruler in Judah after the ten tribes revolted and pulled away from King Rehoboam was Asa, his grandson, who "did what was good and right in the eyes of the Lord his God." He abolished idolatry and sun worship, called for reformation of life among the people, and set an example in godliness. He ruled the nation realistically, for he built up the defenses and increased the army to over a half million soldiers.

When Zerah the Ethiopian marched against Judah with an army of a million men, King Asa drew up his battle lines to defend the kingdom. At the same time he realized that his strength did not lie in warriors and weapons; therefore he prayed, "O Lord, there is none like Thee to help, between the mighty and the weak. Help us, O Lord our God, for we rely on Thee, and in Thy name we have come against this multitude.  O Lord, Thou art our God; let not man prevail against Thee."

This is an appropriate prayer for the modern Christian who is beset with a legion of enemies that would degrade and destroy the soul.  Only as we realize that we are helpless in our sinful condition will we sense our need of divine power.

With divine assistance the armies of Judah defeated the Ethiopians and they fled from the land, the soldiers of King Asa pursuing them as far as Gerar.  The men of Judah captured much booty, including sheep and camels.  With King Asa leading them, the conquering army marched into Jerusalem to the cheers of the waiting citizens.  Soon a day of thanksgiving was proclaimed, when the people assembled to offer sacrifices to the Lord for a glorious victory.

Near the close of Asa's reign, the king of Israel came against Judah, and in panic, Asa made a league with Ben-hadad, king of Syria, who agreed to send military aid to help stop the invaders.  The prophet Hanani gave the king of Judah a message of reproof in these words: "Because you relied on the king of Syria, and did not rely on the Lord your God, the army of the king of Syria has escaped you.  Were not the Ethiopians and the Libyans a huge army with exceedingly many chariots and horsemen?  Yet because you relied on the Lord, He gave them into your hand.  For the eyes of the Lord run to and fro throughout the whole earth, to show His might in behalf of those whose heart is blameless toward Him.  You have done foolishly in this; for from now on you will have wars."

### A Dangerous Alliance

After a reign of forty-one years, Asa died, and his son Jehoshaphat sat on the throne.  The thirty-five-year-old ruler followed the good example of his father, for he "sought the God of his father and walked in His commandments."  The king also appointed men to go from city to city teaching the people the law of God.

An alliance between the royal families of Judah and Israel was made when Jehoshaphat's son married Ahab's daughter. After some years King Jehoshaphat visited Ahab in Samaria, and while he was there the Syrians menaced the northern border of Israel. Ahab urged Jehoshaphat to join him in fighting the enemy, and the king of Judah foolishly pledged his word to assist in the war. But as he pondered over the alliance he had made he became more and more convinced that he should withdraw from it. After he had committed himself to fight, Jehoshaphat decided it was time for him to know God's will. So Ahab arranged for four hundred false prophets to visit the palace, and they counseled the kings to attack Syria. They said, "Go up; for God will give it into the hand of the king."

Jehoshaphat suspected that the message of these prophets was false, and he requested the advice of still another prophet. Finally Micaiah, a man of God who was hated by Ahab, came to the king's palace. When he spoke the divinely inspired message, he said, "I saw all Israel scattered upon the mountains, as sheep that have no shepherd; and the Lord said, 'These have no master; let each return to his home in peace.'"

The warning of defeat was plain; but foolhardy Jehoshaphat, having already pledged to give military assistance to Ahab, did not want to break his word. The armies marched to Ramothgilead, where they suffered a complete rout from the Syrian host. Ahab was wounded by an arrow, and before the sun set that day he was dead. Jehoshaphat returned to Jerusalem crestfallen by the blow of defeat as well as in the knowledge that he had disobeyed God's will. As he was about to enter the city gate a prophet of the Lord met him and asked, "Should you help the wicked and love those who hate the Lord?" Here is a pertinent question that echoes down the centuries. Shall we compromise principle for business success? Shall we help those who do evil simply because they are strong and we are afraid to say No? Should we support industries that produce soul- and body-destroying products?

263

Should we help the wicked and love those who hate God and spurn His word?

Jehoshaphat established an efficient judicial system whereby the people received justice. When enemies threatened the land, the king called for days of prayer and fasting. In a beautiful supplication for divine aid, he said, "We do not know what to do, but our eyes are upon Thee." God was the strength of Judah in the national crisis; her enemies withdrew and "the fear of God came on all the kingdoms of the countries when they heard that the Lord had fought against the enemies of Israel."

## *The Boy Who Became King*

Jehoram, the son of Jehoshaphat, came to the throne with a heritage of temporal and spiritual blessings—all of which he soon squandered. He killed his six brothers because he was afraid they might succeed him on the throne. His wife, Athaliah, the daughter of Ahab and Jezebel of Israel, was cruel and ruthless like her parents. King Jehoram ruled for eight years, and he died "with no one's regret." Ahaziah, the youngest son of Jehoram, became ruler; but he brought only trouble, for he led the people into idolatry. When King Jehu, of Israel, purged the house of Ahab and slew all of its members, King Ahaziah was captured and executed.

Upon hearing of her son's death, Athaliah, the wicked queen mother, determined to wipe out the royal family of Judah. Jehoash, one of her grandchildren, was heir to the throne; but she plotted to destroy the baby. While princes and princesses were being murdered, the baby's aunt snatched him out of his cradle and took him and his nurse to the high priest's apartment, which adjoined the temple of Solomon. The aunt was the wife of the high priest, and she hid the child in the temple for six years, so that Athaliah had no knowledge of the prince regent's existence.

During this period the dissolute queen ruled supreme, leading the kingdom into every form of paganism. In the seventh

At the signal, Jehoash, the seven-year-old prince, was brought before the crowd and anointed king of Judah.

JOE MANISCALCO, ARTIST     © P. P. P. A.

265

18—H.F. 2

year the high priest mustered up courage to meet with the soldiers who guarded the temple treasury. When the captain of the guard heard that the prince was alive he was willing to co-operate in a plot to overthrow the queen mother. With shields, spears, and other weapons supplied them from the armory that King David had once built up, the people stood ready to act. At a given signal, Jehoash, the seven-year-old prince, was brought out to the waiting crowd. A crown was placed on his head, and the high priest anointed him as king of Judah. A copy of the law, which he pledged to uphold, was placed in the child's hands while the soldiers and the crowd shouted, "Long live the king."

When Athaliah heard the people running through the street and shouting, she hurried to the temple court to investigate what was happening. It was unbelievable! There stood the boy king at the temple entrance, while the people rejoiced and the guards blew a salute on their trumpets.

"Treason! Treason!" shouted Athaliah.

Then the high priest gave command to the soldiers, saying, "Bring her out between the ranks; anyone who follows her is to be slain with the sword."

They took the queen mother outside the temple area and executed her. Then the people rushed to the temple of Baal, wrecked it, and pulled down all the heathen images and altars.

Jehoash began a work of reform in Judah that spread to every part of the kingdom. He instructed the priests and Levites, saying, "Go out to the cities of Judah, and gather from all Israel money to repair the house of your God from year to year; and see that you hasten the matter."

The young king ordered a chest to be placed at the temple gate where devout visitors could place gifts for the repair of the neglected house of worship. Judah followed God's commands as long as Jehoash's uncle, the high priest who spared the boy king, lived and gave him good counsel. In later years, Jehoash listened to unwise advice from his courtiers, and the nation was led into idolatry. Jehoash also became rebellious

266

and ruthless in the closing period of his kingship. When the nation did evil, God sent Zechariah, a cousin of the king, to call the people to repentance. Zechariah said, "Thus says God, 'Why do you transgress the commandments of the Lord, so that you cannot prosper? Because you have forsaken the Lord, He has forsaken you.'"

The people became angry when they were reproved, and at the command of King Jehoash they stoned the man of God. Thus did the reprobate monarch forget the kindnesses of his youth and the counsel of those who attempted to save him from disaster. As Zechariah lay dying, he said to the king, "May the Lord see and avenge!"

Retribution came upon Jehoash, for at the end of the same year the Syrian army invaded Judah and made a smashing attack on Jerusalem. In the conflict princes were slain by the sword and the king was wounded, and later he was murdered while helpless in his bed. The son of Jehoash, Amaziah by name, took the throne, and he reigned twenty-nine years. His first act was to revenge the assassination of his father by putting the accomplices to death. Evil were the days of Amaziah's rule, for he defied the God of his people.

## The Leper King

In a war between Judah and Israel, King Amaziah was captured by the king of Israel and marched as a prisoner into his own capital of Jerusalem. The invaders broke down the city gate and some of the city wall, seized the sacred vessels in the temple, and looted the king's treasury. Peace came finally, but there was insurrection in the royal court. When Amaziah learned of a conspiracy to kill him, he fled to Lachish, only to find the traitors closing in upon him there. Soon he was assassinated, even as his father had been twenty-nine years previously.

A wise and godly king—Uzziah, the son of Amaziah— ascended the throne at the age of sixteen. For fifty-two years this man of strong faith and keen judgment guided the destiny

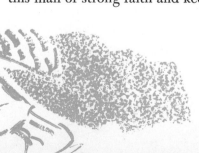

of the kingdom. He strengthened the army, built fortifications, and created new weapons of defense. Nevertheless, success proved the undoing of the good king, for the record states: "But when he was strong he grew proud, to his destruction. For he was false to the Lord his God, and entered the temple of the Lord to burn incense on the altar of incense." A group of priests were shocked at the irreverence of Uzziah in attempting to perform the duties of a dedicated priest in the temple. They warned him, saying, "It is not for you, Uzziah, to burn incense to the Lord, but for the priests the sons of Aaron, who are consecrated to burn incense. Go out of the sanctuary; for you have done wrong, and it will bring you no honor from the Lord God."

The king flared in anger, and he was ready to threaten the priests when they suddenly saw a deadly white spot on Uzziah's forehead. It was leprosy! Quickly the stricken monarch was hurried from the holy sanctuary—a sick, bewildered man. For forty years he ruled as the leper king, shut off from court society because of the dread disease.

After Uzziah died there was a succession of weaklings— two kings who failed God and the nation. Then, at the age of twenty-five, Hezekiah became ruler of Judah. Realizing that the ten tribes of Israel were sinking under the savage blows of enemies from the north, the courageous youth determined with God's help to save his people of the two tribes from a similar fate. As a symbol of the spiritual reforms needed in the nation, he commanded the priests to have the temple cleaned and renovated. He said, "Our fathers have been unfaithful and have done what was evil in the sight of the Lord our God; they have forsaken Him, and have turned away their faces from the habitation of the Lord, and turned their backs."

### Isaiah, Mightiest of the Prophets

King Hezekiah had the admonition and counsel of Isaiah, the son of Amoz, one of the mightiest prophets of the Old Testament. Isaiah prophesied during the days of four kings—

Uzziah, Jotham, Ahaz, and Hezekiah, warning, exhorting, and reproving the nation. It was in the year that King Uzziah died that young Isaiah, worshiping in the temple court, saw a vision of God's glory. He describes his mystical experience in these words: "In the year that King Uzziah died I saw the Lord sitting upon a throne, high and lifted up; and His train filled the temple. Above him stood the seraphim; each had six wings: with two he covered his face, and with two he covered his feet, and with two he flew. And one called to another and said, 'Holy, holy, holy is the Lord of hosts; the whole earth is full of His glory.'"

As the young prophet beheld the majesty of the Lord of all creation, he felt his unworthiness. "Woe is me!" he exclaimed. "For I am lost; for I am a man of unclean lips, and I dwell in the midst of a people of unclean lips; for my eyes have seen the King, the Lord of hosts!"

Then, as a symbol of the blessing of heaven that was bestowed upon his life and work, the prophet saw an angel take a live coal from the altar and place it upon his lips. The angel said, "Behold, this has touched your lips; your guilt is taken away, and your sin forgiven." Then the Lord asked, "Whom shall I send, and who will go for us?"

"Here I am! Send me," said Isaiah, a man with a dedicated spirit. Soon the prophet entered public affairs in the kingdom. He saw the menacing power of Assyria rising like a storm cloud in the north, and he pleaded with the leaders to avoid all political intrigue. Without mincing words, Isaiah described Judah's plight:

"Your country lies desolate,
   your cities are burned with fire;
in your very presence aliens devour your land;
   it is desolate, as overthrown by aliens.
And the daughter of Zion is left
   like a booth in a vineyard,
like a lodge in a cucumber field,
   like a besieged city.
If the Lord of hosts

had not left us a few survivors,
we should have been like Sodom,
and become like Gomorrah."

The Eternal One longed to save the remnant and make His people an everlasting nation. Gracious is the invitation to repent and the promise of forgiveness that has come down to us from Isaiah's message:

"Come now, let us reason together,
    says the Lord:
though your sins are like scarlet,
    they shall be as white as snow;
though they are red like crimson,
    they shall become like wool.
If you are willing and obedient,
    you shall eat the good of the land."

The prophet saw the rich estates of the wealthy, for the land was full of silver and gold; but he knew that the optimism of the age was based on the crumbling foundation of luxury, easy living, and materialism. He despised pride and self-glory, as he saw it exemplified in the flippant young women of Jerusalem. He pronounced this scathing rebuke upon them:

"Because the daughters of Zion are haughty
    and walk with outstretched necks,
    glancing wantonly with their eyes,
mincing along as they go,
    tinkling with their feet;
the Lord will smite with a scab
    the heads of the daughters of Zion,
    and the Lord will lay bare their secret parts."

Although the crisis was grave, it was not a time for Judah to seek help from pagan Egypt. Isaiah warned that "the Egyptians are men, and not God," and that "they will all perish together." To the idol-loving crowds who had rejected the worship of the Lord, Isaiah gave some of his strongest denunciations. He said,

As Isaiah was worshiping in the temple, he saw a vision of God's glory, and he was ready to do the Lord's will.

> "To whom then will you liken God,
>     or what likeness compare with Him?
> The idol! a workman casts it,
>     and a goldsmith overlays it with gold,
>     and casts for it silver chains.
> He who is impoverished chooses for an offering
>     wood that will not rot;
> he seeks out a skillful craftsman
>     to set up an image that will not move."

Then he called men to look at the starry heavens, whose wonders could scarcely be fathomed in those times as compared with our knowledge through modern astronomy, and the prophet gave God's challenge:

> "To whom then will you compare Me,
>     that I should be like him? says the Holy One.
> Lift up your eyes on high and see:
>     who created these?
> He who brings out their host by number,
>     calling them all by name;
> by the greatness of His might,
>     and because He is strong in power
>     not one is missing."

Some of the most faith-building promises in all the Bible are found in the rhapsodies of Isaiah. His words shine like precious gems to the trusting child of God seeking divine truth in the darkness of our modern world:

> "Fear not, for I am with you,
>     be not dismayed, for I am your God;
> I will strengthen you, I will help you,
>     I will uphold you with My victorious right hand."
> "Seek the Lord while He may be found,
>     call upon Him while He is near;
> let the wicked forsake his way,
>     and the unrighteous man his thoughts;
> let him return to the Lord, that He may have mercy
>     on him,
>     and to our God, for He will abundantly pardon."

272

"When you pass through the waters I will be with you;
    and through the rivers, they shall not overwhelm you;
when you walk through fire you shall not be burned,
    and the flame shall not consume you."

"He will swallow up death forever, and the Lord God will wipe away tears from all faces, and the reproach of His people He will take away from all the earth; for the Lord has spoken."
Isaiah 41:10; 55:6, 7; 43:2; 25:8.

The invitation to return to God is given to every prodigal of our generation even as it was offered in Isaiah's day or in the time when Jesus Christ walked among men:

"I have swept away your transgressions like a cloud,
    and your sins like mist;
return to Me, for I have redeemed you."

From the day that Adam sinned, the hope of a Deliverer has centered in the coming of the Messiah. Abraham, Jacob, Moses, David, and a host of other sincere men and women looked for the world's Redeemer. The prophets of Israel and Judah believed that the bondage of sin would be broken by the coming King of kings. Isaiah looked for "the Prince of Peace," when he said:

"For to us a Child is born,
    to us a Son is given;
and the government will be upon His shoulder,
    and His name will be called
'Wonderful Counselor, Mighty God,
    Everlasting Father, Prince of Peace.'
Of the increase of His government and of peace
    there will be no end,
upon the throne of David, and over his kingdom,
    to establish it, and to uphold it
with justice and with righteousness
    from this time forth and forevermore.
The zeal of the Lord of hosts will do this."

The Messiah would "bring good tidings to the afflicted," "bind up the brokenhearted," "proclaim liberty to the captives,"

273

and "comfort all who mourn." Jesus read this prophecy of Isaiah in the synagogue and He declared to the congregation, "Today this scripture has been fulfilled in your hearing." Luke 4:21.

## "The Suffering Servant"

The high-water mark of Old Testament prophecies is the fifty-third chapter of Isaiah, where the prophet presents a pen picture of the suffering and death of the Son of God for a sinful world. We cannot here reproduce the entire chapter, but we suggest that the reader quietly and prayerfully read these poetic lines in his Bible.

Among the magnificent prophetic stanzas are these lines depicting our Lord's suffering and humiliation:

> "He was despised and rejected by men;
> a Man of Sorrows, and acquainted with grief;
> and as One from whom men hide their faces
> He was despised, and we esteemed Him not.
> Surely He has borne our griefs
> and carried our sorrows;
> yet we esteemed Him stricken,
> smitten by God, and afflicted.
> But He was wounded for our transgressions,
> He was bruised for our iniquities;
> upon Him was the chastisement that made us whole,
> and with His stripes we are healed."

To make the love and sacrifice of Jesus more real, may we suggest that the reader place the personal pronouns "me" and "my" in the verses. Then we can say, "Surely He has borne *my* griefs, and carried *my* sorrows." It was that divine love that led Jesus Christ to humble Himself and suffer the basest of deaths. Today the cross towers above our world— the sign of victory over sin in all its hideous forms. The cross has become the symbol of hope, for by the death of the Son of God we have received the precious gift of eternal life with Him!

## *Hezekiah's Dedication to God*

The messages of Isaiah caused King Hezekiah to make a covenant with the Lord. He called the priests to sanctify themselves and stand in the temple as servants of God. In the first service at Jerusalem, Hezekiah joined the priests and Levites in seeking forgiveness for sin. Offerings were made, the musicians played, and the congregation worshiped.

News of the siege of Samaria, with the resulting death and destruction wrought by the Assyrians, reached the kingdom of Judah. It was an hour of serious contemplation, a time to seek God. For many years the Passover had not been observed as a national feast. Therefore, King Hezekiah sent messengers to all the tribes of Israel, as well as to Judah, inviting the faithful to gather for the Passover Feast. The response was so great that Jerusalem was jammed with visitors seeking to offer sacrifices and celebrate the ancient festival. For a week the celebration continued, and then the leaders agreed to continue the festival for another seven days, while the priests taught the people and performed the ritual of the temple.

In the fourteenth year of King Hezekiah's reign Sennacherib, king of Assyria, came against Judah with powerful armies. The enemy required such high tribute of the king of Judah that he was forced to take all the gold and silver from the treasury, and then strip the gold from the doors and pillars of the temple! The Assyrians retired, leaving the people of Judah with the hope that the enemy had been pacified; but it was only a lull in the storm.

About this time a serious malady seized King Hezekiah and he was at the point of death. The prophet Isaiah came to the sick man with this instruction: "Thus says the Lord, 'Set your house in order; for you shall die, you shall not recover.' "

In humility the king turned his face to the wall and prayed, "Remember now, O Lord, I beseech Thee, how I have walked before Thee in faithfulness and with a whole heart, and have done what is good in Thy sight."

275

Isaiah was leaving the palace when he received divine instruction to return and say to Hezekiah, "Thus says the Lord, the God of David your father: I have heard your prayer, I have seen your tears; behold, I will heal you; on the third day you shall go up to the house of the Lord. And I will add fifteen years to your life. I will deliver you and this city out of the hand of the king of Assyria, and I will defend this city for My own sake and for My servant David's sake."

The prophet directed a special treatment for the king—a lump of figs was to be placed on the diseased part as a poultice. Naturally the king longed for an assurance that he was healed, so he said to Isaiah, "What shall be the sign that the Lord will heal me, and that I shall go up to the house of the Lord on the third day?"

"This is the sign to you from the Lord," replied the man of God, "that the Lord will do the thing that He has promised: shall the shadow go forward ten steps, or go back ten steps?"

"It is an easy thing for the shadow to lengthen ten steps," reasoned the king; "rather let the shadow go back ten steps."

Therefore the shadow of the sundial moved back ten degrees as Hezekiah had requested. Then the king wrote a poem of thanksgiving for the wondrous answer to his prayer. He said:

"I said, In the noontide of my days
    I must depart;
I am consigned to the gates of Sheol
    for the rest of my years.
I said, I shall not see the Lord
    in the land of the living;
I shall look upon man no more
    among the inhabitants of the world."

"O Lord, by these things men live,
    and in all these is the life of my spirit.
    Oh, restore me to health and make me live!
Lo, it was for my welfare
    that I had great bitterness;
but Thou hast held back my life
    from the pit of destruction,

King Hezekiah entertained the envoys from Babylon, and he proudly showed them all of his treasures.

> for Thou hast cast all my sins
> behind Thy back."

> "The Lord will save me,
> and we will sing to stringed instruments
> all the days of our life,
> at the house of the Lord."

When the king of Babylon heard that King Hezekiah had been healed of a fatal malady, he sent an envoy to the court at Jerusalem to congratulate him on his recovery. Here was a magnificent opportunity for the ruler of Judah to glorify God and set forth the love and mercy of heaven; but he missed his golden moment! Instead, the king showed the ambassadors the treasures he had gathered—gold, silver, spices, and the weapons of his armory.

When Isaiah heard of Hezekiah's folly, he came to the court and asked, "What did these men say? And whence did they come to you?"

"They have come from a far country, from Babylon," the king explained.

"What have they seen in your house?" asked the prophet.

"They have seen all that is in my house," Hezekiah replied proudly; "there is nothing in my storehouses that I did not show them."

Then Isaiah said, "Behold, the days are coming, when all that is in your house, and that which your fathers have stored up till this day, shall be carried to Babylon; nothing shall be left, says the Lord. And some of your own sons, who are born to you, shall be taken away; and they shall be eunuchs in the palace of the king of Babylon."

The king passively accepted the divine verdict, for he thought, "Why not, if there will be peace and security in my days?"

## The Coming of the Assyrians

The long-threatened crisis broke on Judah when the armies of Sennacherib stormed down from the north. Confident that

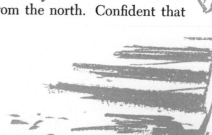

he could quickly swallow up the small kingdom, the Assyrian monarch sent half of his army to fight the Egyptians. Sennacherib sent his commander in chief to the capital, and with him went a crafty politician named Rabshakeh. This man did his best to discourage the people of Judah and persuade them to surrender. He said, "On what do you rest this confidence of yours? You think that mere words are counsel and strength for war! On whom do you now rely, that you have rebelled against me? Behold, you are relying now on Egypt, that broken reed of a staff, which will pierce the hand of any man who leans on it."

Rabshakeh also spoke to the men of Judah, but they refused to answer the enemy. As soon as King Hezekiah heard the Assyrian propaganda, he tore his garments, covered himself with sackcloth, and entered the temple to pray. The king also sent a messenger to Isaiah, asking him to seek God's help in the national crisis.

The brave prophet sent this message of courage back to King Hezekiah, "Thus says the Lord: Do not be afraid because of the words that you have heard, with which the servants of the king of Assyria have reviled Me. Behold, I will put a spirit in him, so that he shall hear a rumor and return to his own land; and I will cause him to fall by the sword in his own land."

Rabshakeh returned to the king of Assyria and reported that the men of Judah had refused to surrender. This caused King Sennacherib to write an insulting letter to Hezekiah, in which he said, "Do not let your God on whom you rely deceive you by promising that Jerusalem will not be given into the hand of the king of Assyria. Behold, you have heard what the kings of Assyria have done to all lands, destroying them utterly. And shall you be delivered?"

When the king of Judah received the letter, he retired to the temple and spread the message before the Lord and prayed, "O Lord the God of Israel, who art enthroned above the cherubim, Thou art the God, Thou alone, of all the kingdoms

of the earth; Thou hast made heaven and earth. Incline Thy ear, O Lord, and hear; open Thy eyes, O Lord, and see; and hear the words of Sennacherib, which he has sent to mock the living God. Of a truth, O Lord, the kings of Assyria have laid waste the nations and their lands, and have cast their gods into the fire; for they were no gods, but the work of men's hands, wood and stone; therefore they were destroyed. So now, O Lord our God, save us, I beseech Thee, from his hand, that all the kingdoms of the earth may know that Thou, O Lord, art God alone."

While Hezekiah prayed, Isaiah sent him an answer from the Lord: "Therefore thus says the Lord concerning the king of Assyria, He shall not come to this city or shoot an arrow there, or come before it with a shield or cast up a mound against it. By the way that he came, by the same he shall return, and he shall not come into this city, says the Lord." In this darkest of dark hours for Judah it required a great and abiding faith to believe this promise.

That night the angel of the Lord went through the army of the Assyrians as it was camped near Jerusalem and slew 185,000 of the enemy. The next morning the men of Judah found the dead lying in the camp. The king of Assyria had fled back to Ninevah, taking with him the handful of men who remained.

This great victory has been described by Lord Byron:

> The Assyrian came down like the wolf on the fold,
> And his cohorts were gleaming with purple and gold;
> And the sheen of their spears was like stars on the sea,
> When the blue wave rolls nightly on deep Galilee.
>
> Like the leaves of the forest when summer is green,
> That host with their banners at sunset were seen;
> Like the leaves of the forest when autumn hath blown,
> That host on the morrow lay withered and strown.
>
> For the Angel of Death spread his wings on the blast,
> And breathed in the face of the foe as he passed;

And the eyes of the sleepers waxed deadly and chill,
And their hearts but once heaved, and forever grew still!

And there lay the steed with his nostrils all wide,
But through them there rolled not the breath of his pride;
And the foam of his gasping lay white on the turf,
And cold as the spray of the rock-beating surf.

And there lay the rider, distorted and pale,
With the dew on his brow, and the rust on his mail;
And the tents were all silent, the banners alone,
The lances unlifted, the trumpet unblown.

And the widows of Ashur are loud in their wail,
And the idols are broken in the temple of Baal;
And the might of the Gentile, unsmote by the sword,
Hath melted like snow in the glance of the Lord.

Thus the prophecy of Isaiah came true, and the little kingdom of Judah was saved from destruction at the hand of the fierce invader! Isaiah called for a return to God as the only hope of the nation. He said:

"For thus said the Lord God, the Holy One of Israel,
'In returning and rest you shall be saved;
in quietness and in trust shall be your strength.' "

The prophet does not teach that God's word will be accepted universally; he sees only a remnant who are faithful in his day, even as John the Revelator saw a remnant people who would be true to God in the final crisis of human history, and would be waiting for Jesus Christ to return.

# The End of a Valiant Kingdom

*2 Chronicles 33 to 36; the Book of Jeremiah*

chapter 24 *

THE kingdom of Judah had struggled through tumultuous times during the reign of Hezekiah; but when he died the people sank into idolatry. Dissolute kings, Manasseh and Amon, ruled successively; superstition and error spread through the land as the kings attempted to worship the gods of Nineveh and Babylon. In his foreign relations, Manasseh was unsuccessful, for he was forced into absolute subservience to Assyria. This vile ruler had a record of bloodshed, and he even offered his own son as a sacrifice to idols. The record says he "shed very much innocent blood, till he had filled Jerusalem from one end to another."

Josiah, the great-grandson of Hezekiah, came to the throne when he was only eight years old. At the same time another youth named Jeremiah was growing up in the village of Anathoth, three miles northeast of Jerusalem. This boy lived in earth-shaking times, for he was to see the fall of Assyria and the rise of the Babylonian Empire, the end of Egypt's power, and the destruction of Judah. He would witness the invasion of fierce and cruel enemies marching and remarching across Judah, ravaging the land, destroying its cities, and taking captive the inhabitants.

Jeremiah was a quiet, tenderhearted youth of the tribe of Levi, trained like Samuel, of a previous age, to be a priest.

When the book of the law was read to King Josiah he was shocked to learn how the nation had disobeyed God.

283

He knew the sad history of his nation, how it had been brought low by the wickedness of King Manasseh and King Amon, and he longed to assist young King Josiah in bringing the people back to the worship of God.

When Josiah was twenty-six years old, he set himself to the task of repairing the temple of the Lord, and while this work was going on, Hilkiah, the high priest, discovered a scroll in the rubbish. This document contained a copy of the law, and it probably contained most of the writings of Moses, including the book of Deuteronomy. When the scroll was read to King Josiah, he was shocked to learn how far the nation had drifted away from the divine commands. When the scribe had finished reading, Josiah said, "Go, inquire of the Lord for me, and for the people, and for all Judah, concerning the words of this book that has been found; for great is the wrath of the Lord that is kindled against us, because our fathers have not obeyed the words of this book, to do according to all that is written concerning us."

Assembling the elders of the land, the king read the words of the law in their hearing, and he made a covenant with the Lord to walk in His commandments and to keep His statutes. As the result of the reformation, altars to pagan gods were broken down, and idol worship was abolished.

### Jeremiah Reproves the Nation

In the thirteenth year of King Josiah, God called young Jeremiah, the son of Hilkiah, to the difficult task of reproving the people for their sins. He longed to be excused from the thankless mission, for he pleaded, "Ah, Lord God! Behold, I do not know how to speak, for I am only a youth."

But the Lord said, "Do not say, 'I am only a youth;' for to all to whom I send you you shall go, and whatever I command you you shall speak. Be not afraid of them, for I am with you to deliver you."

Then the Lord said, "Behold, I have put My words in your mouth. See, I have set you this day over nations and over

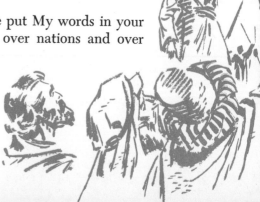

kingdoms, to pluck up and to break down, to destroy and to overthrow, to build and to plant."

## The Mission of Jeremiah

Jeremiah was told to leave his home village of Anathoth and go to the cities where he should speak to the crowds in the market places and in the streets. He must warn them that if they continued in their rebellious ways the nation would be destroyed. The prophet faithfully gave the message, but most of the people refused to listen. Then the Lord gave Jeremiah a picture of the doom facing Judah, a mighty enemy descending from the north and overthrowing the cities and destroying the temple. Because the people would not obey the commands of God they would be taken into exile as slaves of an enemy king.

Again the nation refused to listen to the warnings; and when King Josiah was killed in the battle of Megiddo, many of the bewildered people turned against Jeremiah, calling him a traitor because he had warned of the trouble to come. The prophet lamented the death of the king, and "the hill of Megiddo" became a symbol of Judah's decline and certain doom.

Jehoahaz, the son of Josiah, reigned only three months before Necho, king of Egypt, came up against Jerusalem and took the king of Judah prisoner and installed Jehoiakim, another son of Josiah, as king. He was ordered to pay immense tribute as a vassal of Pharaoh.

During this crisis Jeremiah went to the court of the temple and in an eloquent sermon warned the people of approaching doom. The Lord had instructed the prophet in these words, "Stand in the court of the Lord's house, and speak to all the cities of Judah which come to worship in the house of the Lord all the words that I command you to speak to them; do not hold back a word. It may be they will listen, and everyone turn from his evil way, that I may repent of the evil which I intend to do to them because of their evil doings."

285

When the priests and prophets heard the words of Jeremiah, they became angry. After he had finished speaking, they laid hold of him. "You shall die!" they shouted. "Why have you prophesied in the name of the Lord, saying, 'This house shall be like Shiloh, and this city shall be desolate, without inhabitant'?"

Mobbed by angry religious leaders, Jeremiah was in danger of losing his life. Then the princes of Judah and the common people heard what was happening, and they came to his rescue. At the temple gate, the priests and false prophets made bitter accusations against Jeremiah. "This man deserves the sentence of death," they said, "because he has prophesied against this city, as you have heard with your own ears."

As the angry mob clamored for Jeremiah's death, it seemed that he would have only a few moments to live. The brave prophet, never flinching from his duty, turned to the princes and made a bold appeal, saying, "The Lord sent me to prophesy against this house and this city all the words you have heard. Now therefore amend your ways and your doings, and obey the voice of the Lord your God, and the Lord will repent of the evil which He has pronounced against you. But as for me, behold, I am in your hands. Do with me as seems good and right to you. Only know for certain that if you put me to death, you will bring innocent blood upon yourselves and upon this city and its inhabitants, for in truth the Lord sent me to you to speak all these words in your ears."

A silence fell upon the rabble rousers, while the princes and the common people shouted to the priests, saying, "This man does not deserve the sentence of death, for he has spoken to us in the name of the Lord our God." Jeremiah was saved from death by his own courageous plea, and from that day he became a notable figure throughout the kingdom.

While Jeremiah was saved by the aid of friends, another prophet named Uriah, who also gave a divine warning, did not escape the anger of King Jehoiakim. Although the second prophet fled to Egypt, officers of the king were shadowing him

and they brought him back to Jerusalem, where he was executed and buried in the potter's field.

The Assyrian Empire, long the scourge of Palestine, fell to the conquering might of Nebuchadnezzar, king of Babylon, and his allies, the Medes, in 612 B.C., when Ninevah was taken. Now Judah was a vassal state of Babylon, the new totalitarian empire with an exotic capital on the Euphrates River. This change in the international situation caused Jeremiah to dictate special messages at the hand of his secretary, Baruch.

Jeremiah said to Baruch, "So you are to go, and on a fast day in the hearing of all the people in the Lord's house you shall read the words of the Lord from the scroll which you have written at my dictation. You shall read them also in the hearing of all the men of Judah who come out of their cities. It may be that their supplication will come before the Lord, and that everyone will turn from his evil way, for great is the anger and wrath that the Lord has pronounced against this people."

Baruch followed the instructions of Jeremiah and read the prophet's message in the temple when it was thronged with people. Now when Micaiah, the grandson of Shaphan, saw what was happening, he hurried off to the palace to tell the courtiers. The officers instantly sent for Baruch and ordered him to bring the scroll to the palace. When the king's officers heard the words of Jeremiah, they were afraid and looked at one another anxiously; they knew they must report this matter to the king.

"Tell us, how did you write all these words? Was it at his dictation?" they asked Baruch.

"He dictated all these words to me, while I wrote them with ink on the scroll," explained Baruch, the secretary of Jeremiah. Then the king's officers, who wished to be friendly, said, "Go and hide, you and Jeremiah, and let no one know where you are."

After Baruch left, the king's officers reported the whole affair to King Jehoiakim, and Jehudi read Jeremiah's message to the king. The king was living in his winter palace and a fire was

287

burning in the hearth. As Jehudi read a portion of the scroll, the king would cut it off with his penknife and toss it into the flames. Part by part, as it was read, God's message was consumed by the fire.

King Jehoiakim and his rebellious courtiers were not afraid of the divine warnings, neither did they repent of their sins. After the message had been read, the king ordered the arrest of Baruch and Jeremiah; but these faithful men could not be found, for the princes helped them go into hiding.

Then God spoke again to Jeremiah, saying, "Take another scroll and write on it all the former words that were in the first scroll, which Jehoiakim the king of Judah has burned." In the second message the prophet gave more fearful warnings of the amazing disaster that was coming upon the disobedient kingdom.

### Jerusalem Faces the Army of Babylon

King Nebuchadnezzar marched his armies against Judah and laid siege to Jerusalem. Soon the helpless nation bowed to the Babylonian invaders, and King Jehoiakim was in chains as a prisoner. At this time the farseeing Nebuchadnezzar took some of the brilliant young men of Judah to Babylon to train them for diplomatic service, among whom were Daniel and his three young companions.

For three years Jehoiakim was permitted to be a puppet ruler in the scourged kingdom; but the arrogant ruler decided to withhold tribute from Nebuchadnezzar, thinking he could rely on Egypt for military support. Jeremiah warned the foolish vassal king that his duplicity would bring utter ruin to Judah; but his wise words only angered Jehoiakim so that he sentenced Jeremiah to be put in stocks overnight.

Once more Nebuchadnezzar marched against Judah and besieged the city of Jerusalem. This time the Oriental monarch was in no mood to mix vengeance with mercy. Jeremiah mourned over the sufferings of his innocent people, in language that is deeply moving:

"Who will have pity on you, O Jerusalem,
　　or who will bemoan you?
Who will turn aside
　　to ask about your welfare?
You have rejected me, says the Lord,
　　you keep going backward;
so I have stretched out My hand against you and
　　　　destroyed you;—
　　I am weary of relenting.
I have winnowed them with a winnowing fork
　　in the gates of the land;
I have bereaved them, I have destroyed My people;
　　they did not turn from their ways.
I have made their widows more in number
　　than the sand of the seas;
I have brought against the mothers of young men
　　a destroyer at noonday;
I have made anguish and terror
　　fall upon them suddenly.
She who bore seven has languished;
　　she has swooned away;
her sun went down while it was yet day;
　　she has been shamed and disgraced.
And the rest of them I will give to the sword
　　before their enemies, says the Lord."

During the siege King Jehoiakim died; but Jeremiah scarcely considered the loss, for he condemned the betrayer of his people in these strong words:

"They shall not lament for him, saying,
　　'Ah my brother!' or 'Ah sister!'
They shall not lament for him, saying,
　　'Ah lord!' or 'Ah his majesty!'
With the burial of an ass he shall be buried,
　　dragged and cast forth beyond the gates of Jerusalem."

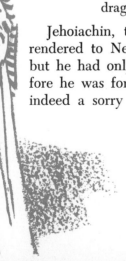

Jehoiachin, the eighteen-year-old son of Jehoiakim, surrendered to Nebuchadnezzar and saved the city from ruin; but he had only three months to play as a puppet king before he was forced to capitulate to the Babylonians. It was indeed a sorry day for the royal family when its members

289

fell into the clutches of the invaders. The young king, his mother, his wives, his nobles, and his officers became captives, along with ten thousand Jewish soldiers and many of the best people. All of them were taken to Babylon—a multitude of displaced persons!

Zedekiah, the uncle of Jehoiachin, was made ruler of the ravaged land, in which only the poorest citizens remained. He was more favorable to the counsel of Jeremiah and sought the advice of the prophet on numerous occasions. About this time Jeremiah sent a message to the captives in Babylon telling them not to be discouraged if they did not get to return to their homeland immediately. He urged them to build homes, plant gardens, marry, and carry on a good life. The letter reads as follows: "Thus says the Lord of hosts, the God of Israel, to all the exiles whom I have sent into exile from Jerusalem to Babylon: Build houses and live in them; plant gardens and eat their produce. Take wives and have sons and daughters; take wives for your sons, and give your daughters in marriage, that they may bear sons and daughters; multiply there, and do not decrease. But seek the welfare of the city where I have sent you into exile, and pray to the Lord on its behalf, for in its welfare you will find your welfare."

About this time the armies of Babylon withdrew from Jerusalem because the Egyptians were advancing across the desert from the southwest. Jeremiah attempted to leave the city to go to the land of Benjamin, probably to visit his home at Anathoth; but a sentry at the city gate arrested him, saying, "You are deserting to the Chaldeans."

"It is false," answered the prophet; "I am not deserting to the Chaldeans."

However, the sentry would not listen to Jeremiah, but took him to the king's officers. The princes were eager to get revenge on the prophet, so they beat him and put him in prison in the house of Jonathan, where he remained many days.

King Zedekiah secretly sent for Jeremiah. "Is there any word from the Lord?" asked the monarch.

"There is," replied the prophet. "You shall be delivered into the hand of the king of Babylon." Then Jeremiah asked, "What wrong have I done to you or your servants or this people, that you have put me in prison? Where are your prophets who prophesied to you, saying, 'The king of Babylon will not come against you and against this land'? Now hear, I pray you, O my lord the king: let my humble plea come before you, and do not send me back to the house of Jonathan the secretary, lest I die there."

Angry because he knew the message of the man of God was true, the king ordered him back to prison with a ration of a small loaf of bread a day as long as there was food in the city.

Jeremiah displayed his faith in the future of his country by purchasing a field from his cousin in the village of Anathoth. The resolute prophet was certain the fields and vineyards would someday be of value in the land of Judah.

When the enemy besieged the city, famine and disease stalked through the streets and haunted every home. Jeremiah warned, "Thus says the Lord, He who stays in this city shall die by the sword, by famine, and by pestilence; but he who goes out to the Chaldeans shall live; he shall have his life as a prize of war, and live. Thus says the Lord, This city shall surely be given into the hand of the army of the king of Babylon and be taken."

When the princes heard this, they rushed to the king with this urgent counsel, "Let this man be put to death, for he is weakening the hands of the soldiers who are left in this city, and the hands of all the people, by speaking such words to them. For this man is not seeking the welfare of this people, but their harm."

"Behold, he is in your hands," said weak King Zedekiah.

The princes threw Jeremiah into a cistern in the court of the prison. The water had been drawn out of the cistern, leaving several feet of filthy mire in the bottom. Jeremiah sank down into the mud, and he would have starved to death had not a

291

friend, Ebedmelech, an Ethiopian servant in the palace, pleaded for him. This loyal friend went to the king and said, "My lord the king, these men have done evil in all that they did to Jeremiah the prophet by casting him into the cistern; and he will die there of hunger, for there is no bread left in the city."

The king was touched at the courage of Ebedmelech, and he ordered three men to rescue Jeremiah. The men went to the cistern, let down some old rags, which Jeremiah could put under his armpits, and drew him up out of the filth.

## The Fall of Judah

Once more King Zedekiah sent to Jeremiah for a secret interview. When asked to tell the truth concerning the future of the country, Jeremiah said to the king, "If I tell you, will you not be sure to put me to death?"

After King Zedekiah had pledged protection to Jeremiah, he made a final appeal to the king to surrender to Babylon. He told the ruler that if he would capitulate he would be saved; but if he held out against the enemy, he would not escape death. Jeremiah said, "If you do not surrender to the princes of the king of Babylon, then this city shall be given into the hand of the Chaldeans, and they shall burn it with fire, and you shall not escape from their hand."

The king believed the prophet, but he did not have the courage to stand against his courtiers. When he refused to surrender, the enemy made a final fierce attack. The walls of the city were broken down, and the Babylonian soldiers swarmed into the palace. King Zedekiah fled, but was soon captured. His two sons were slain, and the king was blinded and taken in chains to Babylon, where he remained a prisoner until he died.

Jerusalem was a waste place and Solomon's temple and the king's palace were in total ruins. Indeed, the entire kingdom of Judah like Israel to the north, was a mass of desolation. Nebuzaradan, the Babylonian captain in charge of the city, treated Jeremiah with kindness. He released the prisoner

The men let down a rope of old rags to Jeremiah and they pulled him up out of the filth of the cistern.

JOHN STEEL, ARTIST                    © P.P.P.A.

from his dungeon and offered to give him a safe-conduct to Babylon if he desired. Nebuzaradan said, "Now, behold, I release you today from the chains on your hands. If it seems good to you to come with me to Babylon, come, and I will look after you well; but if it seems wrong to you to come with me to Babylon, do not come. See, the whole land is before you; go wherever you think it good and right to go." However, the prophet desired to stay in his homeland to cheer the discouraged remnant of the people.

Gedaliah, a man of high principles, was appointed governor; but he was assassinated, and some of the innocent people feared reprisals. They were ready to flee to Egypt, but before leaving, they sought counsel of Jeremiah. After ten days the prophet declared that it was God's plan for them to stay in their own country, separated from the heathenism of Egypt. The group was obstinate, however, and refused to accept the message. A large caravan set out on the road to Egypt, taking the unwilling prophet and Baruch with them. The refugees settled in the land at the east side of the Delta, where they continued to disregard the commands of the Lord, turning away from Him to bow before the hundreds of Egyptian gods. A final message was given by Jeremiah in which he said, "Therefore thus says the Lord of hosts, the God of Israel: Behold, I will set my face against you for evil, to cut off all Judah. I will take the remnant of Judah who have set their faces to come to the land of Egypt to live, and they shall all be consumed; in the land of Egypt they shall fall; by the sword and by famine they shall be consumed; from the least to the greatest, they shall die by the sword and by famine; and they shall become an execration, a horror, a curse, and a taunt."

The days to come were to prove that the prophet's words had been true. Disaster overtook the runaways, but Jeremiah disappears from the scene—a stalwart for God to the last. Through more than forty precarious years the prophet gave an unpopular message that seemed to produce little positive results. While he condemned the sins of Judah he also promised

294

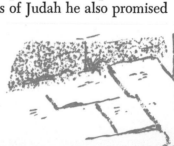

that the Lord would save the people if they would repent. He
said,

> "O Jerusalem, wash your heart from wickedness,
>     that you may be saved.
> How long shall your evil thoughts
>     lodge within you?"

In the short book of Lamentations, Jeremiah expressed his
deepest sorrow over the fate of the chosen nation. He wrote,

> "Judah has gone into exile because of affliction
>     and hard servitude;
> she dwells now among the nations,
>     but finds no resting place;
> her pursuers have all overtaken her
>     in the midst of her distress."

> "Her foes have become the head,
>     her enemies prosper,
> because the Lord has made her suffer
>     for the multitude of her transgressions;
> her children have gone away,
>     captives before the foe."

He called for a return to God, a merciful Father, who is
ready to pardon His wayward children:

> "For the Lord will not
>     cast off forever,
> but, though He cause grief, He will have compassion
>     according to the abundance of his steadfast love;
> for He does not willingly afflict
>     or grieve the sons of men."

> "Let us test and examine our ways,
>     and return to the Lord!
> Let us lift up our hearts and hands
>     to God in heaven:
> 'We have transgressed and rebelled,
>     and Thou hast not forgiven.'"

The prophet Jeremiah was a lonely individual because of
his work. Once he cried out, "I sat alone because of Thy hand."
He attempted to stop the ruinous course of the nation, but he

was spurned and rejected. One commentator writes, "If we want to know the meaning of personal religion at its finest and highest in the Old Testament, we must become, like Baruch, disciples of Jeremiah. In this respect there is no figure comparable with his, nor any of whom the revelation is so intimate and full."

# In the Royal Court
# of Babylon

*Daniel 1 to 4*

AT THE time that King Nebuchadnezzar first laid siege to Jerusalem, four young men of Judah were among those taken to Babylon to be educated in the royal court. They were strong and handsome, skillful and capable of learning—men of royal blood. Daniel was the youth who seems to have led the group, and his three companions were Hananiah, Mishael, and Azariah. To begin their career in Babylon, they were given new names. Daniel became Belteshazzar, in honor of the god Bel; his name means "may Bel protect his life;" while his friends were named Shadrach, Meshach, and Abednego.

These youth had grown up in Judean homes where the true God was worshiped. They had a heritage of faith that knew no compromise when it found itself faced with the pagan philosophy of Babylon. The four princes purposed in their heart that they would not worship idols or enter into the mystical rites and ceremonies of heathenism; they would be true to God in every test.

The first problem they faced concerned the food they ate. The king's officer, Ashpenaz, brought the four Hebrews special food and wine from the royal table, a compliment to them since they were actually exiles. Now the young men had been taught not to partake of food offered to idols, for

297

to eat it would signify that they were honoring the pagan gods. Then, too, there were "unclean" meats that for ceremonial and health reasons were not to be eaten, and the drinking of wine was not in harmony with true temperance.

Daniel resolved, or "laid upon his heart," that he would stand true to his religious convictions. The approval of his God and the peace that came with a clear conscience meant more to him than the command of a mighty king. Men and women are needed today who, like Daniel, will stand unflinchingly for principle in large and small matters of daily life. Where is our absolute loyalty to anything in this age of chaotic standards? Where are those who will be true to their convictions in spite of persecution or death?

Young Daniel, having already gained the confidence of Ashpenaz, requested that he and his friends be allowed to eat simple food instead of the royal dainties. The officer listened sympathetically, but he said, "I fear lest my lord the king, who appointed your food and your drink, should see that you were in poorer condition than the youths who are of your own age. So you would endanger my head with the king."

"Test your servants for ten days; let us be given vegetables to eat and water to drink," urged Daniel. "Then let our appearance and the appearance of the youths who eat the king's rich food be observed by you, and according to what you see deal with your servants."

Finally the officer agreed to the test, although he knew that in so doing he might earn the displeasure of the king. At the end of the ten days Daniel and his companions were better in appearance and fatter than the other young men who ate the food from the king's table. After that the officer had no further question concerning the simple diet which the princes ate. At the end of three years Nebuchadnezzar called for a personal inspection of the young men trained in his court. Upon examining them, he found that Daniel and his three friends were more distinguished in learning than the rest of the group, and most amazing of all, they were ten times wiser than the

Daniel and his three companions were called before King Nebuchadnezzar to see if they would pass inspection.

magicians and astrologers of Babylon! It was not luck or
fortune that brought these youth to the highest achievement.
They had studied diligently; but with their good use of time
and talent, they also added the help of God, for they had
earnestly sought divine guidance in their life. We cannot
know true success without the help of heaven; yet at the same
time we can be sure that "God never inspires a vacuum."

## The King's Forgotten Dream

One night King Nebuchadnezzar had a dream; but when
he awoke he could not remember it and he was much perplexed.
He commanded his magicians and enchanters, the representatives of the wisdom and knowledge of the age, to stand before
him in order that they might describe what he had dreamed.

"O king, live forever! Tell your servants the dream, and we
will show the interpretation," begged the wise men.

That was the difficulty! The king could not remember his
dream, and in his frustration he said, "The word from me is
sure: if you do not make known to me the dream and its
interpretation, you shall be torn limb from limb, and your
houses shall be laid in ruins. But if you show the dream and
its interpretation, you shall receive from me gifts and rewards
and great honor. Therefore show me the dream and its
interpretation."

Again the wise men pleaded with the king to reveal to them
his dream and then they would be able to concoct a plausible
interpretation. The magicians realized that they were helpless in this situation; indeed, there were many questions for
which they did not have the answer. They humbly said,
"There is not a man on earth who can meet the king's
demand; for no great and powerful king has asked such a
thing of any magician or enchanter or Chaldean. The thing
that the king asks is difficult, and none can show it to the king
except the gods, whose dwelling is not with flesh."

One of the characteristics of our time is our growing disillusionment with knowledge. We have fathomed many of the

secrets of the physical world—enough to destroy our civilization; but we have not solved our deepest problems. We have increased the power we control by a million times, but we have not developed spiritual power or found moral controls. We are clever, but we are lost! Sooner or later we must face the essential issues, and, like Nebuchadnezzar, we must find an answer to our nature and destiny. This monarch of Babylon was to learn that "the fear of the Lord is the beginning of wisdom." It would take years for him to accept the divine fiat, but it would eventually strike deep in his soul.

King Nebuchadnezzar was furious when he saw that the wise men of Babylon had failed him. In the true character of an Oriental despot he ordered all of them to be executed. Although Daniel and his three friends were not at the dramatic council, yet since they were classed with the wise men, they were under sentence of death. When the soldiers arrived to carry out the royal decree, Daniel discreetly asked what it was all about. "Why is the decree of the king so severe?" he queried.

When the officers explained the reason, Daniel hurried to the king and requested that the execution be delayed for all the wise men so that he might tell the king his dream. Then the Hebrew youth returned to his house, and told Shadrach, Mechach, and Abednego what had happened. The four young men prayed earnestly, and God revealed the dream and its interpretation to Daniel. Then another prayer was offered by Daniel, a psalm of thanksgiving, for answering their request. Daniel said,

> "Blessed be the name of God forever and ever,
> to whom belong wisdom and might.
> He changes times and seasons;
> He removes kings and sets up kings;
> He gives wisdom to the wise
> and knowledge to those who have understanding;
> He reveals deep and mysterious things;
> He knows what is in the darkness,
> and the light dwells with Him.
> To Thee, O God of my fathers,

I give thanks and praise,
for Thou hast given me wisdom and strength,
and hast now made known to me what we asked of Thee,
for Thou hast made known to us the king's matter."

The next morning Daniel went to the officer of the guard and said, "Do not destroy the wise men of Babylon; bring me in before the king, and I will show the king the interpretation."

The officer hurried Daniel to the palace and, in the egotistical manner of little men, the officer boasted to the king, "I have found among the exiles from Judah a man who can make known to the king the interpretation."

"Are you able to make known to me the dream that I have seen and its interpretation?" asked the king in astonishment.

Daniel humbly explained, "No wise men, enchanters, magicians, or astrologers can show to the king the mystery which the king has asked, but there is a God in heaven who reveals mysteries, and He has made known to King Nebuchadnezzar what will be in the latter days."

In refusing to take honor to himself, Daniel turned the attention of the king to the true God, the Author of all wisdom. Then with courage to believe that he had been given the king's dream, the Hebrew youth plunged into the description:

"You saw, O king, and behold, a great image. This image, mighty and of exceeding brightness, stood before you, and its appearance was frightening. The head of this image was of fine gold, its breast and arms of silver, its belly and thighs of bronze, its legs of iron, its feet partly of iron and partly of clay. As you looked, a stone was cut out by no human hand, and it smote the image on its feet of iron and clay, and broke them in pieces; then the iron, the clay, the bronze, the silver, and the gold, all together were broken in pieces, and became like the chaff of the summer threshing floors; and the wind carried them away, so that not a trace of them could be found. But the stone that struck the image became a great mountain and filled the whole earth. This was the dream; now we will tell the king its interpretation."

302

In his dream the king saw a great image of gold, silver, brass, iron, and clay—a symbol of world empires.

Without pausing for the king to say he was correct in telling the dream, Daniel went on to give the interpretation of it. "You, O king, the king of kings, to whom the God of heaven has given the kingdom, the power, and the might, and the glory, and into whose hand He has given, wherever they dwell, the sons of men, the beasts of the field, and the birds of the air, making you rule over them all—you are the head of gold."

The head of gold! Nebuchadnezzar took a deep breath and gloated over his power. But wait! The young prophet was continuing to speak. "After you shall arise another kingdom inferior to you, and yet a third kingdom of bronze, which shall rule over all the earth. And there shall be a fourth kingdom, strong as iron, because iron breaks to pieces and shatters all things; and like iron which crushes, it shall break and crush all these. And as you saw the feet and toes partly of potter's clay and partly of iron, it shall be a divided kingdom; but some of the firmness of iron shall be in it, just as you saw iron mixed with the miry clay. And as the toes of the feet were partly iron and partly clay, so the kingdom shall be partly strong and partly brittle. As you saw the iron mixed with miry clay, so they will mix with one another in marriage, but they will not hold together, just as iron does not mix with clay. And in the days of those kings the God of heaven will set up a kingdom which shall never be destroyed, nor shall its sovereignty be left to another people. It shall break in pieces all these kingdoms and bring them to an end, and it shall stand forever; just as you saw that a stone was cut from a mountain by no human hand, and that it broke in pieces the iron, the bronze, the clay, the silver, and the gold. A great God has made known to the king what shall be hereafter. The dream is certain, and its interpretation sure."

## A Preview of World Empires

Babylon was the most magnificent capital of any ancient civilization. Its terraced towers rose above the plains, its courts were filled with potentates from every country of the world; here, indeed, were pleasure domes surpassing the glory of Xanadu. The palace of Nebuchadnezzar, portions of which have been restored by archaeologists, was greater than that of any of his successors. There were famous Hanging Gardens built for the Median queen who was homesick for her native hills. The empire, sated with conquest and riches, was the center of pagan sun worship.

How well Babylon fitted the symbol of the golden head can scarcely be realized today, for the capital city drew the wealth of the world to it. Historians declare that the temple of Bel contained cups and vessels of gold worth more than a hundred million dollars!

But how fateful are the words, "After you shall arise another kingdom inferior to you." Babylon must fall! In 539 B.C., the armies of Cyrus took the city of Babylon, and the Medo-Persian empire ruled the world. This second empire was more powerful in armed strength; but it was inferior in wealth and magnificence.

The third empire, symbolized by the belly and thighs of bronze, conquered the Medes and Persians in the battle of Arbela, 331 B.C. This third world empire was ruled by Alexander the Great. The Greek legions swept from one nation to another until the world bowed at his feet. His reign helped bring Asia and the East into the sphere of Western influence.

But the Greek Empire began to crumble before its Roman conquerors at the battle of Pydna, 168 B.C. The armies of Rome, described as strong as iron, brought Greece to her knees. The empire with its capital on the Tiber River rose on the spoils of all kingdoms and nations before her. Rome was cruel and tyrannical in power; but she was finally "broken to pieces" by the barbarians from the north. Generations before there was such a nation, God declared that the iron empire would be divided.

Since the fall of Rome every ambitious ruler has attempted to weld the heterogeneous pieces together into another world

empire. Charlemagne could not bring the dream of glory to pass; Charles V, in his pride and arrogance, failed; and Louis XIV went to his grave a disillusioned monarch. Napoleon died on the island of Saint Helena, a victim of his ambitions. Kings and queens of Europe in the later nineteenth century promoted many blood alliances, and when World War I came, royal brothers and sisters, cousins, and grandchildren were leading armies against one another. Intermarriage did not bring the union of Europe that many a statesman had hoped to achieve. Adolph Hitler planned a state that would comprise all of Europe and would endure a thousand years; but his will-o'-the-wisp destroyed him and his power.

Today Europe is divided into two great camps—Russia and her satellite nations and the Allied powers. There is lack of unity within the two camps, for "they will not hold together." The lack of unity has caused severe losses to the Western democracies since World War II in Southeast Asia, China, and the Middle East. Nationalism and the selfish pride of human hearts block the hopes of a united Europe. The Eternal One saw that these tensions and animosities would exist, and He gave the prophecy to Daniel: *"They will not hold together."*

Yet "in the days of those kings" a great event will take place which will write *finis* to human history. For the God of heaven will establish an everlasting kingdom. The stone that was cut out of the mountain without the help of human hands symbolizes the omnipotent power of God. The kingdom that shall be set up is ruled by Jesus Christ, for He shall come in the clouds of heaven and all men and all nations shall see Him.

In the second chapter of the book of Daniel is presented an outline of world history from the Babylonian Empire to the second advent of Christ. Like mileposts along a highway, the prophecies of God's word tell the Christian that he is living in the period symbolized by the feet of clay, and that soon the King of kings will establish a kingdom of peace that shall never be destroyed. We can be citizens of that land where there shall be no war, no death, no sorrow, and no sickness. The

306

The nations of Europe are broken by disunity, and "they will not hold together," even as the prophecy states.

Saviour invites us to be there, for He says, "Blessed are they that do His commandments, that they may have right to the tree of life, and may enter in through the gates into the city." Revelation 22:14, King James Version.

As the young prophet finished the interpretation of the dream, Nebuchadnezzar was convinced that it was absolute truth. He came down from his throne and bowed humbly before Daniel, saying, "Truly, your God is God of gods and Lord of kings, and a revealer of mysteries, for you have been able to reveal this mystery." The king rewarded the Hebrew with costly gifts and placed him in greater authority in the empire.

## The Ordeal of Fire

As Nebuchadnezzar remembered his dream of the metallic image of a man, selfish pride and political ambition swelled within him. He was not satisfied for Babylon to be the head of gold; he would change the meaning of the dream to make his empire endure forever. Therefore he had a gigantic image, some one hundred feet in height, covered entirely with gold, set up on the plain of Dura. Here was the pagan monarch's challenge to God's will—a challenge that would meet certain defeat.

The king sent for all his governors, judges, counselors, and other high officials to assemble for the dedication of the golden image. On the designated day a herald shouted the king's instructions to the crowd massed on the plain, saying, "You are commanded, O peoples, nations, and languages, that when you hear the sound of the horn, pipe, lyre, trigon, harp, bagpipe, and every kind of music, you are to fall down and worship the golden image that King Nebuchadnezzar has set up; and whoever does not fall down and worship shall immediately be cast into a burning fiery furnace." Tyrants of every age have determined that their subjects shall bow to something they have made; they must be little gods in their phantom universe.

308

As soon as the throng heard the music, all of the people of every nation and language bowed before the golden image, as the king had decreed. That is, everyone except three young government officials—Shadrach, Meshach, and Abednego. They refused to worship the idol of gold. No doubt Daniel would have stood with his companions, but he was evidently not at the celebration. As soon as the Babylonians saw the three men standing in defiance of the royal edict, they hurried to Nebuchadnezzar and said, "There are certain Jews whom you have appointed over the affairs of the province of Babylon: Shadrach, Meshach, and Abednego. These men, O king, pay no heed to you; they do not serve your gods or worship the golden image which you have set up."

The Oriental king revealed his insecurity in that telltale moment, for he flew into a rage and his anger was terrible. He knew he could not fight against God, yet he was determined to demonstrate his power by taking vengeance on innocent subjects. Therefore, he commanded that the three Hebrews be brought before him, and he questioned them, saying, "Is it true, O Shadrach, Meshach, and Abednego, that you do not serve my gods or worship the golden image which I have set up?"

Nebuchadnezzar decided to display his magnanimity to the bystanders. He continued by saying, "Now if you are ready when you hear the sound of the horn, pipe, lyre, trigon, harp, bagpipe, and every kind of music, to fall down and worship the image which I have made, well and good; but if you do not worship, you shall immediately be cast into a burning fiery furnace; and who is the god that will deliver you out of my hands?"

"O Nebuchadnezzar, we have no need to answer you in this matter. If it be so, our God whom we serve is able to deliver us from the burning fiery furnace," said the three brave men; "and He will deliver us out of your hand, O king. But if not, be it known to you, O king, that we will not serve your gods or worship the golden image which you have set up."

309

When the king of Babylon heard this straightforward reply, his face was distorted with rage against the three calm, stalwart men. He ordered the furnace to be heated seven times hotter than usual. Then at his command, certain of his strongest bodyguard bound the three officials and threw them into the fiery furnace, whose heat was so intense that the soldiers who tossed the men into the flames were killed by the torrid blast.

Nebuchadnezzar watched as the bound men fell in the flames, but then he became alarmed. Calling to his ministers, he asked, "Did we not cast three men bound into the fire?"

"True, O king," they answered.

"But I see four men loose, walking in the midst of the fire, and they are not hurt; and the appearance of the fourth is like a son of the gods," shouted the king excitedly.

Edging as close to the inferno as he dared, the king called, "Shadrach, Meshach, and Abednego, servants of the Most High God, come forth, and come here!"

To the amazement of all the watchers, the three Hebrews walked out of the furnace without even a single singed hair or the smell of smoke on their clothing! The impetuous king, who the moment before had been ready to defy the God of heaven, was now earnestly praising Him for protecting the three Hebrews. "Blessed be the God of Shadrach, Meshach, and Abednego, who has sent His angel and delivered His servants, who trusted in Him, and set at nought the king's command, and yielded up their bodies rather than serve and worship any god except their own God. Therefore I make a decree: Any people, nation, or language that speaks anything against the God of Shadrach, Meshach, and Abednego shall be torn limb from limb, and their houses laid in ruins; for there is no other god who is able to deliver in this way." The king promoted the three princes, giving them greater responsibility in the kingdom.

Furthermore, the king demonstrated his faith in the power and greatness of God by sending a message to all the people

The three young men refused to bow before the giant image because of their faith in the God of heaven.

311

JOE MANISCALCO, ARTIST      © P. P. P. A.

of his kingdom. He said, "Peace be multiplied to you! It has seemed good to me to show the signs and wonders that the Most High God has wrought toward me.

> "How great are His signs,
>     how mighty His wonders!
> His kingdom is an everlasting kingdom,
>     and His dominion is from generation to generation."

### The Downfall of the Mighty

The conquests of Nebuchadnezzar were completed and he ruled the kingdom without fear of enemies. The ambitious monarch, while accepting the true God, became proud and arrogant in his sumptuous palace. He forgot that all of his power, his wealth, his strength, yes, and the faculties of his mind came from the Creator. In love and mercy God sent another dream to Nebuchadnezzar to warn him of his careless, soul-destroying course of action.

The king had no defense against this frightening dream; it haunted him the moment he awakened. The magicians and astrologers were called in to hear the dream but they could not give the interpretation of it. Once more Daniel was summoned and once more he gave a divine message to Nebuchadnezzar. The king described his dream in these words: "The visions of my head as I lay in bed were these: I saw, and behold, a tree in the midst of the earth; and its height was great. The tree grew and became strong, and its top reached to heaven, and it was visible to the end of the whole earth. Its leaves were fair and its fruit abundant, and in it was food for all. The beasts of the field found shade under it, and the birds of the air dwelt in its branches, and all flesh was fed from it. I saw in the visions of my head as I lay in bed, and behold, a watcher, a holy one, came down from heaven. He cried aloud and said thus, 'Hew down the tree and cut off its branches, strip off its leaves and scatter its fruit; let the beasts flee from under it and the birds from its branches. But leave the stump of its roots in the earth, bound with a band of iron and bronze, amid the tender grass of the field. Let him be wet with the dew of heaven; let his lot be with the beasts in the grass of the earth; let his mind be changed from a man's, and let a beast's mind be given to him; and let seven times pass over him. The sentence is by the decree of the watchers, the decision by the word of the holy ones, to the end that the living may know that the Most High rules the kingdom of men, and gives it to whom He will, and sets over it the lowliest of men.' This dream I, King Nebuchadnezzar, saw. And you, O Belteshazzar, declare the interpretation, because all the wise men of my kingdom are not able to make known to me the interpretation, but you are able, for the spirit of the holy gods is in you."

When Daniel heard the dream, he was stunned and his thoughts frightened him. How could he tell the king, his friend, that this spelled his doom? When Nebuchadnezzar saw the amazed look on Daniel's face, he said, "Let not the dream or the interpretation alarm you."

"My lord," replied Daniel fearfully, "may the dream be for those who hate you and its interpretation for your enemies! The tree you saw, which grew and became strong, so that its top reached to heaven, and it was visible to the end of the whole earth; whose leaves were fair and its fruit abundant, and in which was food for all; under which beasts of the field found shade, and in whose branches the birds of the air dwell— it is you, O king, who have grown and become strong. Your greatness has grown and reaches to heaven, and your dominion to the ends of the earth."

The tree was to be cut down, leaving only the stump and the roots. The meaning of the dream was all too clear to the Hebrew prophet, for he said, "This is the interpretation, O king: It is a decree of the Most High, which has come upon my lord the king, that you shall be driven from among men, and your dwelling shall be with the beasts of the field; you shall be made to eat grass like an ox, and you shall be wet with the dew of heaven, and seven times shall pass over you,

313

till you know that the Most High rules the kingdom of men, and gives it to whom He will. And as it was commanded to leave the stump of the roots of the tree, your kingdom shall be sure for you from the time that you know that Heaven rules."

As the stunned monarch sat on his golden throne, Daniel pleaded with him to repent and turn from his proud, defiant course. "Therefore, O king, let my counsel be acceptable to you; break off your sins by practicing righteousness, and your iniquities by showing mercy to the oppressed, that there may perhaps be a lengthening of your tranquillity," said the wise counselor.

A year later the king surveyed the magnificent city of Babylon from the roof of his palace. He saw the lofty zig-gurat, somewhat like a giant pyramid, rearing its pinnacle toward heaven as the tallest edifice in the capital. There was the giant Temple of Marduk, the most famous god of the Chaldeans. Scores of temples and palaces could be seen rising above the two- and three-story brick homes. The king could look, too, at the broad avenue flanked with walls of colored glazed brick—a resplendent boulevard lined with monuments and palm trees.

There were the Hanging Gardens, one of the Seven Wonders of the World, built by the king for one of his wives, the princess from the mountains of Media. The homesick girl had longed for hill country, and Nebuchadnezzar had done his best to give her the illusion by creating these lofty terraces on which grew lush flowers, plants, and trees. They were watered by an elaborate irrigation system by which slaves lifted water to the highest level. As the monarch gazed at his human para-dise, he boastfully exclaimed, "Is not this great Babylon, which I have built by my mighty power as a royal residence and for the glory of my majesty?"

While the words were still in his mouth, a divine edict came, "O King Nebuchadnezzar, to you it is spoken: The kingdom has departed from you, and you shall be driven from among men, and your dwelling shall be with the beasts of the

314

As King Nebuchadnezzar looked at the glories of Babylon, pride filled his heart and he forgot his Maker.

field; and you shall be made to eat grass like an ox; and seven times shall pass over you, until you have learned that the Most High rules the kingdom of men and gives it to whom He will."

For seven years the king wandered about insanely, eating grass like an ox and requiring the care of his guardians. It is interesting to note, as Dr. Will Durant points out in his history, that the king's name disappears from the empire's historical records and government reports for a period of years, only to reappear again near the close of his long reign.

When Nebuchadnezzar's reason was restored he gave thanks to the God of heaven, saying,

> "His dominion is an everlasting dominion,
>     and His kingdom endures from generation to generation;
> all the inhabitants of the earth are accounted as nothing;
>     and He does according to His will in the host of heaven
>     and among the inhabitants of the earth;
> and none can stay His hand
>     or say to Him, 'What doest Thou?' "

The haughty monarch of Babylon, "the terrible of the nations," the ruler who had gloated, "Is not this great Babylon, which I have built?" had been humbled in the dust. He had thought of the material grandeur of his kingdom, he had built the golden city to be one of the wonders of the world; but he had forgotten God. Like many other power-crazed men, he had not reckoned with the plans of the Eternal One. Fortunately, Nebuchadnezzar saw the folly of his way, and he repented. He learned that genuine greatness is based upon true goodness.

The Bible account of Nebuchadnezzar's life ends at this point. The once proud and egotistical king had become a contrite child of the God of heaven; he had learned through bitter personal experience that "those who walk in pride" God "is able to abase." Certainly there is an object lesson for our time in the career of Nebuchadnezzar. The insanity of our way of life; the headlong plunge toward destruction that our civilization is taking; the foolish denial of God by millions

316

—all of these are marks of unbalanced reason, the lack of wisdom. It is time that we come to ourselves, acknowledging our Creator and Redeemer, and seeking His salvation. That alone can bring peace and happiness to our generation.

As Dr. Alexis Carrel, Nobel laureate in medicine, pondered the problems of our generation, he gave this verdict: "We are unhappy. We degenerate morally and mentally. The groups and the nations in which industrial civilization has attained its highest development are precisely those which are becoming weaker. And whose return to barbarism is the most rapid. But they do not realize it. They are without protection against the hostile surroundings that science has built about them. In truth, our civilization, like those preceding it, has created certain conditions of existence which, for reasons still obscure, render life itself impossible."—*Man the Unknown,* page 28.

Our prodigal civilization, like the prodigal son of Christ's parable, has wallowed in the pigpen of hedonism. It is not too late for the truly repentant to come to himself and say, "I will arise and go to my Father." We can be certain that a loving God will be ready to receive us with outstretched arms.

# Daniel, an Honored Prophet of God

*Daniel 5, 6*

chapter 26 *

BABYLON, "the most terrible of nations," knew no equal during the reign of Nebuchadnezzar; but after his death the kingdom declined under the rule of his son, Evilmerodach, and two succeeding kings. The final episode in Babylonian history, as recorded in the book of Daniel, took place when the last king, Nabonidus, was absent in Arabia and his weak son Belshazzar acted as ruler in the capital city.

With arrogant pride Belshazzar sat in the palace, caring little that enemy armies of the Medes and Persians surrounded the city. Babylon was located on the Euphrates River, protected by giant double walls and huge gates of brass. Modern excavations reveal that the Inner City had a brick wall about twelve feet thick and a second one twenty-two feet thick at its base. The outer network of fortifications consisted of two walls, twenty-four and twenty-five feet thick respectively. Along the walls were watchtowers and special fortifications.

Babylon, the center of pagan idol worship, had scores of temples, luxurious palaces, and colorful monuments built of glazed bricks fired in many rich colors. In underground storehouses there was food to last the city for months, and the treasure houses guarded the royal wealth of gold, silver, and precious stones. This was a golden city, the prize for an enemy that could defeat the armies of Babylon and overthrow its monarch.

While the courtiers drank and reveled, the fingers of a mystic hand wrote the doom of Babylon on the wall.

319

In the great hall of the royal palace, Belshazzar gave a riotous feast and drinking party for a thousand of his courtiers. They were unaware of the national tragedy that overshadowed them as they lolled on their couches in a drunken stupor. The sacred cups and bowls that had been used in the religious service in Solomon's temple were brought to the banquet, and princes and statesmen drank wine from them and praised their heathen gods. Suddenly, a hush and then silence fell on the crowd. The fingers of a man's hand appeared and began to write on the wall. Belshazzar turned pale, and his knees knocked together; he shouted for his wise men to come to his aid. "Whoever reads this writing, and shows me its interpretation, shall be clothed with purple, and have a chain of gold about his neck, and shall be the third ruler in the kingdom," said the drunken ruler.

When the wise men entered the banquet hall and saw the writing on the wall, they stood helpless before the ruler; they could not read it. When the queen mother heard the cries of Belshazzar and his courtiers, she came into the hall. She remembered how Daniel had interpreted the dreams of King Nebuchadnezzar in days gone by. "O king, live forever!" she said. "Let not your thoughts alarm you or your color change. There is in your kingdom a man in whom is the spirit of the holy gods. In the days of your father light and understanding and wisdom, like the wisdom of the gods, were found in him, and King Nebuchadnezzar, your father, made him chief of the magicians, enchanters, Chaldeans, and astrologers, because an excellent spirit, knowledge, and understanding to interpret dreams, explain riddles, and solve problems were found in this Daniel, whom the king named Belteshazzar. Now let Daniel be called, and he will show the interpretation."

Daniel, now an aged man in the service of Babylon, was brought before the king. When Belshazzar saw the prophet, he said, "You are that Daniel, one of the exiles of Judah, whom the king my father brought from Judah. I have heard of you

that the spirit of the holy gods is in you, and that light and understanding and excellent wisdom are found in you."

### Daniel Interprets the Writing

Wishing to gain the statesman's favor, the frightened ruler promised special rewards. He said, "Now if you can read the writing and make known to me its interpretation, you shall be clothed with purple, and have a chain of gold about your neck, and shall be the third ruler in the kingdom."

"Let your gifts be for yourself, and give your rewards to another," said Daniel bluntly; "nevertheless I will read the writing to the king and make known to him the interpretation."

Daniel reminded Belshazzar of how Nebuchadnezzar made the mistake of forgetting God, and of the terrible punishment that came upon him. Pointing to the writing on the wall, the prophet said, "This is the interpretation of the matter: MENE, God has numbered the days of your kingdom and brought it to an end; TEKEL, you have been weighed in the balances and found wanting; PERES, your kingdom is divided and given to the Medes and Persians."

Daniel was clothed in purple, a gold chain was placed around his neck, and he was proclaimed third ruler in the kingdom. But these Babylonian honors were of little worth, for that night the strong army of the Medes and Persians stealthily entered the city, overcame the guards, and killed the king of Babylon. The words written by the divine hand on the wall of the banquet room had come true!

The fall of Babylon had been daringly predicted by the prophet Isaiah almost one hundred and seventy-five years before the event took place. Not only was the end of the kingdom foretold, but the name of the conqueror was given over a hundred years before his birth! The prophet, through divine inspiration, had written:

> "Thus says the Lord to His anointed, to Cyrus,
>   whose right hand I have grasped,

321

to subdue nations before him
and ungird the loins of kings,
to open doors before him
that gates may not be closed:
'I will go before you
and level the mountains,
I will break in pieces the doors of bronze
and cut asunder the bars of iron,
I will give you the treasures of darkness
and the hoards in secret places,
that you may know that it is I, the Lord,
the God of Israel, who call you by your name.
For the sake of my servant Jacob,
and Israel My chosen,
I call you by your name,
I surname you, though you do not know Me.' "

Once this prophecy had been declared, the enemy of God's truth would make every effort to keep it from being fulfilled. If Cyrus, a Median, could be killed or prevented from doing this work, the divine prophecy would fail. In the annals of the Greek historian, Herodotus, we find the fascinating story of Cyrus. There was a king in Media named Astyages, who dreamed that a great river flowed over Asia. His wise men told him that the dream meant that the children of his beautiful daughter, Mandane, would become conquerors. This displeased the power-crazed monarch, so he arranged for his daughter to marry a Persian prince—a plan that would make the countries friendly, but never united.

After King Astyages had the dream a second time he worried constantly over its meaning. About this time a son was born to his daughter, and to prevent any possible fulfillment of his dream, the ruthless king decided to kill the young heir— whose name was Cyrus. The king secretly took his grandson, dressed in fine clothing, and gave him to his trusted servant, Harpagus, with instructions to kill the child and return the body to the palace. Now Harpagus feared to do the brutal murder, so he endeavored to shift the responsibility to another.

He called a herdsman from the mountains and instructed him to expose the baby in the cold weather, and return the body to him when the child was dead.

The herdsman took the healthy young child to his own house, where he found his wife mourning the death of their newly born son. To see his own son dead and to have the horrible guilt of killing a beautiful child thrust upon him was too much for the herdsman. Dressing the body of his own dead son in the royal clothes, the man took it to Harpagus. Then the king received the dead child, and was satisfied with the thought that the future heir, Cyrus, was dead.

Thus it was that Cyrus grew up in the hut of the herdsman. When he was about twelve years old, he was made "general" while playing a game of war with the other boys. One boy, the son of a nobleman, refused to follow the commands that were given, so Cyrus gave him a beating. The whipped boy reported the matter to his father, who took the incident to King Astyages. The king called the peasant boy into the court to question him about the attack on the other boy. The king and his grandson unknowingly faced one another! However, the nobility of the lad and the strong family features reflected in his face so impressed the king that he determined to make an investigation. The herdsman was called in, and after torture and threats, admitted that he had saved the life of Cyrus. The king punished his officer, Harpagus, for disobeying his commands, by making a banquet in his honor and serving him special dishes of meat. Then the king revealed to Harpagus that he had been served the flesh of his own murdered son!

## The Overthrow of Babylon

Cyrus grew to manhood, and in later years he conquered Media, and dethroned Astyages in 550 B.C. His ascendancy to power prepared him for the greatest conquest of his life —the capture of Babylon. When the time came for him to march against the city on the Euphrates River, Cyrus faced a perplexing problem. How could he capture such an impregnable fortress? Finally he conceived the plan of diverting the river that ran through the city into an artificial lake that had been created previously by a queen of Babylon. On the night of attack, when Cyrus knew that Belshazzar and his courtiers would be reveling, Cyrus divided his army. As the water of the river receded after it had been channeled into the artificial basin, one section of the army waded into the river where it flowed under the thick walls. Thus they gained entrance into the city. Another part of the army waited at the lower side of the city and entered the same way as soon as the water had dropped low enough for them to wade upstream. All of this would have availed little in capturing Babylon, since there were strong walls along the river on each bank, had it not been that the gates leading from the river had been left unlocked and unguarded on that night of feasting. The Medes and Persians surprised the few soldiers in the streets and soon the magnificent capital fell to the armies of Cyrus. Truly, as the prophecy declared, the "gates may not be closed," and thus the way was prepared for the stealthy invaders.

The end of Babylon is written simply in God's word: "That very night Belshazzar the Chaldean king was slain. And Darius the Mede received the kingdom, being about sixty-two years old."

Within thirty years after Nebuchadnezzar died, his golden kingdom, which he had hoped would endure forever, had crumbled to pieces. The doom that the Hebrew prophets foretold had come to pass.

> "How the hammer of the whole earth
> is cut down and broken!
> How Babylon has become
> a horror among the nations."

The complete destruction of the city was accurately set forth by Jeremiah, for he declared, "Therefore wild beasts

and jackals shall dwell in Babylon, and ostriches shall dwell in her; she shall be peopled no more forever, nor inhabited for all generations."

## A Matter of Conscience

The conquering Medes and Persians reorganized the government by dividing Babylon into satrapies with high officials over each. The 120 divisions of the kingdom were supervised by three presidents, one of whom was Daniel. Some of the king's courtiers soon became jealous of the Hebrew statesman as he gained more and more favor with Darius. The ambitious rivals studied the public life of Daniel to find some act of intrigue or dishonest maneuver that they could use against him, but their detective work revealed no weakness in his character. In desperation they finally said, "We shall not find any ground for complaint against this Daniel unless we find it in connection with the law of his God."

All honor to a man who has such strength of character and moral principles that the only criticism anyone can find against him is that he has different religious views! The enemies of Daniel were bigots; they could not be tolerant of differing views, especially in matters of conscience. In the final analysis they cared nothing about Daniel's religion, or their king; they sought only selfish ends—to rise to power and glory by destroying a man of sterling character!

To carry out their sinister plotting these men went to King Darius and flatteringly said, "O King Darius, live forever! All the presidents of the kingdom, the prefects and the satraps, the counselors and the governors are agreed that the king should establish an ordinance and enforce an interdict, that whoever makes petition to any god or man for thirty days, except to you, O king, shall be cast into the den of lions. Now, O king, establish the interdict and sign the document, so that it cannot be changed, according to the law of the Medes and the Persians, which cannot be revoked."

These men knew that Daniel prayed to the God of heaven;

325

but they did not mention this to the king. They knew that if he realized that the law would endanger Daniel's life or rob him of his religious freedom, he would not sign the decree. Darius was proud that his courtiers wanted him to be worshiped as a god, so he signed the decree, and the spies went swiftly to Daniel's house to see what he would do.

When the prophet of God heard that the decree had been signed, he went to his house, which had windows in the upper chamber which faced Jerusalem. Three times a day, as was his custom, the prophet-statesman knelt and gave thanks to God. Daniel's enemies spied on him all through the day; and when they saw him in prayer, they hurried to the king's palace. "Did you not sign an interdict, that any man who makes petition to any god or man within thirty days except to you, O king, shall be cast into the den of lions?" they said.

"The thing stands fast, according to the law of the Medes and Persians, which cannot be revoked," said the king.

"That Daniel, who is one of the exiles from Judah, pays no heed to you, O king, or the interdict you have signed, but makes his petition three times a day," gloated the spies.

When King Darius heard this, he was grieved, for he realized that these officers had plotted their attack on Daniel. The king worked all day trying to save his faithful governor; but at sunset the crafty officers thronged about the monarch, and said, "Know, O king, that it is a law of the Medes and Persians that no interdict or ordinance which the king establishes can be changed."

Darius was forced to issue the royal order, and Daniel was brought to the den of lions. Before the brave Hebrew officer was put into the den, King Darius spoke to him, saying, "May your God, whom you serve continually, deliver you!" Then the pit was closed with a great stone, and it was sealed with the king's signet.

In the royal palace that night there was no sleep for the king. His thoughts were on Daniel in the den of snarling lions. In the morning, at daybreak, the monarch hurried to the den

Three times a day, as was his custom, Daniel knelt and prayed to God. And his enemies watched his devotions.

JOHN STEEL, ARTIST          © P. P. P. A.

and called in a pleading voice, "O Daniel, servant of the living God, has your God, whom you serve continually, been able to deliver you from the lions?"

Would there be an answer from the darkness of the den? Was the God of Daniel able to save him from the savage beasts?

"O king, live forever! My God sent His angel and shut the lions' mouths, and they have not hurt me, because I was found blameless before Him; and also before you, O king, I have done no wrong," called Daniel. The world longs to see men and women who have put God to the test. "Can He save us?" they ask. "He is our only way of salvation!" Are we Christians who can testify to the saving power of God? Do we know he has "shut the lions' mouths" for us?

The happy king quickly gave orders for his friend to be taken from the lions' den. Darius then commanded that the evil courtiers and their wives and children should be thrown to the lions. There was no question about the ferocity of the wild beasts, for this time they broke the bones of their victims before they reached the floor of the den. Then Darius wrote this decree to all nations: "Peace be multiplied to you. I make a decree, that in all my royal dominion men tremble and fear before the God of Daniel."

Daniel, the man of affairs in a great empire, held true to his religious convictions. His political activity was subjected to the severest scrutiny of his critics, but they could find no flaw in his character. He was a man of prayer, who refused to hide his daily devotions because enemies were watching him. As Christians we dare not push aside our devotions and expect to prosper spiritually. In the time of stress and crisis we need more prayer and greater power. We cannot drift along carelessly in our religious life and then meet the emergencies with a right-about-face experience. A crisis merely reveals what prayer, Bible study, faith, and love have meant to us in the ordinary round of life. How important are daily devotions in holding us steadfast to God's truth!

328

There is beauty in an hour of quiet meditation with God when the bickering cares of the world are shut out. We can relax from the anxiety that infests the mind by following the tested admonition, "Be still, and know that I am God."

Yes, there is an escape from the raucous din, there is relief from the ugly realism of our age. It is found in the peace and strength of our devotions.

> "Come, My people, enter your chambers,
>   and shut your doors behind you;
> hide yourselves for a little while
>   until the wrath is past."
>                     Isaiah 26:20.

# Daniel Previews the Future

*Daniel 7*

chapter 27 &

THE last six chapters of the book of Daniel present a series of visions that God gave the Hebrew statesman-prophet during the latter years of his life. The first of these, a dream of world empires, was presented to Daniel after he was eighty years of age. He saw four universal kingdoms symbolized in his vision, the same empires that King Nebuchadnezzar had seen in his dream of the great image many years earlier. The four empires were described to Daniel in order that he might see God's hand in the history of nations. He was to know that "through all the play and counterplay of human interests and power and passions, the agencies of the all-merciful One," are "silently, patiently working out the counsels of His own will." (*Education*, page 173.)

The vision came to Daniel in the first year that Belshazzar was acting king of Babylon, at the time that King Nabonidus was away from the capital city. The account begins with these words: "I saw in my vision by night, and behold, the four winds of heaven were stirring up the great sea. And four great beasts came up out of the sea, different from one another. The first was like a lion and had eagles' wings. Then as I looked its wings were plucked off, and it was lifted up from the ground and made to stand upon two feet like a man; and the mind of a man was given to it. And behold, another beast, a second

In vision the prophet Daniel saw four huge beasts rise out of the sea—symbols of nations of history.

331

one, like a bear. It was raised up on one side; it had three ribs in its mouth between its teeth; and it was told, 'Arise, devour much flesh.' After this I looked, and lo, another, like a leopard, with four wings of a bird on its back; and the beast had four heads; and dominion was given to it. After this I saw in the night visions, and behold, a fourth beast, terrible and dreadful and exceedingly strong; and it had great iron teeth; it devoured and broke in pieces, and stamped the residue with its feet. It was different from all the beasts that were before it; and it had ten horns."

God is here "revealing His secret to His servants the prophets." Amos 3:7. It is evident at once that these are symbolic figures portraying world empires, for we are told that the fourth beast represents the "fourth kingdom on earth." Such composite beasts may seem weird to modern readers, but actually they were familiar enough to that generation since they were constantly used in decorative art and sculpture. For centuries cartoons and pictures have featured animals and birds as symbols of nations. The United States is represented by an eagle; Great Britain by a lion; France by a cock; and Russia by a bear.

In his dream Daniel saw the sea, which in Bible symbolism represents nations and peoples. See Revelation 17:15. The four winds that troubled the sea represent war and strife. See Isaiah 17:12-14; Jeremiah 49:36, 37. Suddenly a lion rises out of the storm-tossed waters, a strange creature with the wings of an eagle. This was a fitting symbol for the Babylonian Empire, since it arose among the nations as the result of wars and ruthless conquest. It may be a coincidence that the winged lion was a common emblem in Babylon, for archaeologists have unearthed monuments and filed pictures of this creature. The prophet watched as the wings were pulled off and the beast stood on two feet. Then a man's heart was given to it, indicating a weakening of the empire. This was the plight of Babylon at the time the Medes and Persians overthrew it in a surprise attack.

332

Then the prophet saw a shaggy bear rise out of the waves, a fierce creature, clumsy but ferocious. The bear, like the silver of the great image compared with the head of gold, was inferior to the lion; yet it was a formidable beast of prey. Medo-Persia, the empire represented by this beast, was a massive force with huge armies and great fleets of war galleys.

Suddenly the bear raised itself up on one side, a lopsided creature lumbering over the sands. This symbolized the dual nature of the kingdom, in which the Persians finally gained dominant leadership above the Medes. The three ribs in the bear's mouth pointed to the savage attacks by which Medo-Persia conquered the three provinces of Media, Lydia, and Babylon.

### The Leopard Symbolizes Greece

The second beast faded as a third wild animal arose gracefully from the water. This four-headed leopard was swift, graceful, and cunning—fit qualities to symbolize the empire of Greece. The wings suggested added speed, for which Alexander the Great was noted. His legions marched over 5,000 miles in seven years, subduing the territory from the cataracts of the Upper Nile in Africa to the broad rivers of India.

The four heads of the leopard represented four parts into which the Greek Empire was divided after Alexander died at the age of thirty-three. After some years four of his leading generals gained supremacy over all rivals and ruled the four areas. Lysimachus took the northern section and built his capital near Gallipoli; Ptolemy ruled the south, which was mainly Egypt; Cassander possessed the west, or Macedonia; and Seleucus took over the east, making his capital on the Tigris River. Thus the Greek Empire began to fall apart, and soon it was an easy prey of ruthless conquerors from the west.

A startled prophet beheld a fourth monster rise out of the deep, a beast beyond the descriptive power of words. It "devoured and broke in pieces" all enemies that attempted to stand in its way. How well this symbolized the Roman Empire,

333

the fourth world kingdom, conqueror of the Greeks! For five centuries Rome held supreme sway over millions of subservient people who dwelt in faraway lands stretching from the British Isles to Asia. Edward Gibbon could write, "The arms of the republic, sometimes vanquished in battle, always victorious in war, advanced with rapid steps to the Euphrates, the Danube, the Rhine, and the ocean; and the images of gold, or silver, or brass, that might serve to represent the nations and their kings, were successively broken by the *iron* monarchy of Rome."—*Decline and Fall of the Roman Empire*, chapter 38.

The prophet noted that this creature had ten horns on its head. If he was puzzled about what they represented, he was soon informed by an angel that the ten horns symbolized ten kings that should rise out of Rome. See Daniel 7:24. The pomp and majesty of the Roman Empire was undermined by civil war, lawlessness, and luxury. The northern frontiers of the empire, weakened by attacks of barbarians, began to disintegrate. From the third to the fifth centuries A.D., "the barbaric tornado was poured out of the north. . . . The great hulk of Rome tottered, fell, and lay dead on the earth, like the stump of Dagon."—J. C. Ridpath, *History of the World*, vol. 3, pp. 28, 29.

Pagan Rome broke into political segments which were the forerunners of modern European countries. There may be some differences of opinion as to the exact ten divisions, but most authorities consider them to be the Burgundians, Anglo-Saxons, Alamanni, Heruli, Vandals, Ostrogoths, Visigoths, Franks, Lombards, and Suevi. In modern history they include France, England, Germany, Spain, Italy, and Portugal. Strong and weak rulers have attempted to unite Europe, but the prophecy holds true—the kingdoms have remained divided.

Then Daniel says, "I considered the horns, and behold, there came up among them another horn, a little one, before which three of the first horns were plucked up by the roots; and behold, in this horn were eyes like the eyes of a man, and a mouth speaking great things."

334

The conquering generals of Rome returned to the capital in triumph with their prisoners and rich treasures.

### The Eleventh Horn

Perplexed by what he saw, the prophet asked for divine help in solving the problems. We know, therefore, that the interpretation of the vision is not of man; it was given by an angel of God.

Of this strange eleventh horn, Daniel said, "As I looked, this horn made war with the saints, and prevailed over them, until the Ancient of Days came, and judgment was given for the saints of the Most High, and the time came when the saints received the kingdom."

The angel gives this specific explanation:

> "As for the ten horns,
> out of this kingdom
> ten kings shall arise,
> and another shall arise after them;
> he shall be different from the former ones,
> and shall put down three kings.
> He shall speak words against the Most High,
> and shall wear out the saints of the Most High,
> and shall think to change the times and the law;
> and they shall be given into his hand
> for a time, two times, and half a time.
> But the court shall sit in judgment,
> and his dominion shall be taken away,
> to be consumed and destroyed to the end.
> And the kingdom and the dominion
> and the greatness of the kingdoms under the
> whole heaven
> shall be given to the people of the saints of
> the Most High;
> their kingdom shall be an everlasting kingdom,
> and all dominions shall serve and obey them."

The Roman Empire had first been a pagan kingdom, but after Christianity spread through the realm the ecclesiastical system of the papacy developed. Thus this eleventh horn which came out of pagan Rome became the papal power, the Roman Catholic Church. This "little horn," according to the prophecy, was not to rise in strength until after the division had been established. Verse 24. History confirms this, for by the end of the fifth century the segments of Rome were established; and in the sixth century the religio-political power of the papacy became prominent and continued for over twelve hundred years.

This "little horn" was to overthrow three kings. Verse 8. This was fulfilled by the overthrow of three "heretical" kingdoms that opposed certain teachings and claims of the papacy. Through a series of wars directed by the papacy the Heruli, the Vandals, and the Ostrogoths fell between A.D. 493 and 554. Thus Arianism (the heretical teaching) was exterminated, and papal Rome became undisputed sovereign of nations and the corrector of heretics.

There are certain characteristics of this power that easily identify it with the description in the prophecy. It was to be different from the other horns, or nations. Verse 24. This is true, for the papacy was a mixture of religion and politics, a religio-political state such as existed nowhere else. It was "to speak words against the Most High." Verse 25. In pride and arrogance it would stand up against God. This powerful ecclesiastical system claims that a man is god on earth. This claim is made by various popes, including Pope Gregory II and Pope Boniface VIII. The latter said, "The pope alone is called most holy. . . . The pope is as God on earth." Quoted by H. Grattan Guinness in *Romanism and the Reformation*, pages 25, 26.

In the papal system priests and prelates assume the place of God over church members by interpreting Scripture, consecrating and offering the "body" of Christ, and claiming to forgive sins. The apostle Paul, seeing the danger of such a system rising even in his day, was led by divine inspiration to declare that there would be apostasy and "the man of lawlessness" would come "who opposes and exalts himself against every so-called god or object of worship, so that he takes his seat in the temple of God, proclaiming himself to be God." 2 Thessalonians 2: 3, 4.

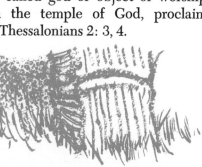

337

This "little horn" would seem "greater than its fellows." Daniel 7:20. True, the papacy became the authoritative power over the kings and princes of Europe. The pope sat as supreme ruler and judge over the nations for hundreds of years.

Again the prophecy states that this power would "wear out the saints of the Most High." History gives ample testimony of the tremendous persecuting power of papal Rome. Through the dark centuries of intolerance the clerical leaders taught that heresy must be blotted out by the sword and physical coercion. The church of Rome defends the horrors of the Inquisition, the Massacre of St. Bartholomew, the extermination of millions of men and women who held religious views at variance from the papal doctrines.

The "little horn" power would "think to change the times and the law." Verse 25. This can refer only to religious observances and the law of God. The Ten Commandment law is an expression of God's nature; it is holy, eternal, and unchangeable. Jesus Christ, in the Sermon on the Mount, declared that He had not come to change the divine law. See Matthew 5:17-19. However, the church of Rome considers itself strong enough to alter heaven's decrees. Here is her boast: "The pope is of so great authority and power that he can modify, explain, or interpret even divine laws. . . . The pope can modify divine law, since his power is not of man but of God, and he acts as vicegerent of God upon earth with most ample power of binding and loosing his sheep."—Ferraris' *Ecclesiastical Dictionary*, art., "Pope."

As to the change of "times," it was the papacy that made Sunday, the first day of the week, the chief religious day of Christendom. In her catechisms this church declares that the change of the day of rest from Saturday to Sunday was an act of the church. See Stephen Keenan, *A Doctrinal Catechism*, page 174. In the Catholic *Information Magazine* of December, 1956, we read, "The Catholic church did change the Lord's Day or the Sabbath to Sunday because of Christ's resurrection on Sunday—and for various other reasons. Christ empowered the

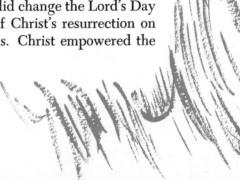

church to teach (Matthew 28:16-20) and we find in its early history mention of the first day of the week (Acts 20:7; 1 Corinthians 16:2) so the change was made through the [Catholic] church with divine authority."

The papacy fits the description clearly set forth in the prophetic vision, for it has attempted a man-made change of the holy day of rest God ordained when the work of creation was finished. The seventh-day Sabbath is specifically designated in the Ten Commandments as the day of rest for man because God blessed and hallowed that day after the six days of creation. Exodus 20:8-11.

The "little horn" power, according to prophecy, would reign supreme for centuries. The exact period is "a time, two times, and half a time." Verse 25. What is the significance of this Biblical measure of time periods? A "time" is a 360-day prophetic year. In prophetic chronology a day stands for a literal year. Numbers 12:34; Ezekiel 4:6. Thus this period of 1260 prophetic days is actually 1260 literal years.

The pope became the recognized authority over the ecclesiastical system of Rome in A.D. 538, by the decree of Emperor Justinian. The papacy held supreme sway over the nations of Europe until 1798, a period of 1260 years. Then, the prophecy declared, "his dominion shall be taken away." Verse 26. The event that closed the domination of Rome was the imprisonment of the pope by General Alexander Berthier, of France. Thus the papacy was given a "deadly wound," but it would revive and later return to power. See Revelation 13:3.

While the prophet was considering the giant beast and the strange machinations of the "little horn," he was given a view of God's throne. Daniel says, "As I looked,

> thrones were placed
>     and One that was Ancient of Days took His seat;
> His raiment was white as snow,
>     and the hair of His head like pure wool;
> His throne was fiery flames,
>     its wheels were burning fire.

THE LAW

I

II

III

IV

V

VI

VII

VIII

A stream of fire issued
    and came forth from before Him;
a thousand thousands served Him,
    and ten thousand times ten thousand stood before Him;
the court sat in judgment,
    and the books were opened.

"I looked then because of the sound of the great words which the horn was speaking. And as I looked, the beast was slain, and its body destroyed and given over to be burned with fire."

According to this prophecy, the judgment takes place soon after the close of the period of papal supremacy. The heavenly tribunal sits in judgment upon the apostate power that has spoken great words against the Most High and has sought to change the divinely appointed times and the eternal law. We read that "the court shall sit in judgment, and his dominion shall be taken away, to be consumed and destroyed to the end." Verse 26.

A court session where a human being is on trial for his life is a solemn scene. How much more majestic and awe-inspiring is the heavenly court where all humanity is on trial before the Almighty! The prophet Daniel was given a view of the supreme court of the universe, and as he watched "thrones were placed and One that was Ancient of Days took His seat." God, the presiding Judge, is clothed in a majestic white robe and seated upon a throne so glorious that it can only be described as "fiery flames." There are many angelic attendants in the court, for "a thousand thousands served Him, and ten thousand times ten thousand stood before Him."

Into the heavenly court comes Jesus Christ to be presented to the Ancient of Days. Christ is the Defense Attorney of all who have placed their case in His hands. "We have an advocate with the Father, Jesus Christ the righteous." 1 John 2:1.

"The court sat in judgment, and the books were opened." Daniel 7:10. There can be no excuse for anyone's not appearing when his record comes up in the heavenly tribunal. A faithful record of every life has been kept, for the books of heaven

Every person's record will be brought to heaven's court, where Jesus Christ offers to act as Defense Attorney.

are a witness to the accuracy of the Almighty, who loves justice and mercy. Paul has said, "We must all appear before the judgment seat of Christ, so that each one may receive good or evil, according to what he has done in the body." 2 Corinthians 5:10.

In the investigation of every case the actual records are opened for proof. There is a book of remembrance where the faithful deeds of the righteous are recorded. Malachi 3:16. In the book of life is recorded the name of everyone who has accepted Christ as his Saviour. What an honor roll this must be of those who have been faithful soldiers of the cross and whose "names are written in heaven!"

Heaven keeps a faithful transcript of every word we speak, every act of our life. If modern science can make a talking motion picture of any event, how easily heaven can record the words, thoughts, and deeds of each individual. Would you care to have your entire life story flashed on a screen in technicolor and stereophonic sound? Jesus Christ explained how carefully the records are kept when He said, "I tell you, on the day of judgment men will render account for every careless word they utter; for by your words you will be justified, and by your words you will be condemned." Matthew 12:36, 37. No hearsay evidence will enter the court.

Here, then, is the court in session. God, the Judge, will hear the case of every individual. Jesus Christ will be the Defense Attorney for all those who have accepted His love and sacrifice on Calvary, and who have given their case into His hands. The standard of judgment is the law of God, the Ten Commandments. We shall be judged by the law of liberty. James 2:10-12.

As each case is considered, either the defendant's sins are erased from his record and his name is retained in the book of life; or the name is blotted from the book of life and the death penalty is written against his record. God promises, "He who conquers shall be clad thus in white garments, and I will not blot his name out of the book of life; I will confess

his name before My Father and before His angels." Revelation 3:5.

No man can stand before the Ten Commandments and say he has kept them perfectly. But, thank God, we have an Intercessor who obeyed all of the divine law, and His perfection will cover our shabby record. "If we confess our sins, He is faithful and just, and will forgive our sins and cleanse us from all unrighteousness." 1 John 1:9. Jesus Christ will continue to plead our case as our Defense Attorney until the solemn tribunal has finished its work. Then He will leave His intercession for man and become king to execute judgment upon the world. Daniel saw this crowning event, for he says, "And to Him was given dominion and glory and kingdom, that all peoples, nations, and languages should serve Him; His dominion is an everlasting dominion, which shall not pass away, and His kingdom one that shall not be destroyed." Daniel 7:14.

A proclamation will then be issued which seals the fate of every human being: "He that is unjust, let him be unjust still: and he which is filthy, let him be filthy still: and he that is righteous, let him be righteous still: and he that is holy, let him be holy still." Revelation 22:11, A.V.

In that hour the final judgments of a just God will begin to fall upon those who have irrevocably turned their backs upon His love. There will be a division between those who obey the Lord of the universe and follow His way of life and those who rebel. The seven plagues described in the fifteenth chapter of the book of Revelation will strike the wicked, God-defying millions. Heaven's door of mercy will be forever closed.

The conflict of the centuries between good and evil will be ended. The enemy of God will have made his last attack and will have been defeated. Then comes the promise of Christ's return to this earth to meet His redeemed people. He says, "Behold, I come quickly; and My reward is with Me, to give every man according as his work shall be." Revelation 22:12, A.V.

At this point the vision from heaven to the aged prophet was finished. Daniel was troubled as he thought of the tremendous events he had previewed. He thought of the trials and persecutions that the saints of God would face. He paled as he considered the enemy's strength; but he gained courage when he remembered that truth will triumph and the faithful followers of God will inherit the eternal kingdom!

# God's Prophetic Blueprint

*Daniel 8 to 12*

chapter 28 *

SOME of the most amazing proof that Bible prophecy is inspired by God is found in Daniel 8 and 9. These prophetic outlines not only foretell the coming of the Messiah, but they project history through the ages to the middle of the nineteenth century. They present a vital message for every man and woman living in these "latter days."

Some two years after receiving the spectacular vision of the four great beasts, symbolizing world empires, Daniel had another remarkable vision. At that time he was living in Susa, in the province of Elam. He recounts his experience in these words: "I raised my eyes and saw, and behold, a ram standing on the bank of the river. It had two horns; and both horns were high, but one was higher than the other, and the higher one came up last. I saw the ram charging westward and northward and southward; no beast could stand before him, and there was no one who could rescue from his power; he did as he pleased and magnified himself. As I was considering, behold, a he-goat came from the west across the face of the whole earth, without touching the ground; and the goat had a conspicuous horn between his eyes. He came to the ram with the two horns, which I had seen standing on the bank of the river, and he ran at him in his mighty wrath. I saw him come close to the ram, and he was enraged against him and struck

345

the ram and broke his two horns; and the ram had not power to stand before him, but he cast him down to the ground and trampled upon him; and there was no one who could rescue the ram from his power. Then the he-goat magnified himself exceedingly; but when he was strong, the great horn was broken, and instead of it there came up four conspicuous horns toward the four winds of heaven. Out of one of them came forth a little horn, which grew exceedingly great toward the south, toward the east, and toward the glorious land. It grew great, even to the host of heaven; and some of the host of the stars it cast down to the ground, and trampled upon them. It magnified itself, even up to the Prince of the host; and the continual burnt offering was taken away from him, and the place of his sanctuary was overthrown. And the host was given over to it together with the continual burnt offering through transgression; and truth was cast down to the ground, and the horn acted and prospered."

Here was the battle of two well-known animals, a ferocious ram and on overpowering he-goat. We realize that these creatures symbolize nations, even as the beasts did in Daniel 7. This is proven when Daniel is told, "As for the ram which you saw with the two horns, these are the kings of Media and Persia."

There are parallels between this symbol and the great bear that raised itself up on one side, for the horn on one side of the ram's head was higher than the other. When Persia became the dominant power under Cyrus and Darius, the armies pushed their conquests "westward and northward and southward." The Persian Empire at its height consisted of one hundred and twenty-seven provinces extending from Ethiopia to India.

But the he-goat came from the west to challenge the prowess of the ram. Its speed was so great that as it charged it seemed scarcely to touch the ground. The symbol of the goat is clear, for the angel said, "The he-goat is the king of Greece; and the great horn between his eyes is the first king."

In his vision Daniel beheld a ram and a he-goat in a gigantic battle. This symbolized Persia and Greece.

JOE MANISCALCO, ARTIST          © P.P.P.A.

Under the leadership of Alexander the Great, the Greek armies attacked Persia with "mighty wrath." At the battle of Gaugamela, near the Tigris River, the final defeat of Persia took place in 331 B.C., and there was "no power to stand before" Alexander. For a few years the Greek conqueror held the supremacy, but "the great horn was broken" when the general died at the age of thirty-three, a dissolute drunkard. Then, as all historians tell us, the kingdom was divided for a time into four parts by four of the strongest generals of the Greek army. Thus there arose "four conspicuous horns toward the four winds of heaven."

## The "Little Horn" Power

Then, out of one of these horns came forth "a little horn" that stretched out with exceeding power. This is the monarchy of pagan Rome, for the Roman legions defeated Macedonia, the western division of Greece, in 168 B.C. It was Rome that struck against God's truth and persecuted His devout followers. The legal power of Herod and Pontius Pilate, officials of the Roman Empire, imprisoned Jesus Christ, and falsely accused, condemned, and crucified Him. Daniel heard an angel ask how long this reign of darkness was to continue. He said, "For how long is the vision concerning the continual burnt offering, the transgression that makes desolate, and the giving over of the sanctuary and host to be trampled under foot?"

Would the enemies of truth always prosper? Would there be no triumph for the message of the Eternal One? The assuring answer, stating the longest time prophecy in the Bible, came to Daniel and is reiterated to every student of God's word: "For two thousand and three hundred evenings and mornings; then the sanctuary shall be restored to its rightful state."

But Daniel did not comprehend the meaning of this long period of twenty-three hundred years. (A day symbolizes a year in Bible prophecy. Ezekiel 4:6.) As he considered the fearful persecution that the Roman Empire would bring upon

the people of God, he could not endure it. The aged prophet fainted and was sick for some days.

In the first year of Medo-Persian rule, when Darius was king, Daniel studied the prophecies of Jeremiah concerning the return of the Jews from captivity in Babylon to Jerusalem. The time of restoration foretold by the prophets Isaiah and Jeremiah was almost due. Furthermore, Daniel was anxious to know the full meaning of the prophecy he had been given, for he had been told that it pertained "to many days hence." Verse 26.

While he was earnestly praying, the angel Gabriel, who had previously instructed him, came and said, "O Daniel, I have now come out to give you wisdom and understanding. At the beginning of your supplications a word went forth, and I have come to tell it to you, for you are greatly beloved; therefore consider the word and understand the vision."

The angel was referring to the vision of the "two thousand and three hundred evenings and mornings," for this was the only portion of the former prophecy that had not been fully explained to Daniel. Beginning with the prophet's desire to know about his own people, the Jewish nation, the angel said, "Seventy weeks of years are decreed concerning your people and your Holy City, to finish the transgression, to put an end to sin, and to atone for iniquity, to bring in everlasting righteousness, to seal both vision and prophet, and to anoint a most holy place."

This period of "seventy weeks of years," or 490 literal years, was "decreed" to the Jewish nation. This allotment must be taken from a longer period of time, namely, the 2300-year period of prophecy. These 490 years were to be a period of test to the Jewish nation; and tragically enough, the rebellion of the chosen people would reach its limit. The Messiah would come and by His death cause sin offerings to be of no avail, and He would make reconciliation for iniquity. The Son of God would bring everlasting righteousness to this earth. Furthermore, the coming of Jesus at the exact time foretold

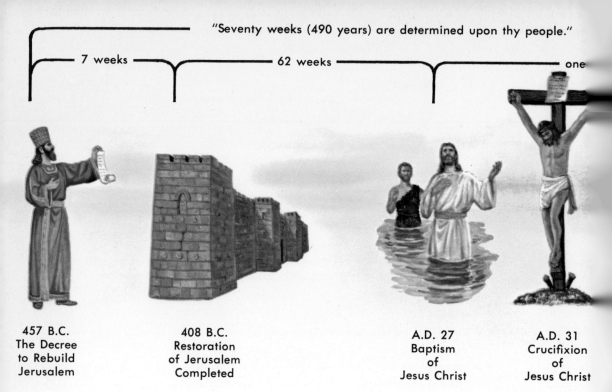

"Seventy weeks (490 years) are determined upon thy people."

7 weeks — 62 weeks — one

457 B.C.
The Decree
to Rebuild
Jerusalem

408 B.C.
Restoration
of Jerusalem
Completed

A.D. 27
Baptism
of
Jesus Christ

A.D. 31
Crucifixion
of
Jesus Christ

The 2300 Days (Ye-

JOE MANISCALCO, ARTIST

by the prophecy would ratify, or confirm, the truthfulness of God's prophetic word.

The prophecy states an amazing series of events; but unless we can determine when these events are to begin, it will avail us little to find the course of its fulfillment. Evidence within the Scriptures gives us the key to the problem. A date always to be remembered by the Jewish people is the restoration of Jerusalem after their return from captivity. This event was to mark the time when the prophecy began, for we read, "Know therefore and understand that from the going forth of the word to restore and build Jerusalem to the coming of an Anointed One, a Prince, there shall be seven weeks. Then for sixty-two weeks it shall be built again with squares and moat, but in a troubled time."

The Bible gives the historical facts concerning this opening date, for Ezra 6:14 mentions the three decrees of Cyrus, Darius, and Artaxerxes Longimanus that fulfilled God's word.

350

A.D. 34
Stoning
of
Stephen

A.D. 1844
Cleansing
of
Heavenly Sanctuary

ıg Bible Prophecy

"And the elders of the Jews built and prospered, through the prophesying of Haggai the prophet and Zechariah the son of Iddo. They finished their building by command of the God of Israel and by decree of Cyrus and Darius and Artaxerxes king of Persia."

This took place in 457 B.C., according to the canon of Ptolemy. This authentic record of Claudius Ptolemy not only lists the kings but verifies their accuracy by the unerring eclipses, solar and lunar, that are listed. These eclipses have been confirmed by modern astronomers, which conclusively proves the accuracy of the canon. Thus we have a threefold proof from Bible, history, and science that the date, 457 B.C., is correct.

Using this date as our beginning, we see the unfolding of the prophecy in the New Testament record, and we are able to project the twenty-three-hundred-year period to its close. The four-hundred-and-ninety-year period was subdivided. There

351

were to be sixty-nine weeks (483 years) to the coming of the Messiah, the "Anointed One." This would leave only the seventieth week (seven years) remaining, and during this seven-year period the Messiah was to be "cut off." Verse 26.

## *The Longest Bible Prophecy*

Sixty-two weeks (434 years) after the city of Jerusalem was rebuilt the Messiah would come. Just forty-nine years after the decree to restore the city had been issued, or in 408 B.C., Jerusalem was again completely rebuilt as the home of the Jews. Adding 434 years to 408 B.C., brings us to A.D. 27, the exact year which history and the Bible record as the date for the baptism of Christ, when the Holy Spirit confirmed the truth, "Thou art My beloved Son; with Thee I am well pleased." Luke 3:22.

This brings us to the final week, or the last seven years of the four-hundred-and-ninety-year prophecy. From the time Jesus was baptized until He was crucified was three and a half years. He died at the time of the Passover, in the spring of A.D. 31. By His death the services of the ancient sanctuary lost their significance; the Lamb of God had died on Calvary for the sins of the world. At that time "the curtain of the temple was torn in two, from top to bottom; and the earth shook, and the rocks were split." Matthew 27:51. This divine omen proclaimed the fact that the services had fulfilled their mission and the work of the earthly priest had been accomplished.

The final act in the four hundred ninety years allotted to the Jewish people came three and one-half years later. In A.D. 34, the leaders of the Jews refused to listen to the gospel story. Stephen, the first Christian martyr, was stoned to death by those who refused to hear the gospel, and the fearful persecution of the young church began. The Jewish nation as such had rejected the Messiah; it would not heed the call to repentance, and, therefore, God sent the apostles to the Gentiles with the gospel.

352

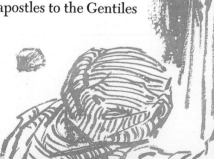

The four hundred ninety years of the prophecy were accurately fulfilled. What of the remaining period of the full twenty-three hundred years? Subtracting four hundred ninety from twenty-three hundred leaves eighteen hundred ten years (2300—490=1810). Adding 1810 to the year A.D. 34, which was the end of the four hundred ninety years allotted to the Jews, we are brought to 1844.

What had the angel Gabriel told Daniel? "For two thousand and three hundred evenings and mornings; then the sanctuary shall be restored to its rightful state." Thus the year 1844 has an extraordinary meaning—the making right of the sanctuary. Could this mean the service of the ancient Jewish sanctuary? No, for this service had accomplished its purpose when Jesus died on the cross.

### The Temple in Heaven

We know from our study of the sanctuary of the Old Testament that there was a Day of Atonement each year when the place of worship was cleansed from the defilement of the sins which had been transferred there by the ritual of the daily sin offerings. On the Day of Atonement a special work was done, which is described in the book of Hebrews as a purifying. Hebrews 9:23. On that day all the sins were removed from the sanctuary. Thus, the Day of Atonement was a time when the sanctuary was restored to its rightful state, cleansed of all sin.

Even as there was a cleansing, or restoration of the earthly sanctuary, so there is a greater work—of which the earthly service was a type—in the heavenly temple where Jesus Christ, our High Priest, now conducts a special work. As the Day of Atonement was actually a day of judgment for every person in Israel, so there is a time of judgment in heaven when the destiny of all men is to be decided. God has appointed a day when the world will come to judgment. Acts 17:31.

The work of judgment, as Daniel saw it in the seventh chapter of his book, began in 1844. May God help us to realize the solemnity of the scene, and to know that if we confess our sins, "He is faithful and just to forgive us our sins, and to cleanse us from all unrighteousness." 1 John 1:9, A.V.

Thus we see that the twenty-three-hundred-year prophecy of Daniel is a blueprint, in which the dimensions of time and predicted events are all minutely and symbolically stated. Within the blueprint is the prediction of the Messiah's first advent, the fulfillment of which seals the authenticity of the whole prophecy. The death of the Messiah was foretold to the exact year. As the New Testament historical account is studied in the light of this prophecy, the inspiration of God's word is revealed to us in all its glory.

## A Prophet of Prayer

Daniel, although burdened by affairs of the empire, was never too busy to commune with his God. One of the great prayers of the Bible is recorded in the ninth chapter of Daniel. Here the prophet seeks the Lord for the forgiveness of his sins and the sins of his people, and he pleads for the restoration of Jerusalem and the Jewish nation, as the prophecies foretold.

The angel appeared to Daniel and strengthened him. He said, "O man greatly beloved, fear not, peace be with you; be strong and of good courage."

Other detailed prophecies were revealed to Daniel in the closing years of his long life. He was shown a vision of the time when Jesus Christ will stand up as King of kings. After the final time of trouble God's people would triumph gloriously. We read, "At that time your people shall be delivered, everyone whose name shall be found written in the book. And many of those who sleep in the dust of the earth shall awake, some to everlasting life, and some to shame and everlasting contempt. And those who are wise shall shine like the brightness of the firmament; and those who turn many to righteousness, like the stars forever and ever."

Daniel was instructed to "shut up the words, and seal the

book, until the time of the end. Many shall run to and fro, and knowledge shall increase." Daniel 12:4. Although he received many divine revelations, the prophet was humble in his knowledge. He never ran ahead of God in seeking to work out the fulfillment of the prophecies. As he wrote some of the divinely-inspired statements, he humbly admitted, "I heard, but I did not understand."

## Seven Reasons for Divine Prophecy

Bible prophecies are not given to man merely to satisfy curiosity; they are ordained for a holy purpose. We may consider seven important reasons why prophecy is given in the word of God.

1. Prophecy confirms our faith in the plans and purposes of the Eternal One. Many prophecies presented to the Old Testament seers gave exact pictures of events hundreds of years before they came to pass. Jesus declared the purpose of such revelations when He said, "And now I have told you before it takes place, so that when it does take place, you may believe." John 14:29. Many of Daniel's prophecies confirm the faith of the Christian in the authority of God's word and His eternal purpose in human history.

2. Prophecy proves the power and identity of the true God. Isaiah presents a challenge to idol worshipers in these words:

> "Remember the former things of old;
> for I am God, and there is no other;
> I am God, and there is none like Me,
> declaring the end from the beginning
> and from ancient times things not yet done,
> saying, 'My counsel shall stand,
> and I will accomplish all My purpose.'"
>
> Isaiah 46:9, 10.

3. Prophecy reveals the truth, whether it be good or bad. Jeremiah lived in a time when there were many false prophets, and it was necessary for him to expose the counterfeit messages.

355

False prophets do not wish to give the truth if it is disagreeable. Therefore, they attempt to offer false security to those who disobey God. Such false predictions are evil because they imply that man may defy divine law without reaping punishment and destruction. The Eternal One reveals the honest facts to His children and then points them to ultimate victory when the controversy between good and evil is at an end.

4. Prophecy leads men to obey God and to keep His commandments. Moses declared, "The secret things belong to the Lord our God; but the things that are revealed belong to us and to our children forever, that we may do all the words of this law." Deuteronomy 29:29. Loving obedience springs from confidence. When men see that God's way has always proved to be the best, when they see that what He has spoken has come to pass, they have faith in His word.

5. Prophecy teaches us to trust in God. Although we live in a world that bears the marks of sin and death, we can be certain that truth will triumph. The Bible brings comfort to the child of God and tells him "to be not troubled." Prophecy points the way to a new heaven and a new earth for the redeemed.

6. Prophecy protects the child of God from error and false doctrine. Before deception comes, the divine message warns of danger. How frequently did Jesus and His apostles warn of coming apostasy, false prophets, and the doctrines of devils. Divine prophecy has always been a shield against the darts of evil. We have a beam of truth to keep us on the correct course, for Isaiah writes, "And your ears shall hear a word behind you, saying, 'This is the way, walk in it,' when you turn to the right or when you turn to the left." Isaiah 30:21.

7. Prophecy helps the Christian to prepare to meet his God. When Nebuchadnezzar heard the outline of future events as they were symbolized in his dream of the mammoth image, he altered his course of action. We, too, may know the trends of our times, the deceptions that will come, the final crisis, and the way God will deliver His faithful followers.

Today as history and prophecy meet in current events, we can say, "In this hour of blackness, destruction, and disillusionment, I see the hand of God working out His salvation. Beyond this moment of tragic history I see by faith the day when truth shall triumph. By faith I see history and prophecy meet in the final victory over evil!"

# Esther, the Dauntless Queen

*The Book of Esther*

chapter 29 *

WHEN Cyrus, the conqueror of Babylon, came to the throne of Medo-Persia, he decreed that the Jews scattered through the provinces could return to their homes in Palestine. However, there were thousands who had lived so long in the foreign land they did not wish to return, and among those who stayed in Persia was Mordecai, a man of the tribe of Benjamin. He was an officer of the king, and in his house at the capital city of Shushan lived Esther, his cousin. When Esther was a young girl, her father and mother died, and Mordecai, a nephew of the girl's father, cared for her as he would his own daughter.

King Xerxes, or Ahasuerus, was now ruler of the Persian Empire. Before setting out on an elaborate campaign against the Greeks, the monarch gave a sumptuous feast at his palace for his princes, army officers, and governors of the provinces. For one hundred eighty days the celebration continued, and the climax was reached at a seven-day banquet. At the same time Queen Vashti made a special dinner for the women in the palace. On the last day of the festival King Xerxes, in a spirit of drunken revelry, commanded the queen to come to his feast so that he could display her great beauty. But the modest Queen Vashti refused to go to the festival which the drunken men had turned into a brawl. The king was angry

King Ahasuerus listened to the request of Queen Esther, and he promised to make her wish come true.

359

because Vashti had the audacity to disobey him, and he ruled that she was no longer to be his queen.

Some time later the king decided to choose another queen from among the beautiful maidens of the empire. Messengers were sent to all the provinces inviting young women to appear at the king's court. Esther was taken to the palace with the other girls. After twelve months of training she was presented to the king, and he chose her to be the new queen of his harem.

Esther was loved by her servants and she soon became a favorite in the women's palace. Mordecai could not visit with her, but every day he walked to and fro in the courtyard near her window.

As Mordecai sat at the palace gate performing his official duties, he overheard the plot of two angry servants to kill King Xerxes. Mordecai sent a message to Queen Esther, and she forwarded it to the king. The men were discovered in their treachery and hanged.

### Race Hatred Flares in Persia

About this time, Haman, the Agagite, a proud prince of the court, was promoted, and the king commanded that the other officers should bow to him. When Mordecai would not bow to this base fellow, the servants reported the matter to Haman. This proud man was filled with rage, but he did not dare lay hands on a loyal officer. Soon he decided upon an evil plan. Since Mordecai was a Jew, Haman stirred King Xerxes with race hatred by saying, "There is a certain people scattered abroad and dispersed among the peoples in all the provinces of your kingdom; their laws are different from those of every other people, and they do not keep the king's laws, so that it is not for the king's profit to tolerate them. If it please the king, let it be decreed that they be destroyed, and I will pay ten thousand talents of silver into the hands of those who have charge of the king's business, that they may put it into the king's treasuries."

Since the king trusted his officers, he did not see the evil

purpose of Haman. Furthermore, he did not know that Queen Esther was a Jew. The royal secretaries prepared an edict which the king signed, commanding the citizens to kill all Jews on the thirteenth day of the twelfth month. Here was anti-Semitism at its worst, and the capital city was thrown into consternation.

When Mordecai heard of the decree, he tore his garments and mourned deeply. He knew that this law doomed his people to destruction. There was only one hope; perhaps Esther as queen could save these innocent and helpless victims of an insane hate.

When Queen Esther learned that Mordecai was mourning, she sent him beautiful garments. Since she was sheltered in the women's quarters, she had not learned of the fateful decree. Mordecai refused to accept the gifts, and finally told the servant to reveal to Esther what was about to happen to her people. The queen was stunned by the message from Mordecai. What could she do? The law said that no one should enter the king's court who was not summoned by him; and unless the monarch held out his golden scepter to the suppliant as he approached the throne, he might be put to death. However, the crisis demanded quick thinking and brave resolution on the part of both Esther and her cousin.

Trusting in the Lord to help his people, Mordecai sent this message to Esther, "Think not that in the king's palace you will escape any more than all the other Jews. For if you keep silence at such a time as this, relief and deliverance will rise for the Jews from another quarter, but you and your father's house will perish. And who knows whether you have not come to the kingdom for such a time as this?"

When Esther received this challenge, she sent a message back to Mordecai, "Go, gather all the Jews to be found in Susa, and hold a fast on my behalf, and neither eat nor drink for three days, night or day. I and my maids will also fast as you do. Then I will go to the king, though it is against the law; and if I perish, I perish." As she penned these words,

361

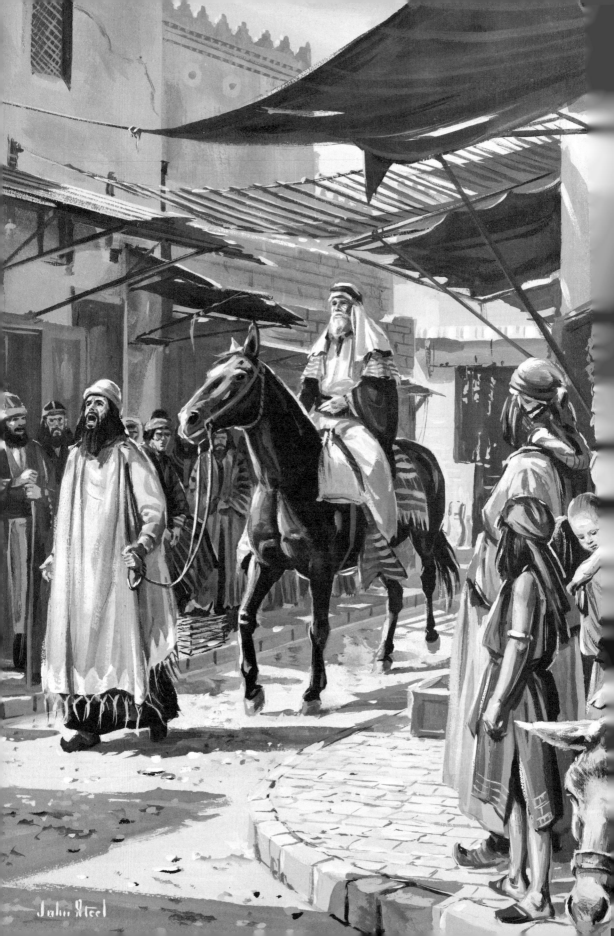

Esther must have remembered how the impetuous king had banished his former queen, Vashti.

On the third day Queen Esther put on her royal robes and went to the door of the audience chamber. King Xerxes, seated on his throne, saw the queen. Her beauty was irresistible, and he held out his golden scepter. Esther drew near and touched it. "What is it, Queen Esther? What is your request? It shall be given you, even to the half of my kingdom," said the king.

## Feasting in the Queen's Apartment

"If it please the king," said Esther, "let the king and Haman come this day to a dinner that I have prepared for the king."

The king turned to his servants and said, "Bring Haman quickly, that we may do as Esther desires."

So the king and Haman came to the banquet that Esther had prepared. Then the king asked Esther what she desired, and again the Queen replied demurely, "My petition and my request is: If I have found favor in the sight of the king, and if it please the king to grant my petition and fulfill my request, let the king and Haman come tomorrow to the dinner which I will prepare for them, and tomorrow I will do as the king has said."

Haman was so proud to be the special guest of the queen that he rushed home to spread the news to his family. "Even Queen Esther let no one come with the king to the banquet she prepared but myself. And tomorrow also I am invited by her together with the king," said Haman. "Yet all this does me no good, so long as I see Mordecai the Jew sitting at the king's gate."

Haman's wife and his friends proposed that a gallows fifty cubits high, or eighty-three feet, be built and that the next morning he ask the king for permission to hang Mordecai. Haman seized the idea with glee, and he had the gallows erected at once.

That night the king suffered from insomnia. To help him

Proud Haman was forced to lead the horse through the streets and see the people paying homage to Mordecai.

JOHN STEEL, ARTIST               © P. P. P. A.

pass the sleepless hours he had his servants read to him from the records of the kingdom. Now in the chronicles there was the account of how two traitors had planned to kill the king and how Mordecai saved Xerxes' life.

"What honor or dignity has been bestowed on Mordecai for this?" asked the king.

"Nothing has been done for him," said the servant, scanning the records carefully.

It was now early in the morning, and Haman had risen early to make his request to the king for the death of Mordecai. At that moment his footsteps were heard in the palace hall. The king, thinking of the traitors who had once almost taken his life, called out, "Who is in the court?"

A servant announced, "Haman is there, standing in the court."

"Let him come in," sighed the king with relief, as the draperies parted and Haman entered.

The king asked a half question, half riddle: "What shall be done to the man whom the king delights to honor?"

Haman said to himself, "Whom would the king delight to honor more than me?" So the proud man attempted to picture all the things he would like to have. "For the man whom the king delights to honor," said Haman, "let royal robes be brought, which the king has worn, and the horse which the king has ridden, and on whose head a royal crown is set; and let the robes and the horse be handed over to one of the king's most noble princes; let him array the man whom the king delights to honor, and let him conduct the man on horseback through the open square of the city, proclaiming before him: 'Thus shall it be done to the man whom the king delights to honor.'"

"Make haste, take the robes and the horse, as you have said, and do so to Mordecai the Jew who sits at the king's gate. Leave out nothing that you have mentioned," commanded the king.

Haman's mouth dropped open in surprise. He was not the

honored one! Instead he must lead a horse through the streets with the detestable Mordecai riding upon it in royal splendor. The honor that he had dreamed should come to him had been heaped upon his hated enemy. Haman rushed home weeping because of what had happened. When his wife heard the news, she intuitively said, "If Mordecai, before whom you have begun to fall, is of the Jewish people, you will not prevail against him but will surely fall before him."

### The Villain Is Revealed

About this time messengers arrived to take Haman to Queen Esther's second banquet. "What is your petition, Queen Esther? It shall be granted you. And what is your request? Even to the half of my kingdom, it shall be fulfilled," said Xerxes, while he and Haman sat enjoying the party.

"If I have found favor in your sight, O king, and if it please the king, let my life be given me at my petition, and my people at my request," pleaded Esther. "For we are sold, I and my people, to be destroyed, to be slain, and to be annihilated."

"Who is he, and where is he, that would presume to do this?" asked the angry monarch.

"A foe and enemy! This wicked Haman!" said Esther, pointing to the cruel officer at the table beside them.

Haman was terrified when he beheld the king's wrath. Xerxes rose from the banquet and strode out into his garden. He now saw how he had been duped by Haman's plot to kill the innocent Jews. At once the king was in a rage; he would punish this prince for his wicked deeds. A servant who stood near the king suggested, "Moreover, the gallows which Haman has prepared for Mordecai, whose word saved the king, is standing in Haman's house, fifty cubits high."

"Hang him on that," said the king curtly, and thus Haman's fate was sealed.

Then Xerxes sent special messengers riding swiftly to all provinces in the empire telling the Jews to gather in groups and fight for their lives on the day that had been set for their destruction. The Jews gathered in armed bands; but when the Persians heard of the king's second decree, they did not dare attack the Jews. Angels of God protected His people. The record states that no one could stand against the Jews, and they "smote all their enemies with the sword."

Esther became the heroine of the Jews in captivity, and her brave appeal to the king was known in Jerusalem, where thousands of exiles had returned to make a new home.

# The Return of the Exiles

*The Books of Ezra and Nehemiah*

## chapter 30

ISPLACED persons! Tens of thousands of Jews were exiled in Babylon and other foreign lands for years, but they never forgot their homeland! Because they had disobeyed the Lord and worshiped idols, He had allowed them to be taken captive by their enemies. In this heathen environment they had the opportunity to see idolatry in all its corrupt and evil forms, so that as a nation they rebelled from it in later generations. After years of exile, the people of Judah realized what it meant to be without a temple where they might worship the true God and offer sacrifices to Him. They wept when they thought of the ruins of the once glorious city of Jerusalem.

> "By the waters of Babylon, there we sat down and wept,
>     when we remembered Zion.
> On the willows there
>     we hung up our lyres.
> For there our captors
>     required of us songs,
> and our tormentors, mirth, saying,
>     'Sing us one of the songs of Zion!' "

When the army of Cyrus surrounded Babylon during the reign of Belshazzar, the Jews took hope. They knew the prophecy that had been written by Isaiah more than a century before the birth of Cyrus, declaring that this man would free the exiles and help them return to their homes. Joyfully they read again these words:

> "Thus says the Lord to His anointed, to Cyrus,
>     whose right hand I have grasped,
> to subdue nations before him
>     and ungird the loins of kings,
> to open doors before him
>     that gates may not be closed:
> 'I will go before you
>     and level the mountains,
> I will break in pieces the doors of bronze
>     and cut asunder the bars of iron,
> I will give you the treasures of darkness
>     and the hoards in secret places,
> that you may know that it is I, the Lord,
>     the God of Israel, who call you by your name.'"

The Lord also told Isaiah that Cyrus would rebuild Jerusalem. This prophecy came to pass in the first year of the reign of Cyrus, the Persian, when he made this decree: "Thus says Cyrus king of Persia: The Lord, the God of heaven, has given me all the kingdoms of the earth, and He has charged me to build Him a house at Jerusalem, which is in Judah. Whoever is among you of all His people, may his God be with him, and let him go up to Jerusalem, which is in Judah, and rebuild the house of the Lord, the God of Israel—He is the God who is in Jerusalem; and let each survivor, in whatever place he sojourns, be assisted by the men of his place with silver and gold, with goods and with beasts, besides freewill offerings for the house of God which is in Jerusalem." Ezra 1:2-4.

None of the Jewish exiles were forced to return to the land of Canaan. Families could choose to go or stay as they wished. Zerubbabel, a descendant of King David, was placed in charge of the caravan, and the high priest Joshua stood by his side to help. "The whole assembly together was forty-two thousand three hundred and sixty, besides their menservants and maidservants, of whom there were seven thousand three hundred and thirty-seven; and they had two hundred male and female singers. Their horses were seven hundred and thirty-six, their mules were two hundred and forty-five, their camels were four hundred and thirty-five, and their asses were six thousand seven hundred and twenty."

The return of the exiles was a momentous turning point in history. "The future of the world lay in this procession to Jerusalem. It rested with it whether we should have a Bible at all as we know it—the Bible, the Jewish faith, Christianity and many centuries of western culture," writes Mary Ellen Chase, noted educator.

Across some 800 miles of hot and dreary desert the caravan made its way. The people carried with them the sacred vessels of gold that Nebuchadnezzar had taken from Solomon's temple. Cyrus gave the vessels to the returning pilgrims to be used in the temple when it was rebuilt. When the people arrived in Jerusalem, they erected an altar on the site where Solomon's temple had stood, and they offered thanks to God for bringing them safely back to their own country.

### Rebuilding the Temple

As workmen began to rebuild the temple, they found some of the immense stones of the former edifice amid the rubble. When the cornerstone was laid, the priests and the musicians sang responsively to the Lord:

> "For He is good,
>     for His steadfast love endures
>         forever toward Israel."

The construction of God's house was encouraged by the prophets Haggai and Zechariah. Many of the returning exiles wanted to build homes and plant their fields before they completed the temple; but the prophets aroused the people to action. Haggai asked, "Is it a time for you yourselves to dwell

369

in your paneled houses, while this house lies in ruins?" Haggai 1:4.

As the work on the temple advanced, the builders were encouraged by the promises of the Lord. The prophet spoke: "For thus says the Lord of hosts: Once again, in a little while, I will shake the heavens and the earth and the sea and the dry land; and I will shake all nations, so that the treasures of all nations shall come in, and I will fill this house with splendor, says the Lord of hosts. The silver is Mine, and the gold is Mine, says the Lord of hosts. The latter splendor of this house shall be greater than the former, says the Lord of hosts; and in this place I will give prosperity, says the Lord of hosts." Here was a direct prophecy of the coming Messiah, the Son of God, who would bring the glory of heaven to the rebuilt temple.

Zechariah spoke to those whose hearts were sluggish with disappointment and discouragement. Since thousands of Jews who returned to Palestine were not finding life easy in the reconstruction period, it was the prophet's duty to comfort and encourage them in their mood of bewilderment and doubt. Zechariah longed for the people to build their lives for God by obedience to His commands and in loving devotion. He said, "Return to Me, says the Lord of hosts, and I will return to you, says the Lord of hosts." Zechariah 1:3.

The cheering promise came from God's messenger: "My cities shall again overflow with prosperity, and the Lord will again comfort Zion and again choose Jerusalem."

As Zerubbabel led out in constructing the temple he was confronted with many difficulties. In that hour Zechariah stood by his side and gave the divine promise: "The hands of Zerubbabel have laid the foundation of this house; his hands shall also complete it. Then you will know that the Lord of hosts has sent me to you. For whoever has despised the day of small things shall rejoice, and shall see the plummet in the hand of Zerubbabel."

In our modern age of titanic power and giant construction projects, let us not despise "small things." The prophet knew

Though beset by difficulties, the returning exiles repaired the walls of Jerusalem and rebuilt the temple.

that it was a stupendous task to rebuild the temple while many people sat and criticized the work; but God was in the small beginning, and He would guide until the work was finished!

Many times we may feel that God's church lacks the power and wisdom of the world; but we are never to forget that Jesus Christ is the foundation of the church "and the gates of hell shall not prevail against it." Matthew 16:18, A.V. To us has been given the message: "Not by might, nor by power, but by My Spirit, says the Lord of hosts."

About four and one-half years after the work was started the temple was completed. Then the Jews celebrated their accomplishment with a dedication service. The altar was set up and sacrifices were offered for the tribes of Israel. The second temple was not as magnificent as the glorious one Solomon had built. No cloud of glory hovered over it as it had at the dedication of the first temple. But the people rejoiced, and they looked for the day when the promised Saviour, the Messiah, would come.

### Nehemiah Comes to Jerusalem

Now in the court of King Artaxerxes of Persia there was a Jew named Nehemiah who was the king's cupbearer. While Nehemiah was at the palace at Shushan, he prayed and fasted, asking the God of heaven to help his people restore the kingdom of Judah. In his prayer he said, "O Lord God of heaven, the great and terrible God who keeps covenant and steadfast love with those who love Him and keep His commandments; let Thy ear be attentive, and Thy eyes open, to hear the prayer of Thy servant which I now pray before Thee day and night for the people of Israel Thy servants, confessing the sins of the people of Israel, which we have sinned against Thee. Yea, I and my father's house have sinned. We have acted very corruptly against Thee, and have not kept the commandments, the statutes, and the ordinances which Thou didst command Thy servant Moses. Remember

372

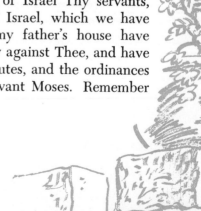

the word which Thou didst command Thy servant Moses, saying, 'If you are unfaithful, I will scatter you among the peoples; but if you return to Me and keep My commandments and do them, though your dispersed be under the farthest skies, I will gather them thence and bring them to the place which I have chosen, to make My name dwell there." Nehemiah 1:5-9.

King Artaxerxes saw his servant's troubled look and asked, "Why is your face sad, seeing you are not sick? This is nothing else but sadness of the heart."

"Let the king live forever!" said the loyal cupbearer. "Why should not my face be sad, when the city, the place of my fathers' sepulchers, lies waste, and its gates have been destroyed by fire?" exclaimed Nehemiah.

"For what do you make request?" the king said.

"If it pleases the king," said Nehemiah, "and if your servant has found favor in your sight, that you send me to Judah, to the city of my fathers' sepulchers, that I may rebuild it."

The king acted favorably on Nehemiah's request and sent him on his way to Jerusalem with an escort of officers and soldiers as well as letters of introduction to the governors through whose provinces he would pass on his long journey. He also carried gifts to assist in financing the cost of rebuilding the city.

After the king's cupbearer had been in Jerusalem for three days, he decided to survey the progress of the work. He describes his adventures in these words: "Then I arose in the night, I and a few men with me; and I told no one what my God had put into my heart to do for Jerusalem. There was no beast with me but the beast on which I rode. I went out by night by the Valley Gate to the Jackal's Well and to the Dung Gate, and I inspected the walls of Jerusalem which were broken down and its gates which had been destroyed by fire. Then I went on to the Fountain Gate and to the King's Pool; but there was no place for the beast that was under me to pass. Then I went up in the night by the valley and inspected

373

the wall; and I turned back and entered by the Valley Gate, and so returned. And the officials did not know where I had gone or what I was doing; and I had not yet told the Jews, the priests, the nobles, the officials, and the rest that were to do the work."

Assembling the leaders, Nehemiah courageously said, "Let us build the wall of Jerusalem, that we may no longer suffer disgrace."

The leaders caught Nehemiah's enthusiasm and they agreeably said, "Let us rise up and build."

The cupbearer of Artaxerxes organized the work, and in spite of enemies led by a villain named Sanballat, who threatened Nehemiah's life, the wall of Jerusalem was repaired in fifty-two days. The dedication of the walls was carried out with elaborate religious ceremonies. Two processions were formed, one led by Ezra and the other by Nehemiah, and they paraded around the wall in opposite directions.

## The Call to the Nation

Although many families from the tribes of Judah and Benjamin returned to Jerusalem, yet thousands of Jews remained in Persia and Egypt after they were released from bondage. Josephus, the historian of the first century, says, "Many abode in Babylon because they did not wish to leave their possessions." (*Antiquities XI*, 1, 3.)

The Jews who returned to Jerusalem no longer worshiped idols, for they loved the God of their fathers and served Him with complete loyalty. Jerusalem once more became the focus of Jewish life as the people came from their homes in distant lands to worship God in the new temple.

As the years passed, prosperity did not return to the nation. Some of the faithful who had made severe sacrifices to come back to Judah began to doubt God's leadership, and their faith waned. Priests neglected their duties, while the people were careless about their vows and offerings to the Lord. In this time, Malachi, the last-known Old Testament prophet, ap-

374

peared in the streets or market places, defending God's truth.

The people asked, "How has God loved us?" and Malachi replied that the Eternal One had not forgotten or forsaken His children; but they had turned from His way. To the priests he spoke God's message: "O priests, who despise My name. You say, 'How have we despised Thy name?' "

God gave this rebuke through His messenger. "I have no pleasure in you, says the Lord of hosts, and I will not accept an offering from your hand. For from the rising of the sun to its setting My name is great among the nations, and in every place incense is offered to My name, and a pure offering; for My name is great among the nations, says the Lord of hosts. But you profane it when you say that the Lord's table is polluted, and the food for it may be despised."

In the final chapter of his book, the prophet gave a fearful warning of judgment to come, when he declared, "For behold, the day comes, burning like an oven, when all the arrogant and all evildoers will be stubble; the day that comes shall burn them up, says the Lord of hosts, so that it will leave them neither root nor branch."

But still there is hope for the repentant, as set forth in this promise: "Behold, I will send you Elijah the prophet before the great and terrible day of the Lord comes. And he will turn the hearts of fathers to their children and the hearts of children to their fathers, lest I come and smite the land with a curse."

Every human being will face the judgment and must give an account for his life to his Maker. Even as the prophets of old pointed out sin and the divine remedy for it, so today we have a Saviour who will plead for us in the heavenly court. Those who come to Jesus Christ will find His exhaustless love and forgiveness if they accept His salvation and follow Him.

### Tragedy Strikes the Jewish Nation

As long as the Persians ruled the world, the people of Judah were safe from invasion. However, Alexander the Great

375

defeated the Persians in the battle of Gaugamela, 331 B.C. Soon the Greek conqueror marched south to capture Jerusalem, for he had decided to punish the Jews for siding with Persia in the long war. When Alexander's army approached the city, Jaddua, the high priest, and all the temple priests marched out through the gates in solemn procession, clothed in white linen robes, to meet the victorious leader. When the Jews surrendered to the Greek army, Alexander was so impressed with their dignity and honesty that he saluted the high priest. Thousands of people saw the kind act of the general, and they shouted for joy. The Greek leader gave the nation many freedoms, and Palestine was secure until Alexander the Great died.

When Antiochus Epiphanes ascended the throne of Syria in 170 B.C., he determined to force the pagan religion and idol worship upon the Jews. After partially conquering Egypt, he led his army to Jerusalem, broke down the walls, massacred thousands of Jews, and burned much of the city. He robbed the holy temple of its golden furniture, and made a mockery of the worship of the Lord and announced that only sacrifices to Greek gods could be offered on the temple altar.

The statue of Jupiter was erected in the temple, and the Jews were forbidden to keep the holy Sabbath. Nevertheless, thousands of faithful men and women stood firm, refusing to disobey the commandments of the Lord.

When officers of Antiochus tried to enforce the tyrant's orders by forcing the priest Mattathias to offer sacrifices on a heathen altar, he fearlessly refused. The five sons of Mattathias stood with their father, grimly determined to gain freedom for their nation at any cost. Enemy soldiers offered the priest riches and honor if he would renounce his allegiance to God, but Mattathias fearlessly said, "If all the heathen in the king's dominions listen to him and forsake each of them the religion of his forefathers, and choose to follow his commands instead, yet I and my sons and my brothers will live in accordance with the agreement of our forefathers. God

376

The five sons of Mattathias stood with their father, grimly determined to restore their nation's freedom.

forbid that we should abandon the law and the ordinances."
1 Maccabees 2:19-22, Goodspeed.

When he stopped speaking, a renegade Jew stepped forward
to offer a sacrifice to a Greek idol, and Mattathias quickly
killed the man. In the fight that followed, he also slew the
king's deputy. As the people rallied to the reformer, he said,
"Let everybody who is zealous for the law and stands by the
agreement come out after me." Verse 27. This started a fierce
revolution, led by the third son of Mattathias, Judas Maccabaeus.

The Jewish revolutionists prospered under the leadership of
Judas Maccabaeus, and he led his followers in many victories.
After defeating the Greek king's regent, Judas obtained religious freedom for his people. This did not stop his attacks
against the Syrians, however, and he was slain in 161 B.C. His
younger brother, Jonathan, successfully led the Jews for almost
twenty years.

About this time the Romans became rulers of the world.
In 63 B.C. the Roman general Pompey captured Jerusalem.
Many faithful Jews were killed defending the city and the
temple, but Pompey did not plunder the holy place nor take
away any of its treasures.

When the Roman governor Herod the Great ruled Judea,
he endeavored to gain the favor of the Jews by rebuilding
the temple. He was an evil, ambitious man, and he chose
high priests who suited his fancy. It was during Herod's
reign that Jesus, the Son of Mary, was born.

For hundreds of years the Jewish nation had looked for
the coming of the promised Messiah. For hundreds of years
they had studied the prophecies concerning the mighty Deliverer who would save His people. Isaiah had sung:

> "How beautiful upon the mountains
>    are the feet of him who brings good tidings,
>   who publishes peace, who brings good tidings of good,
>     who publishes salvation,
>     who says to Zion, 'Your God reigns.'

"Hark, your watchmen lift up their voice,
    together they sing for joy;
for eye to eye they see
    the return of the Lord to Zion.
Break forth together into singing,
    you waste places of Jerusalem;
for the Lord has comforted His people,
    He has redeemed Jerusalem.
The Lord has bared His holy arm
    before the eyes of all the nations;
and all the ends of the earth shall see
    the salvation of our God."

Bethlehem, where David grew up, was to be the birth-place of the Messiah, for Micah, the prophet of God, had said,

"But you, O Bethlehem Ephrathah,
    who are little to be among the clans of Judah,
from you shall come forth for Me

One who is to be ruler in Israel,
    whose origin is from of old,
    from ancient days."

As the Old Testament epic closed, God's faithful souls in Judah were waiting for the coming of the Messiah, who would save His people from their sins. They knew the many prophecies pointing to heaven's greatest gift to the human race—Jesus Christ.

# Prophecies of the Coming of the Messiah

## chapter 31

### The Redeemer Shall Come

"I see Him, but not now;
I behold Him, but not nigh;
a Star shall come forth out of Jacob,
and a Scepter shall rise out of Israel;
it shall crush the forehead of Moab,
and break down all the Sons of Sheth."
Numbers 24:17. (See Revelation 22:16.)

"The Lord your God will raise up for you a Prophet like me from among you, from your brethren—Him you shall heed." Deuteronomy 18:15.

"I will put enmity between you and the woman,
and between your seed and her seed;
He shall bruise your head,
and you shall bruise his heel." Genesis 3:15.

"The scepter shall not depart from Judah,
nor the ruler's staff from between his feet,
until He comes to whom it belong;
and to Him shall be the obedience of the peoples."
Genesis 49:10.

"For to us a Child is born,
to us a Son is given;
and the government will be upon His shoulder,
and His name will be called

380

'Wonderful Counselor, Mighty God,
    Everlasting Father, Prince of Peace.'
Of the increase of His government and of peace
    there will be no end,
upon the throne of David, and over his kingdom,
    to establish it, and to uphold it
with justice and with righteousness
    from this time forth and forevermore.
The zeal of the Lord of hosts will do this."

Isaiah 9:6, 7.

## *"Born of a Woman"*

"Therefore the Lord Himself will give you a sign. Behold, a young woman shall conceive and bear a Son, and shall call His name Immanuel." Isaiah 7:14. (See Matthew 1:22, 23.)

"But you, O Bethlehem Ephrathah,
    who are little to be among the clans of Judah,
from you shall come forth for Me
    One who is to be ruler in Israel,
whose origin is from of old,
    from ancient days."

Micah 5:2. (See Matthew 2:1.)

## *His Ministry to Men*

"The Spirit of the Lord God is upon Me,
    because the Lord has anointed Me
to bring good tidings to the afflicted;
    He has sent Me to bind up the brokenhearted,
to proclaim liberty to the captives,
    and the opening of the prison to those who
        are bound."

Isaiah 61:1. (See Luke 4:16-21.)

"He was despised and rejected by men;
    a Man of Sorrows, and acquainted with grief;
and as One from whom men hide their faces
    He was despised, and we esteemed Him not."

Isaiah 53:3. (See John 1:10, 11.)

### *His Trial and Crucifixion*

"He was oppressed, and He was afflicted,
    yet He opened not His mouth;
like a lamb that is led to the slaughter,
    and like a sheep that before its shearers is dumb,
    so He opened not His mouth."
        Isaiah 53:7. (See Matthew 27:13, 14.)

"They divide My garments among them,
    and for My raiment they cast lots."
        Psalm 22:18. (See Matthew 27:35.)

"And they made His grave with the wicked
    and with a rich man in His death,
although He had done no violence,
    and there was no deceit in His mouth."
        Isaiah 53:9. (See Matthew 27:38.)